Out of Time & Place

volume 1

Out of Time & Place
An Anthology of Plays by the
Women's Project Playwrights Lab
volume I

edited by
Alexis Clements
with Christine Evans

Women's Project
New York, NY

Published by
Women's Project & Productions, Inc.
55 West End Avenue
New York, NY 10023

Printed in the United States of America.

© 2010 by Alexis Clements and Christine Evans

Back From The Front © 2005 by Lynn Rosen, Rewind © 2009 by Laura Eason, The Quiver of Children © 2008 by Charity Henson-Ballard, The Vigil or The Guided Cradle © 2010 by Crystal Skillman, Weightless © 2007 by Christine Evans

"A Thousand Voices" © 2010 by Theresa Rebeck

All rights reserved. No part of this publication may be reproduced or transmitted in any form or by any means, electronic or otherwise, without written permission from Women's Project & Productions, Inc., New York.

CAUTION: These plays are fully protected, in part or in any form, under United States of America as well as International copyright laws and are subject to royalty. All rights, including professional, amateur, motion picture, radio, television, recitation, public reading, and any method of photographic reproduction are strictly reserved. All inquiries concerning amateur and stock performances should be addressed to the parties noted in the "To Obtain Rights To Produce This Play" section preceding each play. General inquiries regarding this publication should be sent to anthology@womensproject.org.

ISBN 978-0-578-06016-3

Design by Alexis Clements

www.outoftimeandplace.com

For all those who inspired us and helped make it possible for us to be here.

Contents

About the Women's Project	xi
Editors' Note	xiii
Preface	
Megan Carter	xvii
Introduction	
Theresa Rebeck, *A Thousand Voices*	xix
Back From the Front	
Connie Grappo, *Entangled in War*	3
Lynn Rosen, *Back From the Front*	7
Weightless	
Ken Prestininzi, *Grounded and Weightless*	91
Christine Evans, *Weightless*	97
The Vigil or The Guided Cradle	
Chris Mills, *Yesterday's Future*	175
Crystal Skillman, *The Vigil or The Guided Cradle*	181
Rewind	
Jessica Thebus, *Laura Eason: My Chameleon Collaborator*	231
Laura Eason, *Rewind*	237
The Quiver of Children	
Louis Scheeder, *The Game Changer*	317
Charity Henson-Ballard, *The Quiver of Children*	321

Acknowledgements 423

Women's Project 2008-2010 Playwrights Lab Member Bios 425

About Women's Project

Julia Miles founded the Women's Project in 1978 to address the conspicuous under-representation of women artists working in the American theater. Even today, only 20 percent of opportunities in the professional theater nationwide are granted to women. The Women's Project continues to combat gender bias with the simple act of job creation.

Under the leadership of Julie Crosby since 2006, the heart of the Women's Project's artistic programming is the Lab, a free, two-year residency program for playwrights, directors, and producers. The Women's Project is deeply committed to its Lab artists and alumnae, who in recent seasons have written or directed most of the theater's mainstage and Hothouse productions, including work by Lear deBessonet, Liz Diamond, Anne Kauffman, Carson Kreitzer, Pam MacKinnon, Saviana Stanescu, Daniella Topol, Joy Tomasko, and Meiyin Wang.

In the past twenty-three years, the Women's Project has staged over six hundred mainstage productions and developmental projects, and published ten anthologies of plays by women. The Ten Centuries of Women Playwrights arts education program inspires over two thousand public school students each year, while the Women's Project's annual Women of Achievement Awards pays homage to luminaries such as Maya Angelou, Eve Ensler, Estelle Parsons, Phylicia Rashad, Vanessa Redgrave, and Chita Rivera, to name but a few. In 1998, the Women's Project became the only women's theater in the nation to purchase its own building, the Julia Miles in midtown Manhattan.

The Lab at Women's Project is fueled by the generous, major support of the Little Family Foundation, the Shubert Foundation, the Andrew W. Mellon Foundation's New York Theater Program, Time Warner Inc., and the Department of Cultural Affairs in the City of New York.

Editors' Note

This anthology, *Out of Time & Place*, in fact comes out of a very specific time and place—two years in the lives of the 2008-2010 Women's Project Playwrights Lab. It offers a snapshot of a particular moment in the working lives of a group of contemporary New York playwrights. The title *Out of Time & Place* also references the peculiar way in which plays (unlike poems or novels) dance in and out of time and place. They travel from early gestation as a dream first grazing the page to the produced and seasoned work, which puts on clothes and a body—sometimes multiple times—with each new production. The plays we offer here are at every point along that spectrum of growth. Our title also reflects that floating sensation, familiar to playwrights in the American theater, of having no fixed address. We write this at a time when the resources for new American plays—and hence a playwriting life—are in real crisis, reflecting the larger economic and political turmoil of our times. Yet this crisis is also compelling many playwrights to take creative action in finding new collaborators, lasting creative homes, and new methods (such as this) for publicly sharing their work.

These two years in the life of the 2008-2010 Lab have been marked by an extraordinary volatility in national and international events. The nation elected its first African American president. Historic health-care legislation passed. The housing and financial markets melted down with stunning speed, bringing a severe recession that has brought ongoing economic hardship to millions. The wars in Afghanistan and Iraq continued. And the nation witnessed one of its worst ever environmental disasters, the catastrophic oil spill in the Gulf of Mexico.

Our own field reflects the larger volatility of the times as old structures come under strain and face intense pressure to change. There is a growing sense that the nation's theaters seriously need to re-imagine their methods, assumptions and models. This has been sparked by a couple of influential studies (Todd London's *Outrageous Fortune: The Life and Times of the New American Play*; and Julia Jordan and Emily Sands' work to quantify the situation of women playwrights) and made urgent by the economic crisis. Part of this reimagining must include confronting the abysmal underrepresentation of women playwrights on the nation's stages.

As you'll read in Theresa Rebeck's eloquent introduction to this book, despite the roughly equal numbers of men and women writing plays today, a mere 18 percent of the nation's produced plays are written by women. Rebeck makes an impassioned call to action in her introduction, and this book is one response to that call. We hope it hammers another nail in the coffin of the specious argument that it is hard to find strong female playwrights. We're here and we're writing plays that are as diverse as we are. They're not "women's plays," which in our view don't exist as a stylistic category. They're plays, period. And they are entertaining their audiences. These playwrights have been commissioned and produced on four continents and dozens of cities, won scores of awards, and been seen on stages ranging from major regional and New York theaters to downtown spaces in Chicago, Minnesota, Rhode Island, Texas, Brisbane, Cape Town, Edinburgh and elsewhere.

Out of Time & Place is also inspired by Diana Taylor's observation in *The Archive and The Repertoire* that what is published can be preserved in the archive, whereas work passed down through living practice tends to disappear along with its practitioners. Plays by women are empirically less likely to be archived, so they vanish at rates disproportionate to their place in the repertoire of their day. Who would know (from the written record) that scores of U.S. women writing in the 1920s, 30s and 40s had critically and commercially successful careers? In purely practical terms, who outside of the few who encounter plays on stage or behind the scenes will be able to find them if they go unpublished? As Marsha

Norman writes, "A theater that is missing the work of women is missing half the story, half the canon, half the life of our time."

Here we present a fragment of that wider view—life in all its luminosity and mess, tragedy and hilarity, as imagined for the stage by our group over these past two tumultuous years. Above all we hope that these plays will entertain, amaze and move you. We offer you this book with that hope in mind.

Preface

Megan Carter

I am amazingly lucky. I get to work with the most talented playwrights working in the American theater today. They are not household names—in fact, many have not yet had their off-Broadway debut—but they are the present and future of the theater, inventing and questioning and encompassing worlds with their writing.

The artists anthologized in these volumes came together through the Women's Project Lab, a residency for playwrights, directors and producers, which is the heart of everything our theater does. It is a vibrant community that connects exceptional theater artists and creates an artistic haven to envision bold new work for the stage.

The 2008-2010 Lab is diverse, brilliant and dynamic, and their range of expression—as evidenced by this anthology—is profound and certainly difficult to sum up. I love Lynn Rosen's gift for moving, outrageous comedies; Crystal Skillman's sepia-toned mysteries; the cadenced and engrossing epics created by Charity Henson-Ballard; Christine Evans' philosophically provocative and stunningly theatrical gems; and the glorious stillness of Laura Eason's evocative narratives.

The Playwrights Lab is a shining credit to the legacy of the Women's Project. Julia Miles saw the lack of production opportunities for women in 1978 and audaciously founded a theater to address the problem. These artists are equally daring and self-motivated. Rather than sit back and lament the dismal statistics for women in theater, they are putting themselves out into the world, not only with this anthology, but also as they invent new modes of collaboration and production.

You may not be familiar with these extraordinary writers' work yet, but I'm sure that soon their work will be lighting up stages all over the U.S. (You read it here first.)

Megan Carter is the Associate Artistic Director & Dramaturg for the Women's Project. Prior to joining Women's Project in 2006, Megan worked as a director, dramaturg and educator in Seattle and New York. Select New York credits include *Freshwater* by Virginia Woolf; *Aliens with Extraordinary Skills* by Saviana Stanescu; *Sand* by Trista Baldwin; *Burial at Thebes* by Seamus Heaney; Mac Wellman's *Sincerity Forever* and *Harm's Way*. Megan has collaborated with Tea Alagic, Anne Bogart, Lear deBessonet, Katori Hall, Carson Kreitzer, Daniella Topol and at such companies as Intiman Theatre, ACT Theatre, and Classic Stage Company. She has an MFA in Dramaturgy and Theater Criticism from Brooklyn College/CUNY.

Introduction: A Thousand Voices

Theresa Rebeck

The following speech was given by invitation at the ART/NY Curtain Call presentation, Laura Pels Theater, March 15, 2010.

Because I am someone who believes in the power of storytelling, I am going to tell you a story. It is the story of a play, and the story of things that happened to me, because of that play.

The play is called *The Butterfly Collection*. I wrote it in 1999. It is about a family of artists, and the tensions that rise between the father, who is a successful novelist, and his two sons, one of whom is a struggling actor, and the other who is an antiques dealer. Tim Sanford at Playwrights Horizons fell in love with this play and said he would produce it in the fall of 2000, and he talked to the guys who run South Coast Rep and they read it and included it in the new play festival that spring, so that we had a chance to work on it out there. The workshop was great, and we were the hit of the festival. When the play came to New York the following fall, we had a thrilling cast—Marian Seldes and Brian Murray, in their first production together, Reed Birney, Betsey Aidem, and the young Maggie Lacey in her New York stage debut. Bartlett Sher directed, and there was enormous excitement gathering around the production. A lot of commercial producers came, as people felt that it could potentially move. Nine regional theaters were circling to produce it. *American Theater* magazine called my agent to ask for the script because they were interested in publishing it (in one of those cool inserts—I was very excited, I've always wanted one of those). Audiences were thrilled with the play. Lincoln Center Library of Performing Arts was filming it for their collection.

When the *New York Times* published its review it was not what anyone expected. The reviewer, who shall remain nameless, dismissed the play—which was about art and family—as a feminist diatribe. He accused me of having a thinly-veiled man-hating agenda, and in a truly bizarre paragraph at the end of the review, he expressed sympathy with the director because he had to work with someone as hideous as me.

The review was horrible and personal and projected all sorts of terrible things onto me. I was shocked. A lot of people were shocked. And there was real outcry in the community. A lot of letters were written to the *Times*—someone told me it was sixty letters, and I don't know how anyone would know that but it made me feel better, even though none of them were published. Apologies were made behind the scenes, none to me but to other people. The heroic Tina Howe went to the Dramatists Guild council and read the review aloud and insisted something be done about this. She and a lot of other people made the excellent point that if anyone at the *Times* had ever dared to publish a review as racist or homophobic or anti-Semitic as this review was, in its bigotry—well, the review would never have been published. So there was a flurry of upset. But with a review that bad, the play closed. All the other productions went away. *American Theater* magazine went away. Everybody knew that it was a crazy mysoginistic review. But no one would produce the play. Ever again. And you should know that many people consider it my best play. Still.

This is what happened to me in the months after that.

People couldn't get over it. For about a year and a half I had people come up to me at least once a week and this is what the conversation would be:

Nice Person Hi Theresa, how are you? I saw *The Butterfly Collection*! Wow it was so beautiful! What a great evening of theater!

Theresa Thank you.

Nice Person That review was crazy! So mysogynistic! Wow, how could he write something like that?

And then this nice person would go on and on and on about that crazy mysogynistic review, so I got to live through it all over again.

I cannot tell you how many of these conversations I had. Maybe two hundred. Then one day I did a joint interview with the great Chuck Mee, and after the interview was over, and the reporter had left, Chuck said to me, "I saw *The Butterfly Collection*. It was really beautiful." And I said, "Thank you." And then I waited, for the rest of the conversation, about that crazy review, and Chuck didn't say it. All he said was, "that play was beautiful," and for a minute, I had my play back.

The other person who repeatedly and heroically gave me my play back was the wonderful actress Lynn Cohen, who was really angry about what happened and who would speak to me with such courage and compassion about it that even though I didn't want to really talk about it, she always made me feel better.

This is another thing that happened—a whole lot of people decided I should change my identity. This is the conversation I had with other well-meaning people:

Nice Person You know, Theresa, everybody knows that your work is terrific but the New York critics don't like you personally.

Theresa How can they not like me personally? They don't know me!

Nice Person Hey! We love you. But you know what you should do? You should produce your plays under a male pseudonym.

Theresa You mean, I should pretend to be a man?

Nice Person That's right. That's the only way they will accept you. Or the plays! They would like your plays, if only you hadn't written them!

Okay I know that sounds crazy, but I swear I had that conversation at least a dozen times. Arthur Kopit, who I love and is really great, thought this was a hilarious idea and he had a lot of fun figuring out for me how I would pull that off, becoming a man. We never went as far as surgery but there were lots of other clever ideas about what I might do to trick people into thinking I was a man. Which is what I needed to do, to make my identity acceptable.

This is another thing that happened to me—one of my friends who was a producer in New York told me that this was all a sign, that I was being told by the *Times* that I am not welcome in New York and I should think of something else to do with my life.

This is another thing that happened—a close friend of mine who is a theater director started screaming at me in restaurants and he told me I wasn't an artist.

This is another thing that happened—my agent said, you know Theresa, how you've always wanted to write a novel? Maybe you should do that. Which is not necessarily bad advice, but it's also not particularly the advice you want to hear from your *theater agent*. He also told me that my next two plays, *Omnium Gatherum* and *Bad Dates*, were unproduceable and that he couldn't represent them.

And, I couldn't get produced. He was right about that. No one wanted to touch *The Butterfly Collection* and no one wanted to touch me. And then I fell off of the map. I got really depressed because of all this, as you might imagine, and I couldn't think anymore, and I was spending way too much time lying on the couch all day, and I was drinking white wine a lot, in one-inch increments. I would lie on the couch and tell myself I wasn't turning into an alcoholic because I was only drinking white wine one inch at a time. And then one day my son, who was five years old at the time, came up to me and said, "Mom, are you all right?" And I looked at him and I thought: *get up*. It is your job to take care of this kid and it's not his job to take care of you and you are not going to turn into this person. So I got off the couch.

And then a bunch of other things happened that were equally or more hideous. It's not like getting off the couch solved everything. I did start writing a novel, although that's a whole different story. But I really was off the grid, for two years, and then one day I went to see my friend Sinan Ünel's play up at the Long Wharf. I caught a ride back to the city with John Eisner, and we talked for three hours and he said, "You should come up to the Lark." And then the next day Arthur Kopit called and told me as well, "You should come up to the Lark." And the Lark saved me. They saved my sanity and they saved my career and I thank them for everything they did for me, and what they do for a lot of playwrights. There is no organization, in my mind, that does more.

And that is the last time I am telling that story. I am never telling that story again. But I tell it today because I don't want to hear from anybody that there isn't, or hasn't been, a real gender problem in the American theater. I really did think about what I might talk to you about today and I had no choice, honestly. I felt like my whole career as a playwright has been so hyper-defined by my gender—sometimes I feel like it is strangely blinding, even. And it's time for all of us to look at this, and talk about it—without just saying, "Oh, there's not really a problem" because there *is* a problem—and then start talking about what we, as a community, are going to do to solve it.

This is an important point to realize: before I came to New York and started working in the theater, I was never told that being a girl was going to be a problem for me in any way that I took seriously. It's not like I was a stranger to conservatism. I know a lot about the Republican Party and the Catholic Church because I was raised, basically, in both. Both my parents were staunch Ohio Republican Catholics until a point when my mother got a clue and switched parties. Now she's a Democrat and my father is still a Republican, and since then they've done nothing but fight incessantly about politics. My father, who is as I said both Republican and Catholic, thinks I'm insane, *but* there was a moment in my childhood when some of his buddies got into ribbing him about having so many daughters. He had four daughters and two sons, and someone apparently even expressed pity one day, the story goes. One of his golfing buddies said something like, "Poor George, what is he going to do with all those girls?" And it pissed him off, and he came home and said to my Democratic mother, "Those girls can do anything the boys can do." And that is what the expectation was in my house.

Then I went to an all-girls Catholic high school where the nuns were all quietly radical liberation theologists who were secretly agitating for women's ordination. Then I went to Notre Dame, which was more traditionally conservative, but I couldn't take it too seriously because they had things like panty raids there. I thought it was just too dumb to be believed. And then I went to Brandeis, where I read a lot of feminist literary theory and considered questions like, "Is the Gaze Male?" This was in the *eighties*; that's more than twenty-five years ago, for people who are counting. And at the time there were fantastic plays being produced all over the country by Wendy Wasserstein and Tina Howe and Marsha Norman and Emily Mann, and I thought it was a cool thing, to be a woman playwright. I thought, I'm not in the Catholic Church anymore, and the world is saying we haven't heard from the women, and now we're ready!

And then I began my career as a professional playwright, where I was told that since I'm a woman, if I write about women, that meant I had a feminist agenda and that's *bad*. I also got told that when I write about men, since I'm a woman, I clearly have a feminist agenda, and that's bad too. I couldn't write about anything without hearing that I had a feminist agenda. It turned out that being a woman playwright was just in itself suspect; if you were a woman playwright by definition you had a feminist agenda, which was so bad, it annihilated the work itself. The other word for woman playwright might as well be "witch."

As an aside, let me add that I would rather be called a witch than a man-hater. Honestly, "man-hater" really does need to be simply *off the table*. It bugs the shit out of me. I have a husband and a son and a lot of men in my life whom I love a lot and it's creepy that people would toss that ugly accusation at anyone in the jovial spirit of name-calling. Someone actually called me that at a party a couple of weeks ago and I wanted to hit him. *But I didn't*. Anyway, if you need to call me a name—the preferred insult would be "witch." Or "madwoman in the attic" is also acceptable.

So those are some of the ways I know there actually is a gender problem in the American theater. This is another way: because so many people—not just Arthur Kopit—have told me, over the years, that in order to have a career that is commensurate with my talent, I should pretend to be a man. This is another way I know there is a problem: because the extraordinary Julia Jordan ran the numbers for us.

Two years ago, in what I think was an act of inspired intelligence and courage, Julia Jordan conducted a series of town hall meetings at New Dramatists, which put the question of gender parity on the table for the American theater to discuss. She invited women playwrights to come and present their situation and they showed up in droves. Then she invited artistic directors and literary managers to come and confront the situation with us. And this is the situation: plays written by women are not being produced. In 2007, the one year I opened a play on Broadway, I was the only woman playwright who did so. That year, nationwide, 12 percent of the new plays produced all over the country were by women. That means 88 percent of the new plays produced were written by men. (Back in 1908 before women had the right to vote, the percentage of new plays in New York, written by women, was higher. It was higher before we had the vote.)

Generally, over the last twenty-five years, the number of plays produced that were written by women seems to have vacillated between 12 and 17 percent.

This is a disastrous statistic, and it is related to another disastrous statistic, which is the number of women writers and directors in Hollywood. This year 6 percent of films were directed by women, and 8 percent of produced screenplays were written or co-written by women. That means 88 percent of all plays were written by men, 94 percent of all movies were directed by men, and 92 percent of all movies were written by men.

Women playwrights like myself have a lot of anecdotal evidence to support some pretty coherent theories about why this is the case. People in the power structure seem more mystified and often they don't seem sure that there is a problem. (One of them actually said to me, not too long ago, "But Theresa, where *are* the women playwrights?" Seriously, he looked me in the face and said that) Several artistic directors have expressed concern at the idea of "quotas." They really don't like the word "quota." I don't like that word either. Other words I don't like are "discrimination," and "censorship," and I wish I could get them to dislike those words as much as they dislike "quotas." "Boys club" is another couple of words I could very well live without. But since there is so much murky territory in language, I think this discussion of numbers is very useful.

Here is what the numbers say to me: if we lived in an ideal world, the balance of new plays produced in theaters all over America would come out to, roughly, 50:50. I am a proud member of the Dramatists Guild, I serve on the council and it's a great organization, everyone who is a playwright should belong—here's a shout-out to Gary Garrison and Ralph Sevush, you are excellent, and so is Stephen Schwartz, our excellent president. Anyway, the Dramatist Guild tracks the percentages of women and men who enter graduate school as playwriting students, and it also tracks the numbers of people who apply for membership, and those numbers either stick to the 50:50 ratio *or* there is a higher number of women. So in the ideal world, those women and men who are over the years developing their craft as playwrights should rise through the system at an even rate. This is not what is happening. Women are being shut out, at different levels of development and production, and you end up with this crazy 17 percent number, which seems to be the highest percentage we can get to, year in and year out. 17 percent of 50 percent is 34 percent of 100 percent. (Bear with me, I'm not making this up, I'm actually pretty good at math) That means that 66 percent of the best plays by women—the plays that *should* be rising to the top, the plays that in a fair world would move into the culture as the stories we are telling ourselves—66 percent of women's stories are being lost. Every year.

And I have to reiterate: the premise of those numbers is that playwriting is *not* in fact a gene on a Y-chromosome, and we are *not* losing women playwrights because they decided to run off and have babies. The reason we lost all those women playwrights is: we buried their work, and we sent them away.

I would also like to note that in January a lot of reports came out about the recent study of the American Council on Education. This study informed us that last year women earned more than half the degrees granted in every category—associate, bachelors, masters, doctoral and professional. The actual numbers nationwide stand at 57 percent women and 43 percent men, and they have stood somewhere in that vicinity since the year 2000. *USA Today* asks, is this "cause for celebration, or concern?"

When I read all these accounts, I thought: 43 percent, wow, women playwrights would be so happy if our numbers got up to 43 percent. We would be throwing parties. But the people who do the studies and write these reports up are in fact *worried* that it's not fair to the boys that they only have 43 percent of the slots in the college population. This is a bad thing, we are told, for a lot of reasons, chief among them that smart girls won't have enough men to date. (That is how the *New York Times* reported the story) A lot of colleges have admitted that just as they might consider race or geographical diversity in building freshman classes, they similarly look for gender parity, which means they are letting boys in over more-qualified girls—which does look like affirmative action, or shall we say "quotas," which apparently are okay when they favor boys.

So women playwrights live in a world where we are told it is a bad thing if women are 57 percent of the undergraduate population because that's too big an imbalance, but it's an okay thing if women are only getting 17 percent or 6 percent or 9 percent of the best jobs in show business (and elsewhere, in America). And if we tried to rectify that it would be unfair because it would involve "quotas."

Now let me tell you something: a lot of people will think that what I just pointed out was a "feminist" statement. But I don't actually see it that way. I see these contradictions as just kind of comical and even, well, stupid. As an indication that there is just something truly, systemically unfair going on here. That's not a feminist agenda. That's the truth.

I never had an agenda. I just wanted to write plays that told the truth. Some of those plays told the truth about what it is like to live on this planet as a woman. Why would that be off the table? Why would that story be something that they only do in fiction, or on cable TV? Why can't we do that in the theater? I just don't think that we theater people want to align ourselves with the backward-looking institutions of culture. We want to see ourselves, I think, as a relevant and intellectually rigorous and culturally progressive community. It's past time to acknowledge the fact that that means welcoming the voices of women into the cultural discussion.

There are a lot of ways to do this. Primarily, I think, we need to encourage theaters and producers and foundations and boards of directors to extend to women playwrights the kind of excellent programs which have been put in place to encourage the work of minority playwrights. All across America, and here in New York, there has been strong and necessary support for these voices, and wonderful writers have emerged because of that support. I have been told so many times over the years that theaters and foundations are interested in "diversity" but that doesn't mean women. That needs to change. We need to stop discussing why the numbers are so bad and stop asking where are the women playwrights. And we need to start recognizing them where they are—which is right in front of us—and hold them up and celebrate their voices, and produce their plays.

In that context, I would like to report that this year, in New York, the following plays were produced:

Circle Mirror Transformation by Annie Baker
Or by Liz Duffy Adams
This by Melissa James Gibson
In The Next Room (or The Vibrator Play) by Sarah Ruhl
The Understudy by me
Smudge by Rachel Axler
Happy Now by Lucinda Coxon

All of these plays have received wide critical recognition; most of them were extended and all of them played to packed houses. In short, there were a lot of plays by women in New York this year, and they were not only fierce and dazzling and interesting: they also made a lot of money. Tim Sanford, over at Playwrights Horizons, who has long been an unacknowledged champion of women's plays, is having a truly sensational season in a worried, recessionary economy. He deserves it. Julie Crosby over there at the Women's Project is also having a sensational season, and she and they deserve it too.

Which brings us finally to another couple of statistics which I think are worth noting: women buy more tickets. They buy 55 percent of movie tickets and anywhere from 60 to 65 percent of theater tickets. So opening our stages and our hearts and our minds to women playwrights is not only cool and relevant and interesting and just—it is also a sound business model.

Sir David Hare recently made news by informing the *London Telegraph* that "many of today's best plays were being written by women, but that 'macho' theater managers were failing to capitalize on the trend." That is a direct quote, and here's another: "I don't think the repertory of most theaters is reflecting what seems to be happening in terms of the most interesting new theater. We would hope to see management in theater reflecting where we think the creativity in playwriting is coming from." A friend of mine was worried about me after all that shit went down with

The Butterfly Collection, so she got me a session with an astrologer named Coral. So Coral did my chart, which was apparently in very poor shape at the time, like me. And she got very specific about the names of the stars and the planets which were passing through my heavens, and apparently there's a planet out there named Chiron. It's not actually a planet. I think it's one of the moons of Jupiter, but Coral informed me that Chiron is the wounded healer, and Chiron was just all over my chart. Then, and now, I apparently have been claimed in every way by Chiron, the wounded healer. And there is no question, I am wounded. But I offer you all this information as a hope that I might actually provide one of the healing voices in this discussion. I really do believe that if enough people stand up and say "this cannot go on," it will not go on. After a season like this one, where so many plays in New York were by women, and were so relevant, and important, and successful, both in what they achieved dramatically and the way they drew in audiences, we will not go back.

There is a Native American saying, "It takes a thousand voices to tell a single story." And Walter Cronkite told us, "In seeking truth, you have to get both sides of the story."

It's time to hear both sides, to hear all voices, to build a culture where stories are told by both men and women. That is the way the planet is going to survive, and it's the way we are going to survive.

Thank you very much.

Theresa Rebeck is a widely produced playwright, novelist and television writer. Past New York theater productions of her work include *The Understudy* at the Roundabout and *Mauritius* at the Biltmore Theatre on Broadway. *Omnium Gatherum* (co-written, finalist for the Pulitzer Prize in 2003) was featured at the Humana Festival, and had a commercial run at the Variety Arts Theatre. Rebeck has published two bestselling novels, *Three Girls and Their Brother* and, *Twelve Rooms with a View*. She has written for many television shows including *NYPD Blue*, for which she won a Peabody Award, and *Law & Order: Criminal Intent*. She lives in Brooklyn with her husband and two children.

xxx

Back From The Front
Lynn Rosen

Entangled in War:
A Conversation About *Back From The Front* Between Connie Grappo and Lynn Rosen

This interview took place in May 2007 before The Working Theater production of Back From The Front *opened, and when the Bush administration was still in power. Connie Grappo directed the production and was then the Artistic Director of The Working Theater.*

Connie Grappo So what prompted you to write *Back From The Front*?

Lynn Rosen Outrage! Also a feeling of helplessness. I was homebound with my newborn son during the run up to the war and found myself watching a lot of TV news. My blood pressure must have been through the roof (maybe this is why my son never napped?) because I could not believe the lies the administration seemed to be feeding us about this warrantless war. I could not believe what was about to be perpetrated in our name—the lives that would be lost on both sides. I was infuriated by the complicity and complacency of both the media and the Democrats. I was appalled that they utilized the threat of terrorism to terrorize their own citizens into submission. I felt the terror too. Like most people, I felt pretty helpless. The only outlet for my anger and concern was, as always, to put it on paper. The tragic absurdity of the lies they told us is what set the tone of this play.

CG Has motherhood had an impact on your views on the current war, or war in general?

LR Imagining what it would feel like to say goodbye to my son—whether in an eternal sense, or simply saying goodbye if he had to ship off to war, especially one as senseless as this—is too painful to bear. Even when my son goes to his grandparents' for the night I feel like a part of me is missing. So while I think that even if I were childless I'd empathize with families who have loved ones involved in this war and who live every day within a shadow of fear and loss, having a child makes my compassion for them and my indignation over this war more intense. Being a mom—and reading interviews with women whose children are entangled in this war—was definitely another catalyst for writing *Back From The Front*. The family in this play, particularly the mother, refuse to abandon the idea that their son is alive and well and that the war is just, no matter what evidence to the contrary might suggest. I can see myself being there…or maybe I'd take the route of Cindy Sheehan. I can't really know and hope I never will.

CG Why have you chosen to use comedy to deal with this subject?

LR I always utilize humor—whether in plays, or in life—to deal with whatever situation is at hand. It's just the way I communicate and get through the day. I think humor is a powerful and subversive way to tell a story and perhaps reflect a point of view. I'm not a fan of hitting someone over the head to make a statement. I'd prefer the audience laugh their way into the world I'm creating. I'd rather everything sneak up on them. But the mood of this play is also dictated by the times we live in. The administration continues to brazenly create their own reality, their own version of the truth, in order to sell this war. It's so absurd and heightened and ridiculous—the tone of the play is a reflection of this. It would be hysterically funny if the consequences weren't so tragic. Likewise, the comedy in *Back From The Front* gives way to what's beneath—the desperate love the family has for their son, and the tragedy they work furiously to deny.

CG You don't let the news media off the hook in this play. Do you think they've done a good job of covering the war and keeping the public informed?

LR Is this a trick question? I think the mainstream media are partly responsible for the war being supported initially by the public, and therefore by congress, and for Bush's reelection and his continued bungling of the war. They did not ask questions. They did not investigate all the claims of the administration (false claims as we know now) in the lead up to the war. They failed to do their job. I'm sure there were a few in the mainstream media who did do their job—but for the most part they failed and it costs people their lives, not to mention billions of dollars.

CG Writing a comedy about a family whose son is missing-in-action, does it worry you that any audience might be offended?

LR Hmm, I never worried about it until you asked me this question. I did a version of this show in the Fringe Festival a few years ago and no one, to my knowledge, was offended. One reviewer, who gave the play a great write-up, also wrote that their brother had just been deployed to Iraq. My own brother was almost sent to the first Gulf War. So even though it's a comedy, it's clearly also a very heartfelt play about a family's love for their son. I trust people will get that. And again, I think humor can be a powerful and subtle way to convey a serious story.

Connie Grappo teaches acting at Yale and facilitates theater workshops with incarcerated men through Rehabilitation Through the Arts. She has directed productions at Yale Rep, Second Stage, WPA, Working Theater, Trinity Rep, Humana Festival, Victory Theater, Theater J, Cleveland Playhouse, San Diego Rep, as well as Fishkill Correctional Facility. She participated in the development of many new American plays at many theaters in NY and regionally. She served three years as Artistic Director of Working Theater, and wrote and directed the short film *Little Feet*, which premiered at Sundance and aired on Showtime.

Characters

Wendy Walker, early 40s, the mother, Caucasian. Well put together, intense and tightly wound, wears the pants in the family, often a mama bear protecting her clan.

Tim Walker, early 40s, the father, Caucasian. Ex-jock, lost his mojo, ego is deflated, removed from the world around him—perhaps purposely so.

Penny Walker, 18-21, the daughter, Caucasian. Dresses like she's stunted at age 12, the age when her family was happy, a dreamer, desperate to please everyone and for everyone to be happy, often escapes to a fantasy world called Elsewhere.

Robbie Walker, early 20s, "the son," Asian American. Dressed in his uniform.

Carlos Sanchez, 30s-40s, the government liaison, says he's Hispanic but this is a lie, so actor should be Caucasian. Suit, tie, a smooth-talker who believes in his purpose—he must.

Hal, early 20s, the neighbor, Caucasian. Army vet, wears fatigues and heavy metal t-shirts, mustache, intense, opinionated, angry as hell, on a mission, loves the Walkers.

Hal2, 18, "the neighbor," Arab. Wears whatever Hal wears, should be harmless looking and very boy-like, he has lost his whole world and is thrown into a new one.

Place

An average Midwestern town. An average working-class living room a bit past its prime.

Time

The present, the day before Thanksgiving.

Playwright's Note

When a slash (/) appears in the dialogue, it indicates that the next character should begin speaking their line at this point, creating overlapping dialogue. Everyone in this play is trying their hardest to deceive themselves. The truth is too painful for them all. Therefore, though the play has a heightened quality, all performances must be grounded in reality. What these people feel is very real.

Production History

Back From The Front was first produced in the New York International Fringe Festival, directed by Giovanna Sardelli. It was subsequently produced by The Working Theater, directed by Connie Grappo.

To Obtain Rights To Produce This Play

Please contact: Seth Glewen, The Gersh Agency, 41 Madison Avenue, 33rd Floor, New York, NY 10010. Telephone: (212) 997-1818.

Back From The Front

The Walker's Living Room

It is completely dark. In this darkness we hear...

Wendy Oh, it's starting? It's starting in ten he says!

Penny *(Excited squeal)*

Wendy Shh. In ten, nine, eight /

Tim Wendy, what if they ask about /

Wendy Six, four, five /

Penny But Mama, what if they ask /

Wendy Five, three, two /

Bright camera lights come up—TV lights. Wendy, Tim, and Penny sit on their sofa. They wear pins that say "Robbie." Behind them is a wall with Robbie memorabilia. There are a few small cracks in their wall. They are giving an interview on TV via an unseen camera in their house. There are a few switchboxes and cables on the floor to indicate the camera equipment. They get questions over an earpiece they hold in their ear, so only they hear the questions of Diane, the interviewer. Having been displaced by all of the unseen camera equipment, a small TV set sits at Tim's feet, facing him. Only he can see the TV image. Penny looks like a deer in headlights. Lines can overlap.

Wendy Yes, good morning!

Tim Good morning! Wow!

Penny Wow!

Wendy Yes, good morning from our living room. Good morning, America, ha ha.

Tim So funny. Ha ha /

Penny Ha ha!

Wendy Thank you. And happy Thanksgiving eve to you too. Let's do it, guys. Like we practiced.

They all do thumbs up and say…

Wendy / Tim / Penny Gobble gobble!

Wendy Well, our pleasure, / Diane.

Penny Pleasure.

Tim Figured you'd never respond to my letter about Robbie, Diane. I wrote it at a low point.

Penny *(Sings in a low voice)* Low.

Wendy But we're not low now. We're high. And we're so proud to be part of your "Waging the War at Home" series. We love it.

Tim Love it so much /

Penny So much.

Wendy It sure was a pleasant surprise to see your crew at our door.

Penny They squashed our decorative Thanksgiving corn. But the Native Americans were slaughtered. That's worse.

Tim Good point, Penny Bird! Way to go!

Wendy Robbie made that corn in sixth grade. It was the best one.

Tim The best.

Penny I made one too.

Wendy Actually, my name is Wendy, Diane…That's ok. Mindy's good too. I mean, you'd know my name better than me being a top-notch journalist and all.

Penny Do another in-depth story on sextuplets, Diane. We need more of those!

Tim *(Pointing to his TV)* There's us! Do I really look like that?

Wendy What gets us through the day, Diane? Well…

Tim I can answer that in one word. Wendy does. Wendy's our Supermom. Superwife.

Wendy Aw, Tim. Sweet.

Penny Oh, it's true, Mama.

Tim She keeps this house in shape. So peppy. Lots of great lists.

Wendy *(Reads list)* One—wake up, think happy thought. Two—watch Diane. Ha ha.

Tim Wendy's also so full of, of, of… Well, I guess you'd call it love.

Wendy Aw, my Tim.

Wendy and Tim kiss. Then she crosses "Kiss Tim" off her list.

Penny Oh, love is good. I like love. More! More!

Wendy *(Annoyed)* Penny!

Tim Never a complaint or a "why me." I mean here's a woman, I'll tell ya, when I met this woman she had such joy. Such a joy about her. *(Starts to cry)* Aw jeez the guys at the plant will have a field day.

Penny Oh, Daddy. Mommy's watching.

Wendy Oh, Sweetie, don't blubber.

Tim She's been our rock during this war nightmare.

We hear loud, screechy feedback from Tim's earpiece at soon as he says "night."

Hello? Diane? My ear thing broke. I can't hear Diane. Should I keep talking or what should I do? *(Shouts)* Mindy's our rock, Diane!

Wendy Let me handle this, Tim. *(To Diane)* Tim can't hear you, Diane.

Tim *(Shouts)* Rock!

Wendy Pardon, Diane?… Yes, Robbie enlisted. Two years ago.

Tim *(Shouts)* Got swept up in it! The fervor!

Wendy She can hear you, Tim. You don't have to /

Tim "Way to go!" I says when he told me he was gonna enlist.

Wendy That was all Tim said. Nothing else. Wish I'd been there.

Tim It was Sunday. The Bears were losing.

Wendy But who could blame Tim for not saying more?

Tim "Way to go." That was all I could think of.

Wendy Well, we thought it was a good cause. Still do.

Tim That's right! Still do!

Wendy Plus he gets the GI Bill. He gets a future.

Tim Why he could become chief of police, Diane, or a CPA.

Penny *(Whispers loudly)* Or a wizard.

Wendy Plus, Tim knew Rob could hack it. Rob's a winner.

Tim Robbie serves on an Apache! Saves people! Expensive piece of machinery! They wouldn't have entrusted that to just anybody.

Wendy Real brave, our boy. Brave and strong.

Tim Strong! Always defended the misfits. Always brought home some kid bleeding from a punch in his funny face cuz he felt bad for him, right? A good boy. Good.

Penny Robbie always had to save me cuz I'm a tad weird. I never know what to do with my hands.

She does something awkward with her hands. Wendy is embarrassed as usual.

Wendy *(Annoyed)* Penny! Yes, Diane, Robbie's Apache crashed over enemy territory. He was missing for a bit, but then he was rescued by Special Ops. He's a survivor.

Tim Special Ops rescued the rescuer! I guess that's what those people call Karma.

Penny Karma larma ding dong.

Wendy *(Annoyed)* Penny! She's so…unique.

Penny Sorry, Mama. I'll go Elsewhere. *(Gets a far off look as she instantly puts her mind Elsewhere)* Lilacs.

Wendy Carlos says Robbie's still in recovery, Diane. But Carlos says he's totally fine. And Carlos would know. Oh yes, we're full of positivity, Diane!

Penny Like a charged ion!

Wendy Come on, guys. Like we practiced.

All do a thumbs up.

Wendy/Tim/Penny Happy almost Turkey Day!

Suddenly, Hal pops his head through the doggie flap in their door. He wears his fatigues, an AC/DC t-shirt, and his purple heart medal. He speaks to the unseen camera.

Hal The only turkey here is this war, Diane! Yum! Ignorance is so tasty!

Wendy Hal! Scram! Tim, do something.

Tim *(Totally ineffectual)* Hal! Wendy says scram!

Penny Thumbs up, see Mama? I wish my thumbs were extra long so I could do it extra well. Mama?

Wendy Hal, you're ruining everything!

Hal finishes crawling into their house via the doggie flap. It was a tough fit.

Hal Oh, I'll ruin things alright, Mrs. W. I'll ruin things so good, America, you'll thank god I'm back. *(Sings AC/DC song in falsetto)* Back in black!

Wendy Like you ruin our property values with your dead lawn? Yeah, that's why the neighbors hate you. If Adelle weren't dead, she'd be horrified.

Hal Don't you talk about my dear Mama! She died of heartbreak when I went to war, Diane! That war killed her!

Wendy Tell him, Tim. Tell him about the dead lawn.

Tim Ok. Your lawn is dead, Hal. And so's your mother. Sorry about that. But try reseeding.

Hal No thanks!!! I got other seeds to sow. Like savin' Robbie! My best pal! Didn't we used to have fun, Penny? Me, you, and Robbie? With our wizards club, and our secret language, *(Secret language)* elfewan thisla friddle dee, Penny, and our *(Secret language)* ixtrath ubervlish ticklish tick!

Hal tickles Penny—holding her in the air. She laughs and laughs. Hal drops her.

But there's no more time for fun. It's time to act! Let's rock this frikkin' casbah!

Wendy Excuse him, America. Hal used to be totally different. A nice Jewish boy. Clean shaven and sweet. We went to his Bar Mitzvah. *(Accent incorrectly on VAH)* But when he came back home he hit rock bottom.

Hal And that bottom's full of shrapnel, Diane! Every time I sit I have a flashback. No joke!

Penny (*Gleeful*) Oh! Have the flashback with the booby-trapped candy!

Penny makes Hal sit. He has a nightmarish flashback. Penny claps—she's delighted by it, not seeing how painful it is for him.

Hal (*In real terror in his flashback*) Is that a candy? Is that a candy? That's no candy!

Wendy Penny! Show Diane Robbie's wall. Distract America while we get Hal out of here. Go! Go!

Camera light follows Penny to the Robbie wall. She talks very loudly to the camera while Tim and Wendy deal with Hal.

Penny Here's where we marked Robbie's growth, America. See? Four feet, then five, then six zillion! That's how I remember him.

Tim Hal. You want your rake back? Huh? You want your rake?

Wendy Oh, did you rake, dear? Oh, very good. (*She crosses "Tim rake" off her list*)

Hal I don't want the rake back! I want my pal back!

Tim Hal! For God's sake! Don't make Wendy make me say something to you!

Penny (*Still to camera*) Robbie got this trophy for making fire using only pretzels and a human hair.

Arabic music begins to emanate from Hal's knee. Hal steals camera focus from Penny.

Hal They put a plate in my knee, America! I still get Al-Jazeera on it! Can't understand a word but I got the feelin' our great nation's getting in deeper and deeper shit, man!

Wendy Tim, he's out of control! Do something!

Tim Like what?

Having to do everything herself as usual, Wendy jumps toward Hal wielding something threatening. Hal runs out the door.

Wendy Diane, I'm back, hi! Tim, over here! Penny, over here! Penny!

Penny *(Whispers to camera)* I'll miss you forever.

Family reforms tableau for the camera. Camera lights shine on the family again.

Wendy Hi, Diane. So sorry about that. I was just going to say…

Hal pops his head through doggie flap again.

Hal That Robbie is bones, and cartilage, and person dust drifting off in a foreign land.

Tim/Penny *(Horrified)* Hal!

Wendy *(Still smiling though shaken by what Hal said)* No. No, I was going to say we know Robbie is fine, and we still believe the conflict is noble and just.

Penny Just what?

Hal Poor Walker family. My poor smiling, Walkers.

Hal exits. We hear Al-Jazeera walk away as Hal walks away.

Wendy A sure way to fail over there, Diane—to fail ourselves and the people who need us, to fail democracy—is to quit. So we will never quit believing. We must stand firm in order for justice to prevail. Right, Tim?

Tim No doubt. Already there was a banner. A dictator in a tiny hole. My son was saved! /

Penny Saved!

Tim And yet, and yet sometimes, I wonder /

Wendy It's ok, Tim. No wondering. Never wondering.

Tim I know, Wendy. It's just it's been a year since my boy was saved. Why isn't he home?

Carlos dressed in a slick suit, Robbie pin, and bloody wad of tissue on his nicked chin, knocks rapidly and anxiously on the door. He realizes about the tissue and removes it.

Carlos Walker family! Walker family! What are you doing, Walker family?

Wendy Yay, Carlos! It's Carlos! That's Carlos.

Tim notices his wife's great enthusiasm for Carlos. He doesn't love it.

Carlos Hey there! Can I come in por favor?

Wendy Hi Carlos! We're on TV!

Carlos lets himself into their house.

Carlos Yeah! I saw in the hotel bar!

Tim *(To Carlos)* You have a key?

Hal tries to barge back inside behind Carlos.

Hal Ramrod of truth!

Carlos Not now, Hal!

Carlos shuts the door on Hal and locks it. Then, remembering he's being watched by America, Carlos salutes Hal via the window in the door.

I mean American hero! I salute you!

Hal spits at him. Spit hits the window. Carlos pulls down curtain on window. Hal exits. Al-Jazeera trails behind him. Carlos whips his ear piece out and talks to Diane—his personal connection to the media. He's smooth.

Carlos Hello, Diane. Hello, America. Carlos Sanchez, U-S-A-F-A-L-O-C-O: US Armed Forces Administrative Liaison Outreach to Civilian Operations. Working to better relations within and without the world. To the lay person or regular Joe, and I consider myself one of those Joes having served two tours of duty and having a father who was a bricklayer or something, that means I keep the Walkers in the loop-dee-loop as we folks in the administration work feverishly to bring their, well make that, *our* sons, home. Say that ten times fast, huh?

Wendy Very good, Carlos. Isn't that good, Tim? Tim?

Tim *(Distracted by TV)* What?

Penny *(Fascinated by Carlos because he's a man)* He's sweaty.

Carlos So how's things Diane? How's shrimpin' today?

He laughs. Then they all laugh really hard at this joke they pretend to get.

Inside joke, guys.

They abruptly stop laughing.

Wendy Diane, Carlos has been our guardian angel, no our *man* angel, during all of this.

Tim *(Oozing dislike for Carlos)* Or maybe a fairy.

Carlos Well, I don't know about man angel, Wendy. Or fairy, Tim. Maybe more of an elf in the workshop.

Penny *(Excited)* Elf? Then you have shoes of stealth, mastery over equine, and a heart so pure?

Wendy Penny. TV. Normal.

Carlos Pardon, Diane?...No, Diane. The administration has no comment on the Walker's rescued missing son. *(Gets call on cell—says without pauses)* Sanchez. Yes. No. Yes. *(Hangs up)* Other than this. On behalf of the administration and myself I am proud to tell you, Walker family and America, that Robbie is coming home!

All What?

Carlos Yes! I was waiting for a more private moment but since you went on TV without getting my approval, not that you should have, yes! Tomorrow morning Robbie will be in your arms. I kid you not! It's real! Thanksgiving indeed!

The next few lines can overlap so it's happy hubbub.

Tim Alive? Alive? Oh my god. Am I dreaming? The cameras are here so it must be real!

Wendy Robbie! Robbie! I knew it! Oh Carlos, you did it! Carlos did it!

Penny Oh wonder! Oh wonder wonder wonder wonder wonder!

All jump around in group hug as Carlos talks to camera. Wendy is especially clingy with Carlos. Tim notices this.

Carlos It is, Diane. It really is. There is understandably a lot of red tape. He must submit to a brief debriefing, but tomorrow morning… *(To family)* Yay! I know! *(Back to Diane)* But tomorrow… *(To family)* Yay! Hugs! *(To Diane)* Tomorrow, Diane, will bring proof that our heroes were not forgotten, or ever in that much peril, or boxed up and buried in the night. We'll start rotating a bunch home and then you'll see. Happy ending indeed…Well, I can't speak for the Walkers, but they say "no" Diane. You may not televise Robbie's homecoming tomorrow. It's going to be an intensely emotional moment, so I don't think they care to televise it. Plus they need closure. And the Pentagon has determined that closure officially takes one year or more.

Wendy It's fine! Televise us tomorrow! It'll be National Robbie Day!

Carlos No no, Wendy, you're just being intensely emotional…No, Diane, I told you it's not a good idea to come tomorrow. *(Using code with Diane)* Shrimpin's not good today.

Wendy It's fine! All the world should celebrate Robbie! Thumbs up, guys! Do it!

They all do thumbs up.

Carlos Well, ok then, tomorrow it is! *(Sarcastic)* Oh thank *you*, Diane! And Diane, dear? I wouldn't buy that gown for the President's ball just yet. I'm just saying. Say goodbye, Walkers!

All Goodbye, Walkers!

All laugh and wave. Camera lights shut off. Hubbub from the Walkers.

Carlos Yay! So happy for you, Walkers! It'll be a long night. I'll order food. *(On his cell, all business—no pauses)* Sanchez. Status Six. Code red. I need a delivery. *(This is code)* White rice asap.

Carlos goes into a corner to talk furtively on his cell.

Tim Alive! Alive! I can't wait to hear his voice! And oh! Smell that baby smell of his! Oh gosh, I'm afraid to believe it!

Wendy Not me. I knew he was alive. If he were gone, I'd feel it. I'd feel like my heart was missing, my nerves exposed. I'd be all pain. But I never felt that. I always felt his life running through my veins. I always felt his life in mine. So let yourselves feel the joy! It's real! At ease, family! At ease!

Tim Yes, sir! Joy reporting for duty, sir!

Tim salutes Wendy while doing a happy heel-click kick in the air.

Penny Joy doth visit Middle earth. *(Plays air harp)* Weeeeeeeeer!

Tim pulls Wendy to him and kisses her with passion. It's been a long time since he did that. Penny squeals with delight at her parents' affection. Wendy pulls away.

Wendy Tim! Carlos is watching!

They look at Carlos on the corner on his cell.

Carlos *(On cell)* I need white rice asap! Christ! *(Sees family watching)* ... is the greatest.

Tim We're back and better than ever! Man, I feel like singing. I feel like singing!

Wendy So let's do it! It's about time! Let's sing!

Penny *(Sings operatically from "Carmen")* Toreadora!

Wendy Not that! Let's sing Robbie's song! *(Sings)* "This train is bound for glory…"

Tim/Penny/Wendy *(Singing together in Gospel fashion)* "This train is bound for glory. This train is bound for glory, children get on board. No more weepin' and a wailin'! *(Penny starts singing off-key)* No more weepin' and a wailin'!"

Wendy Ouch. A little flat. Who was flat on Robbie's song?

Penny *(Beat)* Sorry, Mama. I'll go Elsewhere. *(She looks off and quickly puts her mind Elsewhere)* Sunshine.

Wendy hugs Penny. Penny is thrilled to get a hug from her. It brings her back from Elsewhere.

Wendy No, don't go Elsewhere, darling. Stay here. I love you. I'm sorry. Sometimes I'm just so desperate for everything to be perfect.

Penny Oh, Mama, I know! Oh, Mama!

Tim pulls them both to him and spins them around.

Tim My girls!

Wendy And who cares if you sing like hell, Penny, cuz Robbie's coming home!

All Yeah!

Wendy I know! Let's throw a party for Robbie! I'll make all his favorites. *(Making her list)* Tacos, strawberry Kool-Aid.

Tim And we can play some ball! Go wide, son! *(Weeps)* Go wide.

Penny comforts him.

Wendy Yes! Let's do it! It'll be a bit improvised, but let's be crazy!

Wendy crosses "Let's be crazy" off her list whispering as she does it "Let's be crazy."

Penny Yes! You make a feast, Mama! And I'll wear my sweet sixteen dress that I never got to wear cuz there was no party. And Daddy will do, you know, whatever Daddy does well. Daddy you do something well, I know it!

Wendy Well, watching TV won't help that much.

Beat. Is she insulting him? Then she laughs. Big relief. They all laugh.

Tim I can do other stuff. I used to be good at lots of stuff. Hey, Mommy loved me on that ball field. Five seconds on the clock, the snap to Walker, and the crowd goes wild! Go long, Wend!

Tim throws a cushion to Wendy but it hits Penny in the face instead. Penny goes on merrily, without so much as a pause, as if she's hit in the face with a pillow every day.

Geez. Sorry, Pen. That always / happens.

Penny And I'll put up my famous paper flowers that you think make me seem retarded, Mama. And oh, should we hang Christmas lights, Mama? Mama?

Wendy *(Not listening to Penny as usual)* I know! Let's break out the Christmas cheer! Hang Christmas lights! Light up the sky for Robbie!

Penny Good idea, Mama. And should we make a sign so the neighbors know to come?

Wendy *(As if it's her idea)* Oh! And we should put up a sign about the party! We want a crowd to celebrate our boy!

Penny You always have the best ideas, Mama.

Tim I'll make that sign! Grab me some markers, Penny Bird. Some bright ones. I can do this! I am alive! I can do things!

Tim draws. Penny puts up paper flowers. Wendy follows behind and removes them. Penny puts up decorations. Wendy rearranges them so they're more perfect.

Penny I hope all the new neighbors come! We hardly know them. Like Ms. Weird Turban who moved in next door. And Ethnic Guy. We never asked their names.

Tim Whatever happened to Darkish Girl across the street? *(With lust)* She was interesting.

Penny There's Ms. Weird Turban now! *(Out door)* Ms. Weird Turban! My brother is coming home tomorrow! Come to our party? Well… *(Makes a "fuck you" gesture back to Ms. Weird Turban thinking it's an ethnic "hello")* …to you too! See you at the party!

Tim Ta da! Done! Whaddya think, Wend?

Tim proudly shows Wendy his sign.

Wendy Great job, Tim. If I could just fix one thing.

She rips it up and starts her own sign. Carlos in the corner…

Carlos *(On cell angrily—speaking in codes)* No! The table is set. The people are hungry. *(Whispers)* Diane is coming. I need *white rice* for tomorrow or else…Really? The eagle flies. *(Hangs up)* Walker family! I just got official word.

Tim Robbie's not coming. I knew it.

Wendy Tim!

Carlos No, Tim, he's coming. In fact, he's coming any minute.

They hoot again. There is hubbub as Carlos talks.

Now before he gets here, quickly now, Penny put the air harp away, just a brief briefing. I know we're all happy and will be so forever, but we must remember that Robbie has been through a lot. And even though it's a good war it's been a little roughish on Robbie. He's been exposed to some baddish violence, to a series of new but probably safeish vaccinations, and maybe some benignish blistering agents.

They gasp.

Not to worry. He's still got ten fingers and tenish toes.

They sigh a sigh of relief.

But he may be slightly altered. Hardish times do funny things to people. I know. When I was a bebe, I traveled here with mi Mamacita y Papacita from our beloved Mexican town of Ohyesican with dirty /

Tim *(Not caring)* Dirty coyotes, we know. So tragic.

Wendy Tim! He's sharing.

Tim, wanting to get away, gets up and puts the sign for the party on their door. Wendy mouths what Carlos says having heard it so often. Penny mouths something else entirely, no one knows what—maybe she mouths what he says in her secret language.

Carlos Mamacita y Papacita loved Estados Unodos so much they tunneled under a fence, staggered through the Arizona desert, suffered unbearable thirst, and circling buzzards to get me here.

Penny I'm never going to Arizona.

Carlos We arrived scorched, prone to despair, and calling people "mamí." And I wondered "was it worth it?" But mis parentes said, "America is home of the free and the brave. Never forsake it, never forsake our hopes." And then they died. But with that flame to light my way, and light my way it has, I devoted myself ever after to this great land and yes, it was. Worth it. So in short, if Robbie seems "different," do no act alarmed, or make him feel unloved, because he, like me, he needs time. To heal. And remember, no matter what, he is always your…

Doorbell rings.

All Robbie!

They open the door. They jump all over Robbie, kiss him, hug him. When they climb off of him we see that Robbie is Asian. They are stunned. He is in fatigues and has a duffle bag that says "Walker."

Robbie It's so good to be home! Home to 2040 Dylane Drive! Phone 938-6542! Zip code 46431!

Carlos *(Gets on cell—shocked and angry)* You sent me egg roll? There's no more white rice?!

Robbie Hello dent in the door from dad's bowling ball. Remember, Pops? Go wide! Hello tall wall!

He stands near Robbie's last recorded height on the tall wall and is shorter or taller than it.

Hello, plants, Frodo and Samwise, characters from my favorite book! I love to read! Other books by JRRR Tolkien, *The Hobbit*, *The Lord of the*

Rings, and *The Ring of the*, the… *(Forgets—moves on)* Hello, house! It's me! Strong, brave, integrity-laden etcetera etcetera me! Mom, you cut your hair! Dad, you've still got that mole. You should maybe have that checked out. Penny, your braces are gone! On your teeth too! Ooh! You've got Nintendo? Does this chair recline? *(He reclines)* Sweet!

Carlos This is simply a coping mechanism, Walkers, reeling off facts from long-term memory. It's a way of making himself believe this is real. Totally normal.

Robbie Oh! I want to drink it all in! Drink it in like my favorite drink strawberry Kool-Aid. Remember when mom told me "cool it on the Kool-Aid" and us and Harv /

Carlos *(Correcting him)* Hal.

Robbie Hal, our neighbor Hal, our neighbor Hal, thought that was so funny we laughed till we peed our pants, our matching corduroy pants. My favorite wizard is Merlin. Hello, tablecloth. Hello, chair. Hello, loose change.

He pockets their loose change. He sees photo of the real Robbie. He loses himself in it momentarily.

Hello, you. *(Regains himself)* Meaning hello me!

Carlos begins taking photos of Robbie and the family from the wall. There are bright yellow squares on the wall beneath each one where the paint has not yet faded.

Hello, home! Oh my home! Oh my family! Accept me! Love me!

He holds out his arms. They all stand there shocked and silent.

Mom? Dad? Penny? Maybe I, yeah. Maybe I should just go. Go quickly.

Robbie tries to flee. Carlos pulls Robbie back.

Carlos *(Threateningly)* Don't run away, Robbie. You know that only leads to pain and more pain. So to speak. Now Walkers. Remember Arizona. Remember love.

Tim But I thought you said he was ok-ish, Carlos. I thought you said he was ok!

Tim slams his hand down. Hearing this loud noise, truly scarred by war, Robbie takes cover.

Robbie Take cover!

Carlos This *is* okay, Tim. You don't want to see what not okay looks like.

Robbie It's okay, Señor Sanchez. I understand. I'm different, huh? My face changed. My eyes got weird. I have shrapnel in my body that pops to the surface now and then.

He pulls a piece of metal shrapnel from his neck and plops it in a cup. We hear it clink.

I don't blame you for recoiling from me like I'm Dracula, *(Listing facts by rote)* my favorite scary movie followed by Poltergeist and The Omen.

Penny You're no monster!

Penny touches his face. She and Robbie both feel a romantic charge. Upon feeling this totally new and unexpected sensation she jumps back.

Tingly, tingly!

Robbie Hello. You're cute up close.

Robbie steps toward Penny. Carlos pulls him away from Penny.

Carlos Whatever gasses that mad man sprayed in the air over there, it appears to swell the body. Causes edema, leukocytoclastic Asiaitis.

Wendy Asiaitis?

Robbie *(Whispers to Penny)* Do you like movies?

Carlos The ocular area seems to be most affected.

Tim What about his skin? That's not the right color.

Robbie Yeah. It got all tinted and wrong.

Carlos A side effect, Tim, of the iodine pills and parasites in the water supply. It's surprising but totally harmless. He should revert to his familiar shade in no time. And I'll talk to Diane about putting a blur on Robbie's face tomorrow. For security reasons, not because you're hideous, or Asian. My accountant's Asian. I like him a lot.

Tim He's really different.

Carlos Yes, he got me a ha-uge refund this year. Oh, you mean Robbie.

Robbie I was afraid of this, Señor Sanchez. I should just go pick shrapnel out of my decimated body somewhere else.

Robbie pulls a piece of metal shrapnel from his arm and throws it. We hear it hit the floor. He starts to exit.

Penny/Tim/Wendy *(Desperately)* No!

Wendy approaches Robbie cautiously and gently touches his crewcut hair. She gasps.

Wendy *(Cautiously)* It's his same hair. Definitely the same color, same hair-like texture and everything.

Robbie Except more stylish, right Mama? Not!

Wendy laughs.

Penny He made you laugh, Mama. Only Robbie could do that.

Tim But his voice is different. It's gravelier.

Wendy Is it?

Penny Is it?

Robbie Yes, I uh. I uh.

He tries to think of a lie to cover for this fact. He turns to Carlos.

Carlos Uh oh. They caught us, Rob. The truth is…he started smoking.

They gasp.

Robbie Yeah, I started smoking. I admit it. A filthy habit. I'll try to stop. But hey, I don't think it's affected my singing voice any. Let's see. *(Sings)* "This train is bound for glory! This train is bound for…Mommy!" Oh, mommy!

Wendy Oh, Robbie! It's Robbie! Oh my boy! Sing the rest of it.

Robbie *(Not knowing the rest)* That's ok! Let's not use up all the happiness now! Oh mommy!

Wendy hugs him and cries. She pulls a piece of metal shrapnel out of his neck and drops it in a mug—we hear it clink in the mug. Robbie turns to Penny and holds his arms out to her, wanting her acceptance.

Sis?

Penny He does have that same smiley. Same smiley that can light up the sky. Send shivers through your body from head to… *(She quickly goes Elsewhere)* Daffodils.

Robbie steps toward Penny. Carlos stops him again. Robbie removes one of Penny's trademark paper flowers from his pocket. Still trying to win her back.

Robbie Penny? It never wilted. Even in that heat. I was so glad you sent it to me. I read it a lot. *(Recites from memory as it really did touch him)* "Born of the earth I quickly fade. Yet lovely while living, uniquely made." Penny? Eflewan thisla, Penny. Gwitheni, ditten frittle dee. Frittle dah.

Penny Frittle dah, Robbie. Frittle dah. Oh Robbie!

They hug. They are deeply attracted to each other. Penny feels things she never felt before.

Robbie Oh, that feels really nice.

Penny Really, really nice. Tingly. Tingly. Pringly. Tingly!

She starts to wrap her legs around him reflexively. Carlos pulls Robbie off of Penny. While hugging her, Robbie has stolen Penny's necklace. He pockets it. Penny has taken a piece of metal shrapnel out of Robbie's neck and drops it into the mug—we hear it clink in the mug. Robbie turns to Tim. Time to win him back. This is his duty.

Robbie Dada?

Wendy Tim. Be open.

Robbie Dada? Can I have that hug you promised? Remember? When I left, you said "Come back to us. Come back to us alive and I'll never let you go again."

Tim gasps and hugs him. Robbie steals Tim's wallet while they hug. He is still in survivor mode from being over there.

Tim Oh Robbie! I've got ya now, son! I've got ya! See, I never broke a promise, did I?

Robbie Remember how you also promised me a Saab? That meant you loved me.

Carlos Robbie! Now now.

Tim Of course I remember! Of course! I'll uh, just uh sell something, something big. And then we'll go shopping next week!

Robbie Thanks, Dada. I feel better already. Whiter even. I'm healing!

Tim Hey, but you better not be a bad driver now that you're Asian, ok?

Offended, Robbie lunges at Tim. Carlos holds him back.

Wendy Tim! That's not funny anymore!

Carlos Yes, Tim. Please know we men of color are sensitive at heart. Even if we've only recently acquired it. You should sensitize too. Es mucho major.

Tim Oh, I'm so sorry. I'll learn. I'll get better. We'll all get better together, son. My son! My boy! Wasn't sure you'd be back. Wasn't sure. *(Smells Robbie's neck)* Same baby smell. Yep! Yep! Same Baby Robbie smell. Oh, Robbie!

Tim pulls a piece of metal shrapnel from somewhere on Robbie's body and drops it into the mug. We hear it clink.

Wendy Don't worry about your Asiatus, son. We don't care what you look like. We love you. We are you. You are us.

Wendy puts chopsticks in her hair, flip flops on over her socks so she looks/walks kind of "Asian." This is the first of many transformations she and the family will make to fit the Robbie lie.

We are one person. Under God.

Wendy/Tim/Penny Indivisible. With liberty and justice for all!

Penny *(Launches into a poem—truly moved and moving)* Come to our shores disguised as another, beneath beats the heart, the blood / of my brother!

Wendy *(Interrupting Penny as usual)* Hey! Let's sing Robbie's favorite song! One more time!

Wendy/Tim/Penny *(Sing)* "This train is…"

Robbie *(Jumping in with his favorite song and gestures to match)* "Ooh that dress so scandalous, and you know another niggah can't handle it. So you shakin' that thang like who's the ish. Thong, thong, thong…"

Carlos Robbie! The train song is your favorite song! Not the "Thong Song."

Robbie Well, she said my favorite song, dude! *(Carlos gives him a look)* Sorry.

Wendy No, no, he's right. Where's my head? That was his favorite song. Come on, Gang! Let's do it!

They sing and dance to "Thong Song"—transforming again to fit the lie in their midst.

All *(Sing)* "Ooh that dress so scandalous, and you know another ni / *(They stop at this word. Beat. They start)* You know another ni can't handle it…"

As they keep singing and doing gestures to match:

Carlos Ok! So happy for you, Walkers. Let me give you some closure time…

Carlos exits as they keep singing. Half-second beat. He returns.

How's that closure comin'?

Carlos claps his hands to punctuate the sentence. Again, hearing this loud sound, Robbie takes cover.

Robbie Get down!

They notice Robbie has collapsed. They all run to him.

All Robbie!

Robbie *(Truly upset)* Oh god! The world!

Wendy Mama here, Robbie. Mama here. Feel Mama hand.

Robbie Please don't touch me! Please don't, please please. I don't want to feel! I don't want to feel anything!

Tim What's going on?

Carlos Uh so this is a typical combat stress reaction called WCS, Wussie Crying Syndrome. *(Threatening)* Robbie. Remember you are with family. Remember. Remember.

Robbie I *am* remembering! I'm remembering it all! I wish I could forget!

Carlos Robbie. You don't want to go to the van for M-H-M again, do you? "Mental Health Maintenance?"

Robbie abruptly stops crying. He looks scared.

Everything ok, Hero?

Robbie No everything not ok. Everything super terrific number one son ok!

Hal enters through the doggie flap. He sees Robbie.

Hal Ah man, you ordered Chinese food? And you didn't tell me?

Carlos Hal! Crap. *(Mutters to Robbie)* Plan Dos.

Thinking Plan Dos is to suffocate someone, Robbie grabs a pillow to suffocate Hal.

No! Plan *Dos*!

Robbie grabs two pillows now and goes for Hal.

No! Plan *Dos*! DOS!

Thinking this is Plan Dos Dos, Robbie starts doing a Latin dance.

No, that's plan Tango. Nevermind! *(Change of tactics)* Hal, great to see you, but you have to go, son. I don't want you to excite Robbie. He could have a cerebral chow fun at any moment. *(Mutters to Robbie)* Chow fun.

Robbie Chow fun? Oh right. *(Grabs heart)* Oh my fragile heart! I'm grabbing it!

Family goes to him. Penny touches him. She and Robbie get a romantic charge. Robbie is entranced with her now.

You smell like cherries.

Penny *(Backing off)* Tingly. / Tingly.

Carlos Oh no! Robbie's having a chow fun right now! You better go, neighbor.

Hal What's going on?

Robbie Oh my good friend Harv!

If Robbie calls him Harv, then the family thinks his name must be Harv. No lie can be denied now or the biggest lie of all, that this is Robbie, will unravel. Robbie hugs Hal.

Hal Hey, get off me, Dude! What the fuck?

Wendy Shame on you, Harv!

Hal Harv?

Wendy Treating Robbie that way.

Hal What are you talking about?

Tim This is Robbie, Harv. Don't you want to welcome your best bud home?

Hal Robbie? Robbie? Robbie wasn't Chinese. He rode a bike but that was about the extent of it.

Robbie, Tim, Wendy, and Penny lunge at Hal finding this insulting. Carlos restrains them.

Carlos Harv! How dare you challenge Robbie when he has gone from fighting for his country to fighting for his life! When his illness makes him look Asian and yet he is not so good at math!

Robbie *(Recites by rote)* 680 verbal. 460 math.

Wendy/Tim A disappointment.

Carlos Do you understand the prejudices out there? The ridicule? And you call yourself a patriot!

Hal You're shitting me, right? Am I on some reality show? "Fool the Vet?" Is Diane here or something? Diane? / America?

Wendy Quiet, Harv! We're healing! And we've got a party to plan. Tell him, Tim!

Tim Yeah!

Carlos Well said, Tim. Now for your own good, Harv, please leave and don't return until morning TV is over tomorrow.

Hal Oh, Carlos. Evil doth lurk in the heart of man, eh? *(To Robbie)* Evil doth lurk.

Robbie *(To Hal)* Don't look at me. Don't look at me! I can't take it!

Penny This is Robbie, Harv. He was changed by the chemicals in the air. Parasites in the water.

Hal *I* drank that water. *I* breathed that air. The only parasite I see here is you, Carlos.

Carlos War affects everyone differently, Harv.

Hal You're being fooled, Walkers. You are blinded by despair!

Robbie *(Sing songy, under breath to Hal)* Not good. Not good. Don't do this.

Penny He knows what pants we wore, Harv. He knows his favorite books and Kool-Aid.

Robbie Robbie Walker. Born: 8/02/87. Died…never.

Hal So he knows a few details? So what? I know that stuff too. Maybe Robbie kept a diary. Maybe he spilled his life story to someone. People do that when they want to live on, man. They want their insides out before they're blasted a million directions.

Penny But he knows our childhood language! Lai kenju hasfeth tiswa Robbiel.

Hal Oh yeah? *(To Robbie)* Ai tiswa hasfeth, Robbiel?

Carlos Now is not the time to be a dweeb, / Harv.

Hal Ai tiswa hasfeth? Ai tiswa hasfeth?

Robbie *(Guessing)* Uh friddle dee? *(Carlos kicks him)* Friddleda!

Hal Friddle dee? Friddle dee? That makes no sense at all! I mean come on! You might as well say niny foo! Or jakamond! Don't fall for this, Walkers! It's smoke and mirrors! It's all a distraction!

Carlos Or is it? Abracazam!

Carlos makes a flash of magic fire appear. They are indeed distracted by it.

Wendy/Penny/Tim Ooh!

Hal If you're Robbie, *Robbie*, who were your friends then? Name some of our old friends!

Robbie Ok! Ok! I saw Gina uh… *(Sees sofa)* Sofa…berg on the way here. By the uh building we loved.

Carlos Sofaberg? *(Gets on cell—to HQ)* I said they must have an improv background! *(Hangs up)*

Hal Give me a break! What about *(makes up equally ridiculous name)* Door McWall? He was nice too.

Wendy Oh yes. Gina and Door had such a crush on Robbie. But then who didn't?

Penny I don't, that's who!

Hal There's no Door McWall! That's a made up name too!

Tim *(To Hal)* You never liked Door.

Robbie Too bad it didn't work out with Gina. We Jews have to stick together.

Carlos *(Aside to Robbie)* Harv's Jewish. *He* is. Not you guys.

If Robbie says they're Jewish then they're Jewish.

Wendy No, he's right. We Jews have to stick together. Cuz we're Jewish as Robbie says. If that's Robbie, and Robbie's Jewish, then we're Jewish. So. Yo!

Carlos *(Mutters)* Oy.

Wendy Oy!

They start to act and sound like what they think is "Jewish," transforming yet again to fit the lie started by Robbie. Another lie to insulate themselves in. Wendy puts a doily from the sofa on her head, as do Tim and Penny.

Tim I had a shtinkle I was a shmarty!

Wendy Wasn't Gina Sofaberg the goil who poished you around at scoil, Penelah?

Penny You'll haf to be more shpeshific.

Wendy I'll see if we have any chicken fat for the shiksa mix. *(Sings to "If I Were a Rich Man")* Diddle diddle diddle diddle diddle diddle diddle dim sum.

Hal *(Overlapping her singing)* You are not Jewish! Your blood type is ham!

Robbie Bite your tongue! And put a tiddle of mustard on it! *(To Carlos)* Don't tell me I don't do improv man! I can do improv!

Wendy produces food, Kool-Aid, cups.

Hal Jews don't drink Kool-Aid!

Wendy Sit and eat! Skin and bones you are. A character I am!

Penny *(Sings from "Yentle")* Mama can you hear me?

Tim What for is to hear? Who needs it?

Penny / Robbie *(Harmonize)* Mama can you see me?

Hal This is insane!

Tim *(To Penny)* See you, I can.

Wendy You're not Yoda, Tim!

Robbie and Penny stare at each other.

Robbie I see you. Oh, do I see you, Sis!

Penny *(Like she's seeing fireworks—continuing the "sis")* Boom bah!

Hal Don't see her! Don't touch her!

Wendy Oy! I think I poiled a gezoinkt! Help me to the soifa, Tim, if you can be bothered.

Tim Sit. Watch TV. I think we get it for free since I hear we run the media.

Hal You are not Jewish! Look at your Christmas decorations!

Hal points to a drawing of Santa with a bag that says "toys" they hung up earlier. Carlos crosses out the "t" so it says "oys."

Am I in a fucking fun house? I'll list the churches you went to!

Tim The list is life. Lehymie!

All lift cups of Kool-Aid. Wendy pulls a tiny bottle of vodka from her apron and downs it. Tim sees this.

Wendy must be a thoid Irish!

Wendy *(Angry)* It's just a little boittle!

Tim Still Wendy, this is a proiblem.

Hal I swear on my mother's grave, Walkers! On her beloved heart and soul, this is not Robbie!

All stop in their tracks…could he be right?

Robbie *(Mutters to Hal)* Don't do this.

Penny He swore on his mother. He swore on his dearest of deadest mothers.

Wendy But if he weren't Robbie I'd feel it. I'd feel like the sky was falling. Is the sky falling?

Hal Yes! The sky is falling! The world is crashing in on us! Feel it!

Carlos Ignore him! He's just, he's just, he's just all like, he's just… jealous!

Hal Jealous? Jealous of what?

Carlos Of Robbie's, of Robbie's big, his big… *(Changing tactics)* He's a racist! Don't listen to the racist spewing poison! *(Gets on cell)* Code red.

Tim We don't listen to racists spewing poison! The way you assumed he was the delivery guy!

Hal *(To Robbie)* Sorry, man. Not a lot of Asians here.

Tim You probably even say the word "ni!"

Family gasps.

Carlos So un-American. So anti-veteran.

Hal *I'm* a veteran!

Carlos And I salute you.

Carlos salutes Hal. Hal knocks Carlos's hand down angrily.

OMG! He's violent! He's crazy! Don't listen to him.

Hal I am not!

Carlos pushes Hal down so he has flashback and thus seems crazy. Hal is in real terror.

Is that a candy? Is that a candy? That's no candy!

Wendy See! You're violent and crazy! We're not listening to your lies!

Hal grabs Penny.

Hal Penny, back me up here, Honey. Back me up!

Carlos Molestation! I'm seeing it!

Penny I've been molested?

Carlos Does he touch you in a funny way?

Penny When he tickles me, that feels funny.

They all gasp.

I feel dirty!

Wendy Oh my little girl! Touched in places. This explains so much about you! A shaina!

Carlos Yeah! Don't listen to him. He's a violent, crazy, predator.

Hal I'm telling you the truth!

Robbie I have to say something!

Carlos covers Robbie's mouth or does something to shut him up.

Tim We're not listening to you, violent crazy predator! Go! Go on! Go molest someone else's kid!

Carlos It must be the drugs.

Carlos pulls a pill bottle out of Hal's pocket.

Hal Hey, that's for my allergies.

Carlos *(Reading bottle)* "Heroin pills." He's a heroin user.

Family gasps.

Hal It does not say heroin pills. Show them!

Carlos Druggie! Drug pusher! Druggist!

Wendy/Tim/Penny Pharmacist! Let's stop the pharmacists!

Carlos Protect the children!

Wendy/Tim/Penny Protect us!

Carlos throws the bottle of pills out the door for Hal to fetch.

Hal My Allegra!

Carlos "My Alla.' He said "my Allah." He's an Allah lover.

Wendy/Tim/Penny Allah lover!

Carlos He's dangerous.

Wendy/Tim/Penny *(Step toward Hal)* Danger!

Robbie *(Mutters to Hal)* Play along, play along.

Hal Dig your own grave, with the shovel he gave, man. Not I!

Hal picks shrapnel from his body and throws it at Robbie. Robbie does the same to Hal. They keep doing this. They have a shrapnel fight.

Carlos He's trying to kill Robbie! Defend thine son, Walkers! Defend him from the…

Wendy/Penny/Tim Terrorist!

Carlos Oh my gosh, I hadn't thought of that but yes, terrorist! Terrorist in the house!

Hal Terrorist? I played wizard in your yard. I ate your apple pie! *(To Tim)* You played ball with me on your lawn.

Tim I did? Was I good?

Wendy Tim!

Hal You were a hero! You were Robbie's hero before! Before all this! Robbie was my hero! See me! I'm your neighbor Harv!

Wendy Wait a minute. Our neighbor's name was Hal, terrorist! Get your story straight!

Penny Oh my god! Terrorist!

Tim He was too different with that mustache and that angry face. I knew it wasn't Hal. To say this isn't Robbie! To say that I was my son's hero. *(Beat—he wants to cry but he keeps in control)* Our Hal would never hurt us like that! Our Hal loved us!

Hal I love you! I love you! *(Al-Jazeera sings from Hal's knee)* Oh shit.

Carlos They're sending him messages! Get him! At least get him as far as the curb. *(Gets on cell)* Van. Stand by.

Robbie *(To Hal)* Not the van, Dude.

Hal jumps on the table to escape them as they encroach on his space.

Hal Walkers! The devil drapes himself in the flag to cover his flames and says all who look beneath shall burn! But an angel lets our flag fly, so its stripes, its stars, give us all repose! It hides nothing. Truth is exposed. It's beautiful. Painful but beautiful for it will set you free! Feel the pain, Walkers. It's in your brain! Let it rain!

Robbie The van is coming so for your sake shut up!

Hal You will never shut me up! *(Sings in high-pitch heavy-metal fashion)* Nevah! *(Singing ends)* I am gonna sing about this 'til everyone hears the truth! Victoriath e Robbie! I'll sing it to Diane! To the world! I'll be back with an army!

Carlos Cool! But first, may I have a word with you inside my darkened van?

Hal You may have a word with the authorities, Carlos, inside your dirty, filthy conscience! Cuz it is my duty as a proud American to call a spade a spade!

Carlos As a man of color, a Latino man, I resent that.

Hal gets out of the door and as he runs away…

Hal God Bless Ameri /

Carlos *(On cell)* Now.

Hal *(As he's abducted offstage)* Ach!

Silence. They open the door. They all see Hal has vanished.

Robbie Holy shit.

Carlos *(Also a little scared)* Oh boy.

Penny Where'd he go?

Carlos I, I'm not sure.

Tim Americach? God bless Americach? What's Americach?

Carlos *(Recovering)* Clearly it's Arabic. But don't worry. He won't be back. I alerted officials to his malfeasance and he is now in the custody of los Estados Unedididos.

Carlos begins to caulk the doggie flap shut.

No one will climb in or out of this doggie door anymore. We are a safe, happy family again.

Tim We?

Wendy Oh my god. A terrorist in our house! Can you believe?

Robbie *(Looks at Carlos with new fear)* No joke.

Wendy Thank god for Carlos. Carlos saves the day again!

Penny But but but I didn't see any officials out there. I saw a black van lurking and then he was gone…

Carlos *(Changing the subject—playing on more of their lurking fears)* You saw a black man lurking? Nobody panic!

Wendy and Tim panic.

Wendy Panic? Why would we panic?

Penny No! I saw a black van, black *van*, and then the impostor disappeared.

Carlos I was afraid of this, Walkers. There is a black man lurking. I'm sure he's lovely and wears colorful comfy sweaters, but still.

Tim Maybe we should sing him "The Thong Song" so he feels at home.

Robbie Wow, Dad.

Penny There was no black man! There was a black van! And it appeared and the terrorist pharmacist disappeared.

Robbie Shh, Penny. No more talking. Just listen to Carlos.

Wendy Penny. You must not have seen right. You know that eye of yours.

Penny But if that's not Hal, where is he? Is he missing? Should we alert the police, or maybe tell Diane tomorrow?

Carlos No, Penny. Hal is fine. In fact here he is now… *(On cell)* Now.

On cue Hal's replacement, Hal2, barges through the door. He is Arab and has an obviously fake mustache to match Hal's. He talks a bit as if he's reading lines. He is only a kid, maybe eighteen. He is adorable.

Hal2 Oh my god! Robbie! My best bud. Dy. It's really you!

Hal2 grabs a handful of loose change and pockets it. He too is in survival mode.

Carlos *(On cell—angry, wearying of this)* Now you're sending me hummus? You're importing hummus from over there? Shouldn't hummus be…in the crisper?

Hal2 It is me, guys. And gals for I must be PC! It's me Hal! Not some Islamic, Arabic impostor. Hi.

Carlos *(On cell)* What about our black beans or our pinto beans?

Robbie Dude, those were the first to go.

Hal2 *(To Carlos)* I am Hal! I like the rock. And the roll. Ooh, is that a Rubik's cube?

Hal2 grabs the Rubik's Cube and starts working it.

I live next door. My mother is dead. My lawn is dead. *(Solves Rubik's Cube)* Ooh, food! *(He ravenously eats Wendy's chips)* We had secret language. Friddle dee friddle… *(Sees Penny)* Hello! You are a young lady!

Hal2 lunges at Penny lustily or maybe just because he's lonely and scared and she seems harmless and safe. Robbie pushes him away.

Robbie Hands off!

Hal2 Ok! Sure thing! She is unclean. Oh god, look at your mug, Robbie man. Asiatics, huh man? You'll be fine though. Better than get Arabicitus like me.

Carlos Yes, you see the real Hal here has been under top-secret quarantine for his Arabicitus.

Hal2 You have Playboy Channel? Hal hates Satanic Playboy! But Hal is so curious.

Hal2 turns on TV and watches.

Carlos Arabicitus is caused by a gas that Islamic mad man concocted to turn everyone into him! Makes the skin olive-y. Makes the speech foreign-y. Causes an urge to face Mecca.

Wendy *(Genuinely asking Hal2)* Does it make you wanna blow people up too?

Hal2 stands up angrily, offended. Carlos holds him back.

Hal2 I think *you* want blow *me* up! Me and my land!

Carlos He's very angry. Arabicitus does that. But no worries, right dogs?

Hal2 *(Afraid)* Dogs? Where?

Carlos With enough time, love, and electrodes he should revert to his gentle, clean-shaven self…

Carlos rips the fake mustache off Hal2. Hal2 screams in pain.

…in no time. Does this look more like the Hal you remember?

Hal2 stares at them very angrily, filled with hate.

Wendy He does look like Hal. Right, Tim? The clean-shaven face. The sweet expression.

Tim The the the two ears. The one nose. Oh my god yes! It's Hal!

Wendy/Penny Hal!

Tim We'll get you better too, Hally. We're all getting better together. And we have our Jewish faith to pull us through. We Jews gotta shtick together.

Hal2 Jewish? Not me.

Carlos A little memory loss. Hal. Remember when you were quarantined in your cell? That Shakespeare quote we reacquainted you with? The one every Jew should know?

Hal2 "Ouch my genitals?"

Wendy I love that quote. It's how we express love.

Carlos No. The one that starts, *(Threatening)* "If you prick us do we not bleed?" You do not like to bleed right?

Hal2 Oh no! Oh yes! I remember! "You prick. We bleed." So true. Awesome!

Carlos Very good. Now go home and study that quote. Keep it in mind.

Tim And get some sleep, son.

Hal2 *(Touched—beat)* Son?

Tim Welcome back, Hally. Su casa es mi casa.

Tim hugs Hal2. Hal2 hugs back hesitantly at first but then truly hugs him.

Hal2 *Son.*

Carlos Tim just said "your van is my van." Speaking of which, the van is outside should you decide to leave without telling me. Goodbye, Hal.

Hal2 won't release Tim from their embrace. He enjoys a fatherly embrace. Carlos shoves Hal2 out the door. There is finally silence.

Well, Walkers. You're safe now. You can finally relax.

Wendy *(Writes herself a note)* Re-lax. Done!

Tim Maybe we can get reacquainted now, huh, son? Wanna tell us about what happened over there. Are you up to it or /

Carlos He's not.

Wendy Oh, he's up to it. Look at him all strong. Come sit on the ol' life boat, Robbie. Come sit in your old place of honor.

Robbie sits in what he guesses was his old seat on the sofa.

Tim I've been dreaming of family time with you, son.

Carlos No family time. Robbie needs his sleep. Come on, Rob.

Robbie That sounds nice. What's family time?

Wendy He doesn't remember. Family time is when we are together. Mom, Dad, and son.

Penny And daughter.

Wendy And daughter. And we talk.

Tim I made up my mind to talk to you more, son. I know we didn't talk enough back then. But I thought about it a lot. Priorities you know?

Wendy And we connect and laugh.

Penny Here's my laugh. *(Does a fake robust laugh)* HA HA HA HA!

Robbie No! I don't want that. I don't want to connect with you. Carlos, no connecting.

Carlos See. He doesn't want to. Rob. Bed.

Tim But /

Carlos Look, just let the awkward silence envelop you like usual, ok? I'll start it. Tim, did you see Darkish Girl today? She's wearing those red cowboy boots you like.

Awkward silence. Wendy stares at Tim. Penny looks Elsewhere.

Nice right? Better than connecting. Rob. Bed time.

Wendy But his room isn't ready. I haven't been in there since he left. It's probably a pig sty thanks to daddy!

Tim Wendy.

Wendy He's locked in Robbie's room every night, in the dark, doing god knows what.

Tim Do you have to say that in front of him, Wendy?

Wendy Well, it's true.

Penny *(Distracting herself from another fight)* That stain looks like France.

Tim Maybe if you ever had anything to say to me, I wouldn't lock myself away.

Wendy Maybe if you didn't lock yourself away, maybe if you weren't always so far away, I'd have something to say.

Tim *I'm* far away?

Penny screams in sadness and frustration.

Carlos See where talking gets ya?

Wendy Oh, come on. We're fine. Come on, Tim, show Penny we're fine.

Tim and Wendy try to kiss but can't quite connect. Tim tries to pull her to him but she pulls away as if repulsed by him.

I better get the rooms ready. Oh, I know! Why don't the kids share a room?

Robbie Ok!

Carlos/Penny No!

Robbie Tickle party!

Robbie tickles Penny. Her laugh grows orgasm-like. She pulls away.

Penn Tingle pringle tingle shingle. I don't think so, mama. I don't think so.

Wendy Tim, get Rob his pjs. Penny, move Mr. Pibbles off the bed. I'll get a pillow.

Tim exits to get the pjs—following Wendy's orders.

Carlos Malalo idea, Wendy. Mucho malalo.

Robbie But if we can't share a room I'll, I'll…chow fun! I'm grabbing my heart!

Robbie starts to have a dramatic chow fun.

Carlos Oh come on! That is so fake!

Wendy It's ok, son. You and Penny share a room. You can keep an eye on each other.

Penny and Robbie ogle each other. Wendy sees it.

Not like that. *(Eew)* Shpoikles.

Penny Mama!

Wendy exits, Penny follows. Carlos grabs Robbie.

Carlos You watch yourself, you. Leave Penny alone. I may not be here but I'll be here, got it?

Robbie Have fun far, far away in your hotel, Carlos. Coming, family! Coming, sis!

Carlos We'll see about that you little /

Robbie exits. Wendy enters with blankets. Carlos covers with a sweet act.

Sweet dreams, Robbie, you cutie! Well goodnight, Wendy. See you tomorrow. Been a long day. I'll just head to my dingy hotel room and dream of my dead family.

Wendy God no! I won't hear of it. Stay here. I'll make up the sofa. I'll give you the clean sheets.

Carlos Can't, Wendy. Against agency policy. Closeness of any kind is prohibited.

Wendy Oh, let me do something for you for a change /

Carlos Ok, twist my arm. *(Pretending his arm is being twisted)* Ow! Ow!

Wendy *(She laughs)* Funny.

Carlos Yeah? Nah.

Wendy starts to make up the sofa.

Wendy I'm glad you're staying, Carlos. It's the least I can do. As it is I barely know how to express my gratitude for all you've done. You've given me my life back. And heck, I guess I kinda like havin' ya around.

Carlos Well, heck, I kinda like bein' around, Wendy. Around you.

Wendy Nah. I'm a snooze.

Carlos No way! I think you're...well I'll tell ya, I appreciate your faith in me, Wendy. Don't think it goes unnoticed. Don't think everybody is as appreciative as you. Sometimes I wonder if I…if I will even make a difference…If I will ever be appreciated…by someone. *(Beat)* Anyway, your support really, really keeps this little cog going. It gives *me* faith, you know? And I…Well, it's just really nice. To feel that.

Wendy Ok.

Carlos Cuz it's a lonely road we travel, you know?

Wendy Yes.

Carlos And I'm on that road a lot. You know?

Wendy *(Beat)* So ok. I better go. I'm around the corner if you…*want me*. Don't hesitate if you…*want me*. Here's a blanket I think you'll find it very soft goodnight.

She exits hastily afraid of her feelings for Carlos.

Carlos Goodnight.

Lights down on Carlos. Minimal light—moonlight—comes up on Penny and Robbie sharing a twin bed.

Robbie Mayday. Mayday. Anybody out there, *(Like an echo)* ere, ere, ere?

Penny *(Beat)* I am here, ere, ere…

Robbie So am I, I, I /

Penny That's spooky, I'd like to stop please.

Robbie Ok. Sorry. *(Long beat)* You smell nice again.

Penny Oh. It's just that powder. For my foot thing.

Robbie Oh right. *(Beat—a little concerned)* Is that foot thing contagious? I forget.

Penny You think I'm so gross.

Robbie No. Not at all. I think you're /

She interrupts with a nervous clicking sound made with her mouth.

Gee, that's a funny sound.

Penny Thanks.

Robbie Sounds like a machine gun.

Penny Or like a horse on a beach.

Robbie Horse on a beach. That's nicer. You're all poetic. With your poems and your thoughts. I like that. I wish I were like that.

Penny Tingle.

Robbie But I'm not. Like I bet if I said it's so silent, your next thought wouldn't be ambush.

Penny *(Sings sweetly)* Silent night.

Robbie *(Overlap song)* It's so silent here. So silent.

Penny *(Sings)* Holy night.

Robbie/Penny *(Harmonizing beautifully)* All is calm. All is bright. Round yon virgin, *(Penny sings the words "embarrassing word" instead of "virgin"),* mother and child. *(Just Penny)* Sleep in heavenly…

Robbie Mother and child. *(Beat)* "Silent Night" is nice. Nicer than ambush. Your eyes have a way of seeing.

Penny No, I had that lazy eye. Remember I had to wear the patch to strengthen / it.

Robbie Eyes deep as the ocean. Poet eyes. I didn't meet many poets back at the front. No poet could survive there. No beauty existed.

Penny It was bad, huh?

Robbie So bad. I shut down. I didn't live there. I only survived. I forgot what life was. I forgot that broken figure on the road, that shredded flesh was once a world to someone. A person. A person so special maybe they even got a poem on a flower. That blew my mind. Who's so lucky to get such a thing, I thought. Who is so loved? Not me.

Penny Not you? *(Beat)* "He is a new man. Reborn in a far off land. He… is my brother." A haiku. For you. Since you're loved. And since you're Asian now.

Robbie A poem? For me? Oh. Oh, Penny!

He turns on light. Penny wears an eye patch for her lazy eye. She rips it off.

I want to give you back something.

He gives her the gold "Penny" necklace he stole from her earlier.

Penny Wow. Wow, it's even engraved with my name!

Robbie *(Entranced by her innocence)* Oh, Penny. *(He gazes at her)*

Penny Don't look at me like that! Don't see me! No one ever sees me. After you left the only voice we heard was yours. Especially Mama. And I'm used to it. I like being alone in my own world! *(Robbie turns her to him)* Don't see me.

Robbie Penny.

They are about to kiss. She pulls away.

Penny Oh god! What's wrong with me? If you are my brother—oh, horrible horrible. If you're not—oh, tragedy, tragedy, worse, worse. Just stone me! Gouge my eyes out! Kill me! I'm so afraid. *(Going Elsewhere)* Lilacs, rose petals!

Carlos jiggles their locked door.

Carlos *(Offstage)* What's going on in there, kids?

Robbie *(Quickly—Carlos is coming)* Penny, I was gonna pretend here too. Just like you. I decided I wasn't gonna feel bad in this house or feel anything. See a gold necklace? Take it. Pawn it. In case I need to escape. Gotta do what you gotta do.

Carlos *(Offstage)* Que Dos Passos?!

Robbie But then I met you. And you give me poetry and and life, and I didn't want to feel but I do. I feel! For this family…For you. And if we feel certain things we can't pretend anymore. We can't see lilacs where there are none. Or see a brother who is not there, a brother who is…

Penny No! You're my brother Robbie and everything is perfect.

Carlos *(Offstage)* No hablablaing!

Robbie Ok. Start small. Look around. What do you see? *(Points to cracks in wall)* What are those?

Penny Winding rivulets.

Carlos *(Offstage)* Let me in, Hero!

Robbie Feel them, Penny. Really feel!

Penny No! I don't want to feel! We should all just stop feeling!

Robbie Feel! Is that a winding rivulet?

He guides her hand over the rivulet on the wall. She feels it's a crack. She feels the crack's intricate trail up the wall, the ceiling, down the wall, to the door. He opens the door between her and Robbie's room. She follows the crack into Robbie's room. Tim sits in the dark on Robbie's bed watching his tiny TV with his headphones on so as not to wake anyone with the sound. A photo of the real Robbie, a ten-year old Robbie, in a football jersey sits near him. Robbie hangs back a bit in the doorway. Upon seeing this Asian man in the door, forgetting, Tim jumps.

Tim Dry Cleaner Guy! *(Then realizes it's Robbie)* Oh sorry, son. So sorry. I don't know why I did that. Our dry cleaner isn't even Asian.

Penny Daddy! Daddy, there are cracks in our walls!

Tim Cracks? What are you talking about?

Penny They're everywhere! Like veins. Like arteries.

Carlos bursts into Robbie's doorway and tries to divert Penny into her Elsewhere fantasy world again before she says anything more.

Carlos Yes, like arteries of the beautiful river Nile. And there are slaves by the Nile. Happy slaves. Happy to be of use.

Penny *(Being led into pretend world a moment)* Yes!

Robbie No!

Penny No! Like cracks in a house! Like a house in disrepair!

Carlos Ok. Tim, Penny suffers from Post-Service Sibling Trauma or PSST which causes compulsive lying. She may need M-H-M for her PSST.

Robbie But I say she doesn't and they'll listen to me cuz I'm Robbie, rash and brave and good!

Carlos No you're not! I mean yes you are! I mean…shit. Wendy!

Carlos runs off down the hall. Tim still watches his TV.

Penny Daddy! We're falling apart! Look!

She turns on the light. Cracks run everywhere. Even under the few superhero posters on Robbie's wall—i.e., Superman, Lord of the Rings. *The cracks are like veins and arteries that lead to this room—as if it were the literal heart of the house. Tim turns off the light.*

Tim Turn that off! That's not how I like it in here.

Penny But Daddy /

Tim That's not how I like it!

Penny But you've got to see /

Tim Not now. My show is on.

Tim turns back to the TV.

Penny Daddy! Listen to me!

Tim What? What? What do you want from me? What do you want from me? I don't know what to do! We're a family again! Everything's fine!

Penny Are you sure? Are you sure we're fine?

Tim turns up the volume on the TV.

Tim I'm trying to watch this!

Robbie picks up a photo of Robbie and Hal.

Robbie Is this me? Me and Hal?

Tim grabs the photo from Robbie.

Tim Put that back!

Robbie Is it?

Tim You're making a mess!

Penny Something's wrong, Dad.

Tim Nothing's wrong! Nothing's wrong! Can I just watch my show!

Robbie notices the real Robbie's little league football jersey hanging on the back of the door. It says "WALKER" on it.

Robbie I played football?

Robbie grabs the very small jersey. Tim grabs it back violently.

Tim *(Finally bursting)* Don't touch that! It's Robbie's! *(Tim realizes what he just said)* I mean…oh god.

Lights down on Tim, Penny, Robbie. Lights up on Wendy in her bed, under her sheets, asleep. Carlos sits over her on her bed, slightly creepy.

Carlos *(Gently)* Wendy? Wendy? Wendy? *(Harshly)* Wendy!

Wendy wakes with a start. We see that, like Penny, Wendy still wears an eye patch at night.

Wendy Carlos! I'm not...! You're in my... *(Pulls off eye patch)* I'm not prepared.

Carlos Are you wearing the flannel nighty with the footballs? No worries. Very maternal.

Wendy How do you know I wear a football nighty?

Carlos Uh, because I have cameras everywhere ha ha.

Wendy Oh, you.

Carlos Yes me. Speaking of me. I was thinking.

Wendy About yourself?

Carlos Yes. Well, no. Well, yes about you and me.

Wendy Oh! Me too. I was hoping you'd come.

Carlos I need you to do something. My job, my life sorta depends on it.

Wendy I figured out how to thank you for giving me my life back.

Carlos No need. Now listen /

Wendy pulls off the sheet to reveal a very sexy nighty.

Wendy Thank you!

Carlos *(Staring at her breasts)* Those aren't footballs, Wendy.

Wendy It's new. I bought it. For a special occasion.

Carlos I see.

She covers herself again—embarrassed.

Wendy Oh god. What's wrong with me? Something's wrong! I'm awful! I'm horrible!

Carlos No, you're not. You're lovely. You're human. So terribly human and lovely.

She pulls off sheet and reveals herself again.

Wendy So are you! And strapping, and manly, and you smell good!

Carlos But but but remember Diane is coming.

Wendy *(Lovingly to him)* Ouch my genitals.

Carlos Remember your family. You are a perfect family again.

Wendy covers up and bunches into a ball again.

Wendy Oh god! What's wrong with me? Why am I doing this if everything's perfect? Why can't I be happy? What is it? What is it?

Carlos Because at times of joyous tumult your id is in your yang and so yeah ok? So I need you to help me get everyone to do what I say. Robbie needs to be quiet and heal but he won't listen. And Tim isn't helping. Tim is being /

Wendy Namby pamby? Tim is being wishy washy? Tim is being Tim?

Carlos I don't want to disparage our Tim, but yes. So will you help me get everyone in line so America can see the perfect family and I can keep my job and other things? Don't disappear on me. Say yes, Sweetheart.

Wendy Yes, Sweetheart!

Wendy pulls off sheet and reveals herself to him again.

Carlos That won't play in Peoria, Wendy.

Wendy curls into a ball. Tim pounds on the door.

Tim *(Offstage)* Wendy! I have something to tell you!

Carlos Wendy, listen to me. I've put all of me into bringing Rob home to you, and I don't want all of my hard work, each muscle straining and swelling to bring you happiness with no regard for my urges, or my pent-up longings, to be for naught! And I just thought that you of all people—trusting, faithful, surprisingly-toned you—would get that!

Wendy I do get it! Don't worry, we'll be the perfect family for America. I'll do anything for you. You brought my son back. You brought my life back. *(She takes his hand)* You're my savior, Carlos.

Carlos Oh Wendy.

Carlos caresses her face. Tim pounds on the door.

Tim Wendy!

Wendy puts on a robe as Tim enters the bedroom. He grips the photo of Robbie and Hal. Wendy furtively takes a swig from her bottle of liquor.

Tim Carlos! You're in our bedroom?

Carlos No.

Tim You don't get to come in here! I don't even get to come in here!

Wendy Tim. Calm down. Robbie is sick and your hysterics aren't helping. We must remain calm. Listen to Carlos and do as he says, you hear me?

They follow Wendy to the living room. She prepares for the party and tries to ignore Tim.

Tim But Wendy, there's something terribly wrong here!

Wendy Quiet, Tim. Celebration zone.

Tim I don't think anything is what it seems!

Wendy Like what? Like you're not a big, spineless, diaper baby who blubbers like a little girl at the drop of a hat?

Carlos Ouch.

Tim Like Hal is missing, Wendy! *(He holds up the photo of Hal)* This is Hal. This is what he looked like, before the war, before today—happy. And this Hal is missing!

Carlos Oh yeah?

Carlos pushes a button on his cell—Hal2 screams offstage.

Sorry. Wrong button. Oh yeah?

Pushes another button on his cell. Hal2 enters.

Hal2 Hey, Amir! Hey Dad! *(Carlos pushes the bad button again—Hal2 screams)* I mean, hey, Tim. It's me. Hal.

Tim This is not Hal!

Carlos Let's ask the expert. Robbie?

Robbie enters living room. Wendy jumps upon seeing an Asian guy.

Wendy Computer Guy! *(Remembering it's Robbie)* Oh whoops. Sorry, son. Don't know why I did that.

Carlos Robbie. Tell us. Is that Hal?

Robbie No! It's /

Carlos twists Robbie's arm. Robbie falls to floor.

Carlos So clearly it's Hal. Case closed, Amiho.

Tim Listen to me, Wendy!

Wendy *(Imitates Tim in fake tough voice)* "Listen to me, Wendy!"

Tim Wendy! That is not Hal.

Hal2 *(To Wendy)* You show too much skin. I will stone you! No, I will put money in your underwear and buy sexy video because I can. I am so confused!

Hal2 sits on the couch with his head in his hands—confused and torn about his identity.

Tim And I don't think we're Jewish either! I mean hello!

He produces a Santa doll.

Wendy Shandazoit, Tim! Of course we're Jewish. Get with the pogrom!

Carlos Program. Program.

Hal2 *(To Tim)* We to have another hug? I be "son" again?

Tim No! Who are you?!

Hal2 Exactly! Who am I? I question everything! Maybe I *am* Jewish! I am so confused!

Tim And Wendy. Oh god, I don't know how to say this. Wendy, I don't think Robbie… *(Turns to Robbie)* I don't think he's… *(To Robbie)* Who are you? Where's my son?

Wendy Tim, have you gone crazy? Don't listen, Robbie.

Robbie I'm sorry. I'm so sorry. Oh god the world!

Hal2 Where's my world! Where's my family? I want my world!

Hal2 escapes down the hallway. Carlos pursues him—they both exit. Tim grabs Robbie.

Tim Tell me where my boy is!

Wendy Tim, our friends are coming. America will be watching us. Don't you do this!

Carlos enters. He sees Tim grabbing Robbie.

Carlos Hey! What's going on!

Carlos shoves Robbie in a corner.

Tim *(To Carlos)* Tell me where my son is, Mr. Angel! Mr. Man! Tell me! You are in *my* house!

Robbie Yeah! Fight it! Fight it! Fight back!

Carlos Wendy. Sadly, the disease is embedding in Robbie. For his own good, I'll put him to refreshing sleep through gentle hypnosis.

Robbie That crap never worked on me. I'm too damn /

Carlos claps twice. Robbie falls asleep and falls to the floor. Carlos exits down the hall again to look for Hal2.

Carlos Hal!

Wendy See, Tim. He needs his sleep. Carlos knows. *(Starts to follow Carlos)* Carlos?

Tim Wendy!

Penny enters wearing Robbie's superhero cape.

Penny Mama! Listen to Daddy! Please!

Wendy What are you wearing?

Penny Robbie's cape. I also found his bag of ten-sided dice. *(She holds the bag)*

Wendy Put that back!

Tim Remember how he loved all that hero stuff? Remember how he always wanted to be a hero. I told him…I told him he'd never get a girlfriend that way with those dice and costumes. Why'd I tell him that?

Wendy Indeed. Sorry he wasn't a football player like you. Sorry he wasn't a hero like you! *(Beat)* I have a party to prepare. Excuse me.

Tim A party? How could we have a party in this house? This dead, broken house? With our dead broken family!

Wendy What are you talking about, Cuckoo?

Tim Come in Robbie's room. Come see!

Tim tries to take Wendy into Robbie's room. She won't go.

Wendy No! I don't want to see the mess you made in there.

Penny Our walls are cracking, Mama. Our yard is brown and dead. You put out fruit magnets for our guests to eat! We're a black hole on the block! Our neighbors hate us! We don't even know their names. We never even bothered! We're scared of them and they're scared of us! Nobody is coming to our party, Mama!

Wendy Well, just go Elsewhere, Penny, if it's so awful here.

Penn I don't want to go Elsewhere. I want Elsewhere to be here. I want a garden here.

Wendy Alright, so maybe we need a little maintenance, but that's daddy's fault. It was his job to fix the house and the yard, but he never read my memos. I tried.

Tim Your mountains of lists and to-do's were never going to fix us!

Wendy Carlos!

Wendy starts to look for Carlos. Tim pulls Wendy to him.

Tim Wendy!

Wendy Oh. Big man. Grabbing me.

Tim Can we please be honest? At least with each other, let's be honest. We're falling apart.

Wendy I'm not listening to you, Tim. You gave up on Robbie long ago. You thought he died and you died with him. I saw it. I saw you slip away into the TV. I saw you stare out our bedroom window at Darkish Girl as if I weren't here. As if you wanted out. Oh yes, I had to hold it all together every day, every day, Tim, with Penny falling apart—I can't bear to see it—and this house falling apart, while I watched you stop caring.

Tim That is not true. I care. I care so much. I just feel so helpless! I don't know what to do!

Wendy How funny. You were the one who let him enlist yet you were the first to give up on him.

Tim Forgive me, Wendy!

Wendy You could have stopped him, but no. Way to go, Tim. Way to make a man out of him.

Tim Forgive me! Forgive me! Why can't you forgive me?

Wendy *(Explodes)* Because you fucking ruined everything! *(Regains composure)* I mean you almost ruined everything. And now you refuse to be happy, because it's Carlos who saved us, not you. It's Carlos I can depend on, because you are dreary and weak and stuck in your dreary weak world, with your question this and wonder that, and I won't be dragged there with you. Can't you see our family is whole again? What more do you want?

Penny Oh, Mama.

Tim I want to remember Robbie. Remember him for real. Not forget him or replace him. No more pretending, Wendy!

Carlos enters.

Carlos Robbie's disease is infecting Tim, Wendy. I must quarantine this house. No one in or out. In the name of National Security.

Carlos unrolls yellow hazard tape and tapes it across the door.

Tim Our boy is gone, Wendy! Wake up!

Robbie awakens.

Robbie Where am I? *(He remembers)* Oh.

Carlos claps twice and puts Robbie to sleep again. Robbie falls to the floor.

Carlos Tim. Please. I don't want to go down this path. I truly don't.

Tim opens the door, breaking the hazard tape, and shouts outside.

Tim I want my baby boy! Where's my baby boy! Baby boy, where are you?! I'm sorry!

Carlos shuts the door.

Carlos Tim, as your USAFALOCO, and your friend, I insist that you shut up and be happy!

Tim You're not my friend! Liar! Get the liar before he gets us! Come on!

Carlos You leave me no choice but to say, can't we work this out civily… inside my darkened van?

Tim No! Fuck you and your dark fuckin' *fuck* van!

Wendy My God, who are you? I don't recognize you any more. What's happened to my Tim? *(On cell)* Now.

Carlos Right! That's it! Who are you? What happened to our beloved, malleable, distant Tim?

Doorbell. Door bursts open to reveal a clown, Tim2, with a dangling cigarette and handcuffs hanging from one wrist. They are obviously scraping the bottom of the barrel for replacements now.

Tim2 It's me. Tim.

Carlos shuts the door on Tim2.

Carlos *(On cell)* You're sending in the clowns? You're killin' me!

Tim Penny! Wendy! Come on! We're getting the heck out of here! We're gonna find our boy! We're gonna tell the world!

Carlos blocks Tim.

Carlos I'm sorry. I can't let you leave, Tim. America wants to see you on TV.

Tim Then you get the heck out of here!

Carlos I can't have that either, Tim.

Tim Who the fuck do you think you are? Mr. Decisions?

Carlos I am Mr. Decisions. I am the protector, the strong one, the cut one. The one trying to make everyone happy! Whereas you're the selfish /

Wendy Weak, disappointing one.

Carlos Who does nothing but hurt and terrorize people! Hey! You're a terrorist! Terrorist!

No one reacts to the terrorist alarm anymore.

What? Once too many?

Tim Who do I hurt?

Wendy Me! You're breaking my heart!

Carlos I'll save you, Wendy! I know CPR! Clear!

Everyone moves away including Carlos.

Whoops. Sorry. I should stay. Clear!

Carlos goes to Wendy to perform CPR, Tim pulls him back.

Tim I'll save her! I'm the man of this house!

Carlos No, I'm the man!

Tim / Carlos *(Simultaneous—in each others face)* I'm the man! I'm the man! I am! Wendy?

They look to Wendy. Wendy is frozen. She kneels down to Robbie.

Wendy Robbie?

Tim He isn't Robbie, Wendy!

Carlos I say he is Robbie. I say our boy is alive and well. No pain in this house, no pain!

Beat. Wendy chooses Carlos over Tim. She kisses Carlos madly. He stops her. Beat. He kisses her. On the table, the wall, on the couch. Tim is stunned and broken.

Tim Wendy.

Penny Mama no!

Tim Wendy!

Carlos Quiet! I am in charge now! I am the savior here!

Tim Then who am I?

Carlos You? You're nothing.

Tim Yes. Nothing.

Penny No!

Tim Nothing.

Penny No! Don't go away again, Daddy!

Tim Nothing.

Tim turns on his little friend, the TV, puts on his headphones and slips away into TV world.

Penny Dad! Dad!

Carlos Yes, sweetie?

Penny Not *you*!

Penny slaps Carlos across the face.

Carlos Use your words, sweetie.

Penny Wake up, Mama! Wake up!

Robbie wakes up. Groggy.

Robbie Where am I? *(Remembers)* Oh.

Carlos *(Seeing Robbie wake up)* Now you've done it, Penny! Wendy, I have to quarantine Penny's larynx. A matter of national hygiene.

Carlos gags Penny and ties her arms back. Robbie approaches him.

Robbie Don't touch her, Carlos!

Carlos Stand back, Robbie. I swear to god!

Wendy walks up to Robbie with a platter of fruit magnets.

Wendy Fruit, dear?

The magnets stick to his shirt because of the shrapnel in his chest.

Robbie It's all falling apart, Carlos. You're panicking.

Carlos I am so not panicking! Everything's so totally under control! So just sit down and shut the fuck up!

Carlos hears a beeping noise—he jumps.

What was that?

Wendy Oh! It's the beeper, Carlos. It's Diane. It's time to turn the cameras on!

Carlos Shit! You all play along you hear? Anyone disobeys? Van. Darkened. You.

Robbie Fuck you!

Carlos Or Penny will go to M-H-M and don't you know I'll get Mama's permission!

Penny Mama!

Penny has freed herself of the gag, but Wendy re-gags her.

Wendy Keep your gag on, Pen. I don't want you to get sicker. Shall I braid your hair?

Seeing Carlos' hold over Wendy, Robbie backs off.

Carlos That's right. It's TV time! *(Carlos puts his handkerchief over Robbie's face like a mask)* Robbie sit here. Wendy sit here. Penny stand here.

He stands Penny behind the sofa with her back turned to the camera.

Great. Sexy. Hot. And Tim…

Carlos sees Tim staring vacantly at the TV with headphones on.

Perfect. Don't change a thing. Let's keep America hopeful!

TV lights come up. Carlos sits on sofa between Wendy and Robbie. Penny stands behind the sofa—her back to the camera. Tim is next to the sofa in his recliner, lost in his TV world. This picks up mid-interview. Carlos and Wendy have ear pieces in through which they hear Diane.

Happy Turkey Day to you too, Diane. Let's do it, guys!

He does thumbs up alone and shouts by himself…

Gobble gobble!

Tim has begun watching his family on TV—unaware it's his own family.

Tim Oh, it's Diane.

Wendy A favorite holiday memory, Diane? Well, after dinner we'd all play a game. Sorry or Yahtzee. It was so nice being together on our little sofa. Our little life boat I'd call it. We'd always joke that no one wanted to be on Robbie's team because he always lost.

Tim *(Watching them on TV)* What a sad family.

Wendy Well, he didn't *always* lose.

Carlos He obviously won this time. I mean look, Robbie's alive and well.

Wendy Yes, and his service has done him good, Diane. I'll tell ya, he's stronger for it. And he gets the GI Bill now. He gets a future.

Tim *(Watching TV)* What a sad lady.

Carlos Yes, we all feel elated, Diane. And as you see we're all set for our party.

Wendy Oh yes, we're ready to get down Robbie style. We may have eggrolls. And latkays *(Meaning latkas)*.

Tim *(Watching TV)* Whatever happened to Donahue?

Carlos A mask on Robbie, Diane? No, no. It's a uh, a uh, a germ-catcher. Just for little germs.

Suddenly, Robbie takes off his mask. Carlos sees this.

Actually, ok, well the truth Diane, is that Robbie suffers from Asiaitus, a rare but totally safeish disease caused by parasites. But he'll revert to his old white self in no time.

Tim *(Watching Carlos on TV)* He's sweaty.

Carlos *(Wiping his sweat)* Sure, Diane. Robbie. Tell them the harrowing yet ultimately victorious tale of your crash and rescue.

Robbie Ok. It was a typical day for us heroes. After a warm shower, a letter from home, and gifts from the indigenous, my buds and I, men and women who love being there, climbed into our Apache for routine reconnaissance. We were at five hundred feet, sure of our mission. And then a bang. We crashed. But then we were rescued and here I am, mission accomplished, the end.

Carlos Happy ending indeed. Good boy!

Robbie But on the ground a nobody, a grunt, saw it differently.

Carlos No he didn't.

Robbie The Apache was doing recon above, but below it was silent. Too silent.

Penny *(Hums)* Silent night, holy night…

Robbie *(Overlap song)* And then an explosion, a repercussion shatters my bones, heat sears my flesh, metal is falling. /

Carlos He's medicated, Diane.

Robbie Stars falling. Stripes falling. People falling!

Carlos He's hallucinating.

Robbie I take cover but when I open my eyes in front of me—a boy. Damaged boy. Broken boy.

Carlos See what that mad man did to our boys?

Robbie I say a prayer for the boy. And then I start running! But where do I run? No place is safe! I'm so scared!

Wendy *(Holds Robbie's hand)* Shh son. It's ok.

Carlos Diane, the AWOL rate in this war is practically nil. And those who do run are thrown in the brig.

Robbie That's right! And then they get an ultimatum. Carry out the plan, they said. Just 'til there are no more questions.

Carlos No. And then they are dealt with according to what we see as the law.

Robbie *(To Wendy)* The families will believe it, they said. People see what they want to see.

Carlos Or do they? Abracazam!

Carlos tries to distract them with magic fire again. The fire doesn't work this time.

Robbie A chance to save myself they said. Spare the family. I believed it. I had to. But /

Penny turns around, takes off her gag and gets close to "camera" or audience. Crying, she says in her and Robbie's special language...

Penny Robbiel disvanisheth. Robbiel disvanisheth. He nevernever. He nevernever!

Carlos This disease is spreading, Diane.

Wendy Don't cry, Penny. This is Robbie, honey. I'd die if it weren't. I'd know!

Penny Oh, Mama. Illyriloss illyriloss.

Wendy She's not well, Diane. Should we send them to M-H-M, Carlos?

Carlos Good idea. *(On cell)* Van. Incoming.

Penny No Mama! Don't listen to him! He's no elf! He's no patriot!

Tim *(Still watching them on TV)* Kick him off the island.

Carlos How dare you say that when mis parientites dijameemamay to meemay on these shores /

Penny That is not Spanish! I bet you're not Mexican! Or Ohyesican!

Carlos Diane, this interview is over!

Carlos pulls plug on camera. TV lights go out. Tim's TV goes out. Tim flips channels frantically, bangs TV.

Tim Uh oh. Cable's out.

Wendy Carlos wouldn't lie about something like this, Penny. You and your fantasies.

Tim I can fix it. I'm gonna get my tools.

Tim exits.

Penny I bet your family isn't even real, Carlos! I bet you made them up!

Or the agency made them up! Or the agency made *you* up. Ohyesican? Ohyesyou*can't*!

Robbie Good one, Penny!

Penny We've been tricked, Mama! We've been fooled!

Carlos Ok! Maybe the Sanchez story is someone else's story and I just really really liked it. But who can blame me? Sanchez is a great guy. Strong and good. You need a cover like that in my line of work, and you gotta go in deep. Heck, I don't even know who I am anymore, I'm so deep in Sanchez. But surely you understand we can never truly reveal ourselves. It's too dangerous. So the details of Sanchez's story are not mine, but the heart of it is. I love this country.

Penny Cynic! Liar! Grishlath frivelfosh!

Robbie English, Penny. But you're doing great.

Carlos I am not lying! I fought for this country. I watched many friends die for this country. That cannot be in vain!

Penny Or was that Sanchez's story?

Carlos No, I…No, I…Look, everything we have done has been for the greater good! And things will be different now. We're getting back on track. We are surging forth. Armies of people are on our side, filled with the hope we offer.

Wendy As are we! *(To Penny)* Be full of hope, Penny! Please!

Penny It's false hope, Mama! I want real hope. We have to arm ourselves with the truth, with our pain, with our magic lassos, and fight back!

Robbie I'll fight for you, Penny!

Penny You will?

Robbie Oh yes. Oh yes. Oh yes.

Penny And I for you.

Penny and Robbie start kissing passionately.

Wendy Aw, who loves her brother?

Penny *(To Robbie)* We've got to get out of here.

Penny grabs a bag she has already packed from the hall.

Carlos Penny! Penny, you may not leave please!

Carlos goes toward Penny. Robbie holds Carlos back by the neck.

Ouch. Windpipe.

Penny Dad! Where's Dad? We've got to find Robbie and Hal!

Carlos *(On cell)* Van! Where's the van?

Robbie *(Grabbing Penny)* The van's gone, Penny. This is our chance. We've got to go now!

Penny We'll get help, Mama. We'll be back!

Robbie Cover my back, Penny! I've got your front. No my back your front. No, your front my back. Stop spinning, sweetie. Nevermind. Just go!

Penny I love you, Mama!

Carlos Can't you wait just one sec, guys? Free van service.

Robbie and Penny run out holding hands. As they run off Penny says—her battle cry.

Penny I had a brother! I had a neighbor! I'll have a garden!

Carlos *(On cell)* Van! Where are you? They're getting away! Fuck!

Wendy Wear your sweaters, kids, it's cold out! Be back for the party!

The van pulls up outside. Maybe we see headlights or hear the motor.

Carlos *(On cell)* Now you come? They're gone! What's your fucking… What?…No, I'm not getting in the van…No, I don't want to talk privately in the van! *(Hangs up)* Uh oh.

Wendy Where is everybody? So rude. Should we call people about the party, Carlos?

Wanting to escape furtively, Carlos tugs frantically on the doggie flap he caulked earlier.

Carlos Shit! The caulk dried! The tube says twenty-four hours! Law suit!

Wendy I want the party to be perfect for Robbie. What if it's not perfect? What if no one shows?

She goes to Carlos for comfort, but Carlos walks away to answer his ringing cell.

Carlos *(On cell)* Sanchez…No, *you're* not Sanchez, *I'm* Sanchez…No, you're not, *I* am…Then who am *I*?

He hangs up but the cell keeps ringing. He stuffs it under a sofa cushion frantically. We see the photos of the family and Robbie that he hid under there earlier.

Wendy It's very strange. Something's off here, Carlos. Something's wrong. Hold me?

She tries to hold Carlos. He pulls away from her.

Carlos Not now, Wendy.

She clings to him.

Wendy Hold me. Why can't you hold me? Hold me!

He pushes her off again.

Carlos I said not now! I'm in trouble!

Wendy Oh yeah? Oh yeah? Well, if you're going to ignore me then you better as hell fix the toaster!

She starts angrily writing chores for him on post-its like she did for Tim.

Carlos But Wendy, I think I'm in hottish water. I think I need help.

Wendy Oh now it's all about you, right? Fix the blender too. The pulse button's stuck! I can't even fucking pulse!

There is an alarmingly aggressive knock on the door. The doorknob rattles from the outside. Wendy goes to open it.

Finally! It's our friends!

Carlos Don't open it! We have no friends!

Wendy What are you talking about?

Knocking.

Carlos What do we do? I don't know what to do anymore. I don't even know who I am.

Wendy What?

Carlos Oh god, I fucked it all up. I ruined it all. I'm so sorry, I'm so sorry.

Wendy You're not gonna cry, are you?

Carlos And Robbie. And Robbie. Oh, Wendy. I'm so sorry. I'm so sorry.

Wendy I'm not listening to you. You're crazy.

Carlos Don't say that. Tell me you still believe in me.

Wendy Someone told me you were a liar and a crazy! I heard about you!

Carlos Tell me I'm still your Sanchez. Sanchez could save us. Sanchez could make it all ok, right? Tell me I'm your Sanchez and I can do anything!

Wendy opens the door.

What are you doing? Don't go out there. The van's out there.

Wendy pushes Carlos outside and locks the door. Carlos bangs on it.

Wendy! Wendy let me in! The van!

Wendy You will not ruin everything with your hysterics and your questions, you hear me! You're not the man I thought you were!

Carlos Wendy, let me in!

Wendy I don't want to hear it! I don't want to hear it! No doubts! No questions!

Carlos Wendy please! Wendy please! Wendy! Wendy *ACH*!

She opens the door. Carlos is gone. Snatched into the van. As she looks outside, Hal2 emerges from the hallway. He had been hiding from Carlos in Robbie's room. He wears Robbie's little league football jersey that says "Walker." Wendy is startled.

Wendy Robbie? Oh. Hal. Where did you... Are those Robbie's clothes?

Hal2 He is gone?

Wendy Yes, he /

Hal2 Shut the door. *(Beat)* Shut the door.

She does. He is menacing. He is angry, trapped, sad, and desperate. She feels it. She tries to ignore it. She talks nervously.

Wendy Well, I'm glad you're here. Everyone else is late. It's very strange. Or maybe it's good cuz I'm low on nuts. Robbie loves nuts. Do you? Or are you allergic? Someone was allergic? Who was it? I can't recall. It all fades so, doesn't it? So many children ran through here, I, I can't recall. Can you?

No answer. He just looks at her.

Well. It'll come to me. Come back to me. So. Enjoying the party?

Hal2 I. Am. Noooooooot!!!!

Wendy Ok. That's fair.

He approaches her. She retreats. Even Wendy can't deny she's in trouble.

So the kids are rounding up some friends. They'll be back any second. Is that them?

She tries to run to the kitchen, away from him. He blocks her. She retreats again.

Maybe Gina and Door will stop by. Wouldn't that be…I'm so…Have you tried the chips?

Hal2 angrily knocks the chips out of her hand.

Hal2 We did not eat this. This is not our food.

Wendy How about some Kool-Aid?

She picks up an empty cup, he knocks it out of her hand.

Hal2 This is not our things! This is not our life! My father, Amir, sit here. And I by his side. And mother here. By me. *My* mother. *My* mother. My home! I want my home! Take me home!

Wendy You're scaring me.

Alarmed, Wendy picks up phone to call for help. Hal2 pulls the cord out of the wall.

Hal2 I scare you? I scare you! *(Repeating the quote he had to learn in captivity from* Merchant Of Venice*)* "But are not I just like you? Do not I laugh like you? Do not I bleed like you? If you poison me, do I not die? If you wrong me shall I not revenge? The villainy you teach me I shall execute. It shall go hard. But I will better the instruction!"

Wendy Hal. Calm down. We're all friends here.

He yells in her face.

Hal2 I am not your friend! You are not mine!

She starts to flee, he grabs her hand.

No! Help me. I am lost. I am so lost.

He falls to the sofa crying. There is a long beat as she watches this young boy, who has also lost his family, suffer. Then she begins to timidly, gently pat his head. She "shhs" him. Then she begins humming the train song.

Wendy I sang this for Robbie when he was a little boy. It always soothed him.

She puts her arms around Hal2 as if he were her own boy. She sings gently...

"This train is bound for glory, this train is bound for glory, this train is bound for glory, children get on board." Shh. You'll be fine, son. I'm here. I am you and you are me. *(Sings)* "No more weepin' and a wailin'. No more weepin' and a wailin'. No more weepin' and a wailin'. Children get on...Children get on..."

Holding this boy who is not her lost son, but is lost just the same, and singing this song—the truth hits her. Grief for her son begins to pour from her. She rocks the boy in her arms and cries. Long beat. Tim enters—perhaps to grab his headphones. But as he is about to exit with them, he sees this young boy in Robbie's jersey being held by Wendy. He is reminded of Robbie. He hears Wendy's grief. He feels her agony. All of this awakens him, awakens him to his own grief again. He goes to Wendy and finally holds her firmly in his arms. He is finally present.

Tim I'm here, Wendy. I'm here. I'm here.

All three sit on their sofa—their lifeboat—together. Tim, Wendy, and Hal2 cling to each other. They are all in pain together.

End of play.

Weightless
Christine Evans

Grounded and Weightless:
An Introduction to Christine Evans' Playwriting

Ken Prestininzi

Even before I met Christine Evans in person, she came to my rescue. In our institution-valuing, man-numbing world, attentive rescue is a basic need. It is also a main impulse behind Evans' playwriting as she reveals play-worlds constructed from the shards of a broken Pandora's box.

But instead of Pandora, Evans invents scrappier, more innovative characters to lead us out of our quagmires. In her plays, there is always a character that insists on compassion against all odds. These select characters act on faith, even before alliances are firm, before there are guarantees of payback or safety. A faith-act is the only possible generative response to an indifferent disaster. Acting on faith is both a tactic and a trait of Ms. Evans, both as a person and as a bold, assertive playwright.

As Evans' plays reveal, small gestures in desperate situations matter. I was looking for an apartment to rent in Providence, Rhode Island, a place new to me. Though we hadn't met, Evans offered her third floor walk-up as a place to crash—a characteristic act of kindness to a stranger. Like many of Evans' characters, I was disoriented. I arrived in Providence and found my way to her apartment. But it was not an easy night. The August heat was unbearable. Windows opened to the dry heat, I fell on the bed exhausted, only to realize I had a visitor. A brown bat had flown into the room and was zooming back and forth against the edges of my dream state.

Like the nonhuman creatures and objects in Evans' evocative plays, whether they be slow-falling birds, doll parts, or crossword puzzles full of dark spaces and missing words, my night companion bat animated and witnessed the first step of my transformation. I realize, years later, that liminal night in Providence could have been a poetic scene from a Christine Evans play. And like her characters, I learned to embrace its strange anxiety and tenderness with a dollop of humor—and gratitude for the bat's strange company.

Evans' plays continue to work on me like that night's visitation. With precise language, fierce intelligence, theatrical daring and darkly brilliant imagery, Evans reminds us that forces larger than us will consume us as fuel and leave us as waste, if we do not act as the attentive rescuers of each other. Christine Evans is the most precise *banshee* I know in the playwriting world. I use the term *banshee* to illustrate the spiritual and kick-ass nature of her imagination. The *banshee* is a keener. She arrives to warn us that we must take heed; that someone or something may be dying. A *banshee* can speak to us through a delicate song or a rattling gust. She is a hybrid battle goddess, mourner, and streetwise troubadour. She is trying to wake up the living to the deadening happening inside them, no matter what the overpowering social reasons may be.

Evans' witty plays tell us we are too often forced, tricked or seduced into becoming exiles from our own bodies. In her play *Weightless*, the son is a "problem" and must be drugged into a constant state of exile. Arrende, the foreigner and indentured servant, wants her agency returned to her along with her missing "woman's parts." Marion, the hired nanny, is the one who most realizes the crime of the family and its false institutions and rationale. Everyone is investing in a Ponzi scheme of no emotional return. Intimacy has been forgotten. But the growing need for true intimacy finally cracks open the edifice of their lives.

In *Weightless*, communion between people is atrophied or mislaid, along with Arrende's "woman's parts." Substitutes—mood-enhancement drugs, disfiguring body operations, sexual role-playing—fill the void.

The void cannot hold. It expands until the entire high-rise building cracks and shatters. The grounded Marion escapes disaster with a stolen credit card, but without her loved one. The estranged and weightless Arrende, however, dreams a different kind of survival.

That dream of ascendance, escape and survival is both shocking and irreducible. It works on me as powerfully as fairy tales and fables worked on me as a child.

Like a revolutionary of the streets, Evans' plays pick up whatever is at hand in the ruins and hurl them at us. Her plays are stubborn activists in the political realm of our collective imaginations. They ask us to examine our behavior from a fantastical viewpoint, so that we may be shocked out of our stupor and reject that which is outrageous and dehumanizing. We ask, along with her characters, who would want to live without access to imagination and intimacy? When and why did we surrender our bodies to others?

At this year's Whitney Biennial I saw a video of an artist in a colorful frock and steel-toed work boots trapped in a small, enclosed box of white sheet walls. Using fists and feet, she kicked holes in the walls so she could climb out of the lifeless trap. In such a way, Christine Evans' characters use their fists and feet, their language and objects, their beauty and truths, to fight entrapment, to poke holes in it and climb out of it.

Christine Evans loves the stage and the permission it gives her artistic, hard-earned, well-toned muscles. Her faith in the stage and her fury at all systems that try to cripple or shut down the imagination is indomitable. She uses the fragile power of words and the recovered beauty of the marginalized human body to create complex stage images and play actions that can break down the walls of prisons we no longer need to call home.

She, like every successful playwright, is a miraculous paradox: grounded and weightless.

Playwright/director Ken Prestininzi's work has been produced in Brighton, Cambridge, Chicago, Edinburgh, Kalamazoo, Los Angeles, Mexico City, New York City, Philadelphia, Prague, Providence, San Francisco and Washington, DC. He is the Associate Chair of Playwriting at the Yale School of Drama. His plays *AmeriKafka*, *Beholder* and *Chaste* were recently produced at Chicago's Trap Door Theatre. Beholder received the 2008-2009 Joseph Jefferson Award for Best New Play. He has received theater awards from ACTF, Brown University, California Arts Council, Djerassi, Gerbode, Goethe Institute, LEF, Rockefeller Foundation, Millay Arts Colony, National Endowment of the Humanities and the San Francisco Cultural Equity Office.

Characters
Lillian, late 40s, looks 25. Plastic surgeon.
Horace, mid-50s, looks rich. Married to Lillian.
Seth, 17. Horace and Lillian's son.
Marion, 23, looks 30. Seth's nurse (and lover) from rehab.
Arrende, 30, looks ageless. A foreign maid of ambiguous gender, played by a beautiful male actor of color.

Place/Time
A slightly twisted mirror-universe, a little in the future.

Setting
The penthouse of Lillian and Horace, perched high above Manhattan. The penthouse has a sparse, steel modular feeling to it.

Music
Seth's songs and the air-guitar music he plays can be invented for each production. However, the song "Junco Partner" (which Marion sings and Seth reprises) is a New Orleans classic—according to Dr. John's liner notes for the album *Gumbo*, it's "the anthem of the dopers, the whores, the pimps, the cons."

Playwright's Note
A slash (/) indicates the interruption point in a line by the following speaker. And with regard to Horace, chicken suits are out of the question.

Production History
Weightless premiered at Perishable Theatre, RI, in November, 2007, under the direction of Vanessa Gilbert.

To Obtain Rights To Produce This Play
Please contact: Peregrine Whittlesey Agency, 279 Central Park West, New York, NY 10024. Telephone: (212) 787-1802. Email: pwwagy@aol.com.

Weightless

Scene I

Arrende Ladies and Gentlemen, welcome to tonight's performance. Every night, it is almost the same and yet—something can always go wrong. Horribly wrong. Perhaps even tonight. For this reason I have been asked to point out the exits to you—here, and here. In the event of an… an event, you could just walk through them. You could go home. You are as free as the birds. *(Beat)* Ladies and Gentlemen, consider the pigeon. *(Pulls rather dead bird from apron)* The humble pigeon will always find its way back home, despite wars, floods, earthquakes and other Events. Somewhere in this bird's body is a little organ that knows where home is. Not all of us are so lucky.

Lillian *(Offstage)* Two minutes Arrende!!

Arrende *(Stuffing the pigeon hastily back into her apron)* Ladies and Gentlemen, my name is Arrende and I welcome you to the penthouse. Please turn off all beeping and flapping devices and remember the location of those exits. Burn them into your memory banks. If you do these two things you will be ready to escape in an emergency without wasting time phoning for help. —Thank you.

During the above, Arrende walks over to her pedestal, removes her maid's costume and stands bionically still on it. In another space we see Seth, unnaturally still, holding the crossword. Lillian enters; lights fade on Seth. She walks round Arrende with a marking pen.

Lillian I'll put on the heat. *(Snaps fingers)* —Are we thinking Grace Jones or something a little more identifiably female?

Arrende You're the artist.

Lillian makes some chalk marks on Arrende's thighs.

Lillian I think thigh implants might be fun, don't you?

Arrende *(Shrugs)*

Lillian I think we're past that very anorexic moment, the gazelle thing. Back to those ancient fertility sculptures but with a Sigourney Weaver twist—

Arrende *(Coughs)*

Lillian Did I offend you?

Marion enters.

Lillian *(To Marion)* Later.

Marion Oops. —Later.

Marion exits.

Arrende I've worked hard for you, haven't I Ma'am. And we've tried a lot of new things haven't we. And I have never complained. Not when the stitches / burst—

Lillian We're at the "cutting edge" of live modeling—and I pay / you very well for that—

Arrende It's not / the pay

Lillian We help your whole village. And we do all your paperwork so that / Immigration—

Arrende Yes Ma'am. You do all that.

Lillian Well, then—

Arrende I would just like…I know you are highly highly trained in Medicine and you know the human body inside and out—

Lillian Well, yes, but—

Arrende —and you have the cat—delicate touch of the Devil himself, I've seen his business card—I don't judge—a soul is a messy thing especially for Christians…madam, your skill is…if anyone can, you can…that is, I am…requesting…

I have a problem with my female parts.

Lillian What do you mean?

Arrende They seem to have disappeared.

Horace enters.

Horace Lillian, where are my silk boxers? They should be in my top… Sorry.

Horace exits. Beat.

Lillian Arrende.

Arrende Yes, Ma'am.

Lillian You must be mistaken. They don't just disappear.

Arrende I am sure they could be recovered. By a skilled detective / of the body.

Lillian Arrende, imaginary problems cannot be resolved by surgery.

Arrende So you won't do it.

Lillian I can't. It can't be done.

Lillian and Arrende change gears and begin The Game.

Arrende In that case, Ma'am, I'm afraid I must terminate my employment with you.

Lillian Oh no! Please do not terminate your employment with us.

Arrende I am afraid I must terminate my employment with you…

Lillian Arrende. Please. *(Beat)* Don't make me beg.

Arrende But I must make you beg.

Lillian Oh no! Please don't make me beg.

Arrende I'm afraid Madam must resort to her knees.

Lillian kneels. Arrende takes the felt pen and pushes Lillian's head forwards.

Arrende *(Her hand following her words)* Now, here. Here is the "string of pearls." And here…is the center line of the body. If you cut along here, why every organ is available to your outstretched hand. And *one* organ… one little organ…is right in harm's way. The Spanish Inquisition called it The Devil's Teat. *(Beat)* Do you want me to stop?

Lillian *(Mumbles)*

Arrende What's that? Speak up Madam. I can't hear you. Do you want me to stop?

Lillian *(Quietly, head bowed)* No, don't stop.

Arrende continues tracing a line down Lillian's body. We hear Lillian breathing, then the sound of the building, groaning.

Scene 2

Seth looks at the crossword. Marion looks at herself in the mirror. There is a thin crack in the floor.

Seth "Hedge your bets, the enemy's loaded." —*Marion?*

Marion Is that a new song, sweet pea?

Seth Nah, it's a clue.

Marion I dunno. Cryptic crosswords are bullshit—Do you think I should get a boob job?

Seth Yeah, when we get our own place. They can have their own room—

Marion You watch your mouth—

Seth But I'll visit so they won't get / lonely—

Marion Shut up!

Seth *(Teasing)* Gonna make me?

Marion Hah! You wish—

Arrende enters.

Arrende Breakfast is served.

Seth *(Returning to crossword)* Hedge. Loaded. Enemy.

Arrende *(Glancing at crossword as she leaves)* Hegemony.

Beat.

Seth Hah! I've got it! "Hegemony!" *(Writes it in)*

Marion Clever boy!

Seth Do you think I should get a cock ring?

Marion Sure, sweet pea. But later. Like after breakfast. —We should get moving.

Marion efficiently prepares Seth's morning medication.

Seth *(Rejecting the pills)* Yeah, later.

Marion Come on, angel dung. We've got a deal, right?

Seth Drop it, Marion.

Marion *(Softly)* Take the fucking pills.

Seth You want my balls whole, or on a plate?

Marion Either way. Now swallow.

Seth Mmmm, breakfast.

Seth bites her breast. She slaps him, hard.

Marion Sweetie? Come on.

Seth drinks the water, eats the pills.

Marion That's better. *(Stretches)* I love Sundays.

Scene 3

There is a noticeable crack in the floor; the table sits over the top of it. Lillian pours coffee; Horace reads the paper. Marion goes to light a cigarette; Seth breaks it in half.

Lillian Darling, Marion can smoke if she wants to.

Marion I can wait.

Marion smiles at Lillian. A sexy moment between them.

Lillian *(To Horace)* Big week at the Home Office darling?

Seth *(To Lillian)* Smoking's bad for your skin, isn't it. Mother—

Horace *(To Lillian)* This week is pretty crazy.

Lillian *(To Seth)* —Lillian. It's not as bad as sunlight.

Horace *(To Lillian)* Actually I thought I might even—you know—venture out and see how the Outside Office / is doing—

Lillian *(To Horace)* Surely that's not necessary.

Seth *(To Lillian)* It gives you wrinkles. I read that.

Lillian *(To Seth)* Smoking *is* a factor—

Seth *(To Lillian)* —Fucks your lungs—

Lillian *(To Seth)* —But sunlight is the prime cause of aging.

Marion Time is kind of a factor / too.

Horace *(To Lillian)* In that case, it seems strange that we have not evolved to live in burrows undergound. That we don't glow in the dark.

Lillian *(To Marion)* Some of us do.

Seth And the rest of us are fucking mushrooms. Left in the dark and / fed on shit.

Horace Big week at the Home Office, darling?

Lillian This week is complete madness. On top of the back to college lipo-rush, there's a free promotional trial on Botox and Derma-blast, and the lines! I've been / online all day trying to cope.

Arrende appears on the balcony. She seems to be trying to persuade a pigeon to fly. Nobody at breakfast notices.

Marion *(To Seth)* There's a lot of rich ladies want their faces paralyzed—

Seth *(To Marion)* Or rearranged.

Horace Watch it young lady.

A pigeon falls from above and lands with a thump.

Seth Fuck!

Arrende *(From the balcony, looking down at dropped bird)* Rats!

Seth sees Arrende; no one else does. Arrende disappears.

Horace Language, son.

Beat. Seth stares up at where Arrende was.

Lillian The new software's fabulous though. Very tactile. Once you put the gloves on, it feels like real skin.

Seth You should go down and do it yourself.

Lillian Seth, you know very well that I do all my own surgery. Onscreen. Once the client is hooked up, it's more accurate *and* more hygienic. Remote-control surgery is the cutting edge of / the profession.

Seth *In person.* Get some fresh air—

Horace *Seth.*

Lillian You know I have allergies.

Seth When did you last go Outside, *Mother?*

Lillian It's / *Lillian.*

Horace *Seth.*

Seth She can't. She's too good to get her hands dirty.

Horace Seth. Your mother has lovely hands.

Marion I have good hands.

Lillian *(To Seth)* Darling. When you're good at something you get promoted. That is why the best models become actors and the best actors become President.

Seth It's why everything sucks.

Lillian —And besides, I stay hands-on with Arrende.

Seth *(Nastily)* Yeah.

Horace Come on, Son—

Marion *(To Lillian)* I've always wondered. That ice cream cone thing with boob jobs. How do you stop them pointing up at the sky?

Lillian Excuse me?

Marion You know, at the beach.

Horace 9 Down, Seth: "Transgression" in 3.

Lillian *(To Marion)* Oh, that was back in the Stone Age. The next generation of silicone is really undetectable.

Seth *(To Horace)* "Sex."

Marion *(To Lillian)* Really.

Horace *(To Seth)* Could be. —No, the second letter's "i."

Lillian *(Silkily, to Marion)* And not just to look at.

Beat.

Horace Where Is Arrende?

Lillian Arrende!

Arrende enters in waitress uniform, with a silver tray with pill cup and glass of water. At some point in the scene, she surreptitiously scoops up the dropped pigeon (unobserved by all except Marion).

Horace Excuse me.

Horace takes the pills and water. Arrende looks at the crossword.

Arrende "Sin."

Lillian *(Referring pointedly to Horace's chest)* Darling, I think you've put on weight.

Seth *(To Horace)* I've got it. It's "sin."

Lillian *(To Horace)* I suspect it's the imported chicken.

Horace *(Fills in "sin" on crossword)* Well done, son.

Lillian We should make sure we get free-range, Arrende. Boys as young as twelve near chicken factories in Brazil are developing gynecomastia—

Marion What?

Seth Growing boobs.

Horace Lillian, where do you get these ideas?

Arrende National Geographic. August edition, page seventeen.

Marion *(To Arrende)* Who asked you?

Horace Lily, we don't have hormones running round in the wild. If it's not cling-wrapped, it doesn't get into the country.

Seth takes out a knife and starts carving into the table.

Lillian Even plastic has hormones in it. *Especially* plastic.

Marion *(To Seth)* Come on sweetie, give / me that.

Horace Lillian, there is no interspecies hormone connection. There is a blood-brain barrier. There are hygiene controls and border patrols, and workers in white plastic boots with disinfectant sprays and disposable cleaning items. There are well-designed cages—

Lillian Everything is connected, Horace.

Seth *(Nastily)* —*Yoga Journal*, September issue.

Marion Seth!

Horace *(Quietly)* —A whole series of cages.

Lillian Well, you looked better on the Atkins diet.

Arrende clears the table. The others sit waxwork still.

Arrende Lunch will be served cold.

Scene 4

Horace is alone with the mirror, shaving. He shaves half his face. The other is covered in cream. He explores his chest with his hands. He is visibly growing breasts. Unseen by Horace, Marion is watching. Horace adopts a manly "gym" type pose. Then tries something else—a Marilyn, girly pose to push the breasts forward. Suddenly, he sees Marion.

Horace What the hell are you doing?

Marion Looking for Seth.

Horace He's not here.

Marion No.

Horace smears over his reflection with shaving cream.

Marion I could assist you with that Sir.

Horace Get out. Go play your mind-fuck games with my son.

Marion "If you use that language with me, Madam, I'm afraid I must terminate my employment with you."

Horace You *have* been getting around, haven't you.

Marion I try.

Horace What do you want?

Marion I want to help you, Horace.

Horace You need help. Not me.

Marion *(Looking at his breasts)* Are you sure?

Horace *(Frosty)* What are you implying, Miss?

Marion Sometimes even the best marriage hits…a speed-hump. Sometimes, an outside eye can…smooth it out. Do you want me to talk to her for you? Find out / what's bothering her?

Horace You watch it, Miss—

Marion The thing is, Lillian likes breasts. In the right context.

Horace —If it weren't for Seth you'd be out on your ass so fast, I could have / you…

Marion You couldn't "have" me. *(Beat)* You're a chemical eunuch, Horace.

Horace goes to hit her; Marion easily catches his arm.

Horace I love my wife.

Marion I know. I could help you.

Scene 5

Seth, alone in a steel room. The walls groan.
There is an empty cardboard box. He starts kicking it idly.
The kicking gets more intense.
Seth works up to a frenzy of demolishing the box.

This goes on for longer than you want it to.

Seth is jumping up and down on the box, making those soccer fan type roars of rage, when Marion enters. She rushes over and holds him in a practiced grip.

Seth Let me go let me go let go let me fucking—

Marion injects Seth in the neck. He folds.

Seth Oooooh.

Marion That's better.

She rocks Seth and sings the chorus of "Junco Partner," ending on the line about Heaven. Seth listens.

Seth Marion? I want to go to Heaven.

Marion I know baby. A basement room and a credit card. I'm working on it, I promise.

Seth Marion? Is it still Sunday?

Marion It just feels that way.

Scene 6

Lillian reads the paper, Horace fidgets. The crack in the floor has disappeared.

Lillian Property rates have more than doubled downtown since '97.

Horace Hmmmmph. Do you think Seth is all right?

Lillian Of course, why?

Horace Can't hear anything.

Lillian We have to let that go Horace. We can start expecting *not* to hear things now.

Horace It seems unnatural.

Lillian Dr. Sanders says we have to stop walking on eggshells. If this whole *Home Parole* thing is / going to work

Horace What would he know, he only ever walks on shag carpet. Seventy floors above street level.

Lillian So do we darling. —Your point is, exactly?—

Horace Forget it. *(Beat)* Do you think Marion does the job with Seth?

Lillian She interviewed well.

Horace So did Arrende.

Tight spot on Arrende, up on the balcony.

Arrende I come from a long tradition.
I am discreet.
I can see in the dark.
I don't get tired.
My English is almost imperfect.
When I walk, I make no sound.
All my joints are articulated.
You will never have to meet my family.
I sleep upside down, like a bat.

Horace stares at Arrende, who begins to fade from view like the Cheshire Cat in Alice in Wonderland—smile goes last.

Lillian We didn't interview Arrende, darling. She came with the apartment. Or the second parking space, I forget which.

Horace I thought we did.

Lillian *(Checking the newspaper)* Seth's half-finished the crossword already. —But you're right, Marion was excellent.

Marion appears on the balcony, in a different space to where Arrende was. Lillian sees her; Horace doesn't.

Horace I don't remember.

The crack in the floor re-opens.

Marion I'm very fond of my clients. I have a lot of experience in the caring professions.

Lillian She was very / professional.

Marion *Professionally* fond.

Lillian And well-organized.

Marion When I worked at Fort Knox Nursing Home, none of my clients. Ever. Escaped.

Marion slowly fades from view as Lillian watches her, entranced.

Horace *(Looking out the window)* Hmmph. —Why do you think they call it "Battery" Park? After Edison?

Lillian Hmmm?

Horace Or maybe for all the muggings. Assault and Battery Park.

Lillian Mmmmm.

Horace Or maybe back in the Dutch days there was a farm there. Farms all over the Island. Hard to imagine now. Maybe they had a farm. A battery farm.

Lillian Batteries are made in factories, not farms.

Horace *Lillian*—Do you really believe I'm a moron? —It says in our free-range egg box that battery farms are inestimably cruel. The chickens never see daylight and they're fed on excrement and hormones. They're just cooped up and expected to do nothing but produce, produce, produce....

Lillian Horace, are you feeling all right?

Horace Yes, fine.

Lillian I think it might be an idea to see Dr. Sanders again. He could do a home visit.

Horace If I want to bleed money I'll find a way to have fun doing it.

Lillian Therapy is not undertaken for pleasure.

Horace What is, Lillian?

Lillian Darling. *(Referring to his chest)* I know you won't consider a reduction. But *(Referring to his crotch)* have you thought about an implant?

Horace No.

Lillian I think it would help you own your power. You should think it over.

Horace Mmmm.

Lillian returns to the newspaper.

Horace *(Quietly)* Actually, what I think is, the sky is this brilliant color even though it's freezing outside. You would never know it's winter. And the window is no barrier to us at all Lily. Arrende keeps the glass so clean that even the birds can't see it. And it's insulated so we don't hear them when they thud into it and fall noiselessly down, down, down all the way to the sidewalk. At least, that's the only explanation I can think of.

Lillian I really think—

Horace —The only reason why, in a cloudless blue sky, in a perfect window, there are sometimes tiny bloodstains and feathers trapped in the corner. They're always gone the next day. But you've seen them, haven't you Lily?

Lillian —I think we can learn from everything, / and if—

Horace —Unless Arrende hunts at night, like an owl—

Lillian —and if the world offers us an image, why not invent from it? Birds are great! Think about peacocks, Horace.

Horace Oh I do. I do.

Lillian *(Smiles at Horace)* Good.

Horace Peacocks. Right. I could get all of our money out of the bank. Fluff out my tail feathers and roll around in it every morning. I'd save big bucks on aftershave—the scent of money drives women crazy.

Lillian It's not / about money, dammit—

Horace Children would clutch at my trouser legs, hoping it would / rub off.

Lillian It's the courage to live! It's easy to pine away and refuse to change—but art *is* change. You get out your paints—or your scalpel and latex gloves—and just do it! Seth can't change and look at him!

Horace You can't say that yet. We have to try—

Lillian Horace, I *am* trying! I've done a sketch for you...Subtle but enhancing...We can work with what's already there, like Michelangelo releasing David from his block of marble...

Horace Oh, so you think I'm a lump / of stone

Lillian No, no, I'm not imposing / some stupid—

Horace I have / feelings you know—

Lillian —Schwarzenegger ideal on you, darling—the body is a reflection of the mind and we have the power / to alter—

Horace And men are from Mars and women are / from Venus.

Lillian Fine.

A tight pause.

Horace I can't talk to you about anything.

Lillian Especially my art. Fine.

Horace But you're so beautiful—

Lillian —"When you're angry."

Horace When you're alive. All blue and silver.

Lillian and Horace look at each other, thawing. But Arrende enters.

Arrende The elevators are no longer functioning.

Lillian So, order lunch in from the Internet.

Lillian returns to the newspaper. Arrende drops a coffee cup, which disappears soundlessly into the crack in the floor. She stares after it. The others don't notice.

Horace We should get out more—

Lillian —Ah, here's one.

Horace —Go for a walk, even—Just a walk in the / park.

Lillian —One across: "High pitched lover, safe and courtly."

Horace —We could wear the gas masks like we / used to.

Lillian —Darling, focus! I'm hopeless at these.

Beat. Horace gives up on the subject of going Outside.

Starts with C…

Horace Casanova

Lillian It fits. But "high pitched?" Cas…Cass…

Arrende Castrato.

Lillian *(As if thinking of it herself)* Mmmm…I've got it! Castrato—

Lillian goes to fill in the word.

Horace Don't do that.

Lillian What?

Horace You know he likes to do it himself.

Lillian Eggshells, Horace. We cannot live like this.

Horace But we do.

Arrende *(Clearing throat modestly)* It's best not—

Lillian *(To Horace)* No.

Horace I said, leave it for Seth.

Lillian I will not be / bullied

Horace Fuck Dr. Sanders. It's better to walk on eggshells than smash them underfoot.

Arrende *(Removing the newspaper from the fighting pair)* It is best not to put all your eggs under one boot. *(Beat)* Oops. Sorry for my English.

Arrende folds the newspaper neatly.

Scene 7

Marion is trying to decide how many buttons to leave undone on her shirt for her visit to Lillian. We see Lillian preparing too, in a separate light; she brushes her hair, then tousles it to look casual. They both want to look sexy, but like they haven't tried.

During the above (and continuing through the dialogue) we hear the sounds of heavy breathing and murmurs of sexual pleasure from Horace's regular appointment with Arrende.

This is a split scene: Horace / Arrende (Offstage); Marion / Lillian (Visible).

Marion So, thanks for making time to see me. I know you're busy and all.

Lillian Not at all, in fact I'm glad to have the opportunity.

Horace Oooh—yeah—

Marion You were mentioning how boob jobs had got a lot better since the Stone Age.

Lillian Oh my God, yes! You'd be amazed. Enhancements, reductions—implants of all sorts. Some of the really cutting-edge set are starting to get their pets done too.

Marion Wow. *(Very seductively)* —Well, I wondered if you might like to take a look and give me a quote.

Horace Ooohh—yes—

Marion —Or we could perhaps do some kind of trade.

Lillian Anything I can do to help. In fact I'm glad you came in. I wanted to thank you personally for taking the position at such short notice. "Home Parole" isn't the easiest job for a therapist—

Horace *(Sounding very fake)* Oh baby, that's it.

Lillian I realize that Seth is a 24-hour job—

Marion —Person.

Lillian Good distinction, yes. You seem like a very caring person.

Marion I try. It's my profession.

Horace Tell me you looove it.

Lillian I like that in a woman—

Arrende *(Through inconveniently full mouth)* I looove it.

Lillian —Professionalism.

Marion I like that in a woman too.

Horace Ohhh yes…ooh harder baby…Ooh…

Lillian How about this! I'll offer you a complimentary procedure—to show my appreciation—of your professionalism.

Horace *(Sounds of attempted pleasure)*

Lillian And perhaps I could bother you for a…shoulder rub some time. Just when you get a moment of course.

Horace You're not trying. Talk dirty to me.

Lillian Because I know you have a challenging, full-time job—

Horace Tell me I've got a beautiful…*big*…

Marion —Actually it's pretty average—

Arrende —Oh what a big one.

Marion Loads of wealthy people have psycho kids.

Lillian My son is not a psycho. He has an—

Lillian / Marion "Anger Management Disorder."

Arrende Oh it's so…mmmm…

Horace *(Sounds of attempted pleasure)*

Lillian Anyway, of course I'll take a look for you. It's best to deal with little blemishes while they can still be erased.

Horace Oh…*Fuck it.*

Marion Like anger.

Lillian Especially anger. Unresolved anger can cause cancer.

Marion Really.

Lillian In mice. They've done tests.

Marion How do they make the mice angry?

Lillian Oh, it's…It's quite scientific.

Horace, defeated, enters tucking his shirt into his trousers, followed by Arrende who is getting up from her knees.

Horace Don't we pay you enough?

Arrende I'm sorry, sir. I tried.

Arrende moves behind Horace and massages his shoulders.

Lillian Anyway, if you want to book in a free procedure—

Marion Thanks.

Horace I'm so stressed.

Arrende Even concrete gets stressed.

Horace We're all human, aren't we.

Lillian We can improve on Nature very gently, you know.

Horace Better than being robots.

Lillian So if you want me to look at those breasts for you—

Horace Though I think my wife might prefer a robot.

Lillian —just let me know.

Marion I will. Don't worry.

Horace *(Enjoying shoulder rub)* Oh, that's good.

Lillian Good.

Arrende Good.

Marion Good.

Scene 8

Seth is in his room, staring into the middle distance. For some moments.

Arrende slowly materializes, watching Seth from the balcony. She has three bedraggled and strangely-placed chicken wings grafted on to her shoulders and torso. The effect is Frankensteinian rather than angelic.

Seth Wow. Can you fly with those?

Arrende Of course not. They are a design feature only.

Seth Are you real?

Arrende Not all that often.

She disappears.

Seth I knew that.

Lights down and up. Seth is alone. He holds the newspaper, stares into the middle distance. A feeling of moving underwater, slowly.

Lights down and up.

Marion is standing beside Seth. He holds his arm out. She takes his pulse. She releases his arm. She goes to leave—thinks again—turns the page of the paper for him.

Marion Look, a whole new page. *(Kisses him on the cheek)* Be good now.

Seth *(Very slowly)* I can't…I can't …

Marion Yes you can. You just sit tight and I'll be back.

Marion exits.

Seth …I can't see the clues now.

As if wrestling underwater, Seth turns back the page to the crossword.

Three down. *(Puzzles, gives up)*
Four down. *(Puzzles, gives up)*
Five down. *(Puzzles, gives up)*
Six down. *(Puzzles, gives up)*
Fuck it.

Seth lets the paper fall, and stares at nothing.

Scene 9

Arrende practices her job application from the balcony. She holds a pigeon. With each new "Good morning," she tries a different attitude.

Arrende Good morning, I am applying for the position of, the position of…

Good morning, my name is Arrende and I would be happy to service your every need.

Good morning.
I am very strong.
I don't need much sleep.
I will not disturb you unless you are easily disturbed.
My rates are very reasonable.
I have opposable thumbs and excellent teeth.
I have no nationality to speak of; I am almost American now.
I have no human needs but one: I would prefer to work in a basement.

There is one small obstacle to my attending an interview: I am in a gravitationally challenged state. My passport and memories are locked in the ground floor lobby, along with my vernacular language, as a security deposit.

If I had those in hand I am confident I could regain enough gravity to ride the elevators down; however as things stand, I may need to be airlifted from my current employment.

Replies may be sent by return pigeon. My contact details / are on—

Lillian *(Offstage)* Arrende!! Three minutes!!

Arrende, startled, drops the pigeon. We see it has a scroll attached to its foot. It plummets.

Arrende *(To herself)* Rats! *(To Lillian)* Coming, ma'am.

Scene 10

Lights on just the pigeon. Marion enters, sees the pigeon, stops. Walks over and picks it up—removes the scroll—then carefully puts the pigeon back where it was.

Scene 11

Lillian and Arrende are in Lillian's studio. As before; Arrende in body stocking, Lillian appraising her with felt-tipped pen in hand.

Lillian How's the temperature, Arrende?

Arrende It's fine, ma'am.

Lillian Are you sure you're not cold?

Arrende No, I am fine, ma'am.

Marion enters.

Marion Is now a good time? —No.

Lillian Later.

Marion exits.

Lillian I'm all at sixes and sevens today. Can't make up my mind. *(Beat)* We've done androgyny. We've done the fertility big thigh thing. —Do you have any suggestions?

Arrende I'm not paid for them.

Lillian Oh come on, you're almost one of the family. Just—off the record.

Arrende You could amputate my legs.

Lillian Pardon?

Arrende Ha. Ha.

Lillian Oh a joke—ha! Yes I see. *(Beat)* Is there something you're not telling me, Arrende?

Arrende In regards to what, ma'am?

Lillian I wish you would call me Lily. —I don't know, I'm wondering if I'm not detecting a teensy bit of passive aggression?

Arrende I'm sorry if I offended you, Ma'am. I am not passion-aggressive. In fact since I misplaced my female parts I do not feel violent things / very much.

Lillian Not this again.

Arrende I don't mean to complain. After all, there are many things I enjoy now that I was not able to enjoy before. On account of the gravitational difference. For instance I can sleep standing up, and only need an hour a night. My hair has relaxed. I could probably dismember a person in public without experiencing fear.

Lillian You're scaring me.

Arrende We could do a leg reduction if you wish. I could wheel myself around just as well as walk. And as I perform my more intimate duties on my knees it would save some wear and tear.

Lillian I don't understand your attitude, Arrende.

Arrende I live to please you. You have all my paperwork. Does that please you?

Horace enters.

Horace Sorry.

Horace exits.

Arrende Ma'am if I could have my female parts restored—

Lillian Arrende, I cannot, *cannot* help you. We live in a civilized country; I've never even seen the results of the kind of operation you're referring to.

Arrende There was no operation. There was a slow and parasitic infection—

Lillian I don't think that is medically possible.

Arrende An infection of the organs that control hope.

Beat.

Lillian We just do surface work.

Scene 12

Lights on pigeon. Marion walks deliberately across toward it as Arrende crosses toward it from the other side of the room. Marion gets there first and picks it up, hands it to Arrende.

Marion You dropped something.

Arrende snatches it from her. Lights.

Scene 13

Horace is alone with his mirror. He practices talking to (absent) Lillian.

Horace "Lillian, my love, is there anything bothering you?" —No, hopeless. Be assertive. Don't start with the negative. "Lily love. Perhaps we need a holiday alone. We could find somewhere indoors. With nice dim lighting." —She hates dim lights.

Beat.

"Lillian. I've been thinking things over, and it seems our Seth levels—our *stress* levels—are getting out of hand. We need some…fresh air. We need to go Outside." —Don't even go there…"Lillian, I want to talk about our marriage." —huh—"Do you like my breasts? I'm growing them for you."

When you look at me, even now,
your blue glance makes me shiver.
I turn into feathers and bone marrow.
I wish you would touch me.
It's years since you touched me.
I'm not counting the sex.

I hold my breath when you're sleeping Lily,
just to hear you breathe.
Your ribs imprison my heart.
Cage it like a tree around a bird.

My lost silver planet Lillian, I am the hopeless moon.
Lily my love.
My only love.
Embalmed like a fetus in alcohol
Eyelids never to open
and the tender lashes still unformed.

Horace stares at himself in the mirror.

Why is the light so bright in here?

Scene 14

Seth lies semi-slumped, still sedated, in the position we last saw him. Moments later we see Arrende, in waitress costume, standing with a tray. Arrende watches Seth. Seth watches something fascinating in the far distance.

Lights down and up.

Seth and Arrende. As before, except Arrende has removed her top garments and breasts are visible. Seth blinks.

Lights down and up.

As before. Arrende is in only a thong. She has no breasts.

Lights down and up.

As before. Arrende is fully clothed, still holding the tray

Seth What time is it?

Arrende It is lunch time.

Arrende approaches Seth, who takes the tray. She kneels on all fours. Seth goes to place the tray on her back—pauses—

Seth Arrende? Where's your wings?

Arrende Pardon?

Beat.

Seth What time is it?

Arrende It is lunch time.

Seth I thought so.

Seth lowers the tray onto Arrende's back.

Seth Arrende?

Arrende Yes, Seth.

Seth Can you hear the building cracking?

Arrende When there are cracking noises, I hear them. When there are not, I don't.

Seth Oh. *(Beat)* You don't exactly *hear* it—It feels like bones breaking.

Beat.

You know there are riots on TV. Down there. We don't get any ground noise up here. Nothing. They could've blown up all the bridges and renamed it Blood Island and we'd never fucking know. Unless they cut off our credit cards.

(Sing-song) Peace and quiet, need a riot—
Higher than the trees. Higher than the breeze.
Higher than the stink of gasoline body-jam sidewalk Ant-land.

(Spoken) Do you think I should get a cock-ring?—

(Sing-song) Higher than disease. Higher than the seas.
High high in the sky. Like an Evil Eye.

Arrende Some of us. Are higher. Than others.

Seth That's evolution baby!

Arrende ———

Seth Not by much though.

Arrende No.

Beat.

Seth Arrende? —Peace.

Arrende Peace, Seth.

Seth finishes. Arrende begins to leave smoothly on all fours.

Arrende?

Arrende *(Tartly)* There's no dessert.

Seth Yeah, I figured.

Arrende stands in one smooth movement, catching the tray.

Seth Sweet.

Scene 15

Lillian's studio. Marion pauses at the door. Unseen by the others or audience, Seth is curled up asleep under the trestle bed.

Marion No commitment, OK.

Lillian Relax.

Marion Where is everyone?

Lillian Oh, they're busy. *(Beat)* Just a preliminary exam. So you know what options are available.

Marion approaches warily. Pauses.

Lillian Oh, never mind the mess. *(It's immaculate)* —Take off your shirt.

Marion does.

Reductions aren't difficult these days. Honestly, you'd be walking around again by lunchtime…without the bounce. This…would be the first incision. Right here. The finest possible blade, thinner than a hair. Hardly even bleeds. Then…down…to the areola…where we could draw a circle right…around the nipple like so. And it would just lift…

Marion kisses her.

I love your breasts. Don't do it.

They fall onto the trestle table. The bump wakes Seth, who shoves his way out and runs from the room. The table spins.

Lillian My God.

Marion Oh *fuck*. Fuck fuck. Seth's medication!

She rushes out.

Lillian Marion?

Seth *(Offstage)* Get me out of here! Get me out, get me the fuck—

Sound of a scuffle offstage as Marion grabs and sedates him.

Oooooh.

Marion Sweetheart. Settle down now, OK? OK? Eeee-aa-sy now.

Seth Marion?

Marion Shhh now… *(Sings the first verse of "Junco Partner." Her song continues offstage until indicated)*

Seth *(Offstage)* You still my girl?

In a cold gray light, Lillian listens to Marion singing. Straightens her hair. Her clothes. Resets the surgical table exactly where it was. Puts on her lipstick and regards herself as if in a mirror.

Lillian *(To her reflection)* There.

Seth *(Offstage, between Marion's sung lines)* She never sang to me.

Lillian All right then.

Lillian takes out a hairbrush and begins to brush her hair, slowly and methodically. Marion's singing (Offstage) becomes a soft hum, which continues until Horace speaks.

Arrende from the balcony, drops another pigeon she is trying to persuade to fly. It falls near Lillian, but she doesn't notice it.

Horace appears behind Lillian. The light around her changes to a beautiful color. Horace watches her like a lonely sailor watching a mermaid. Lillian brushes her hair, showing no sign of hearing Horace as he speaks.

Horace Lily my love. I've been thinking things over and I think—that is, we—perhaps we should... *(Beat)* It seems that our...*stress*...levels are somewhat, you know, above the norm. Or the norm has got more stressful. Or stress has leveled, has leveled out. I mean got worse. You know. *(Beat)* I think...I think we need...It wouldn't have to be far. We could do mostly indoor things. We could go somewhere very clean. *(Beat, then with all his courage)* We need to go Outside. —Lily?

Lillian looks at her brush. Sees it is full of hair. She snaps on a pair of latex gloves and takes out a comb. She methodically combs the hair from the brush, removes it from the comb and drops it into a Zip-loc bag, and the gloves in after it. She drops the bag without looking down; the crack in the floor swallows it.

Lillian *(Still to the mirror)* What is it, Horace?

She turns. They stare at each other.

Horace Nothing.

Scene 16

Marion enters, sees the dead pigeon on the floor. Arrende enters from the other side of the room, hurries toward pigeon—sees Marion and stops.

Marion walks deliberately over the pigeon and picks it up. She holds it out to Arrende.

Marion You dropped something.

Arrende snatches the pigeon. They stare at each other.

Scene 17

Seth, alone in his room. He stares into the distance. For some moments. Arrende enters.

Arrende Afternoon tea is being served.

Seth You look different.

Arrende That is my job.

Seth What happened to the wings?

Arrende What wings?

Seth Forget it. *(Beat)* They looked like crap anyway.

Arrende Cross-species transplants are very difficult.

Seth Yeah, like pigs' hearts.

Arrende Actually, humans are well suited to pigs' hearts.

Seth That's totally depressing. *(Beat)* How about that mouse with the human ear? They sewed a fucking human ear on to its back. Sick. I just think, what does it hear?

Arrende The ear?

Seth The *mouse*, fuck it. The poor fucking mouse.

Arrende Hah.

Seth Does it hear, like human sounds through that ear? Does it have to listen to all the shit we get, the "War on Everything"—

Arrende I doubt it. From my limited experience with wings, I was unable to flap. There was no way to interpret the data pouring in. It was like static. A gray hissing of incomprehensible sensation.

Seth Yeah, I get that when Dad talks to me.

Arrende I don't think / that's the same.

Seth *(Starting to pace)* It's the same fucking thing. They're trying to graft me back on and my immune system is going, woah danger, fucking fight or flight—

Arrende Cookies with your coffee?

Seth *(Running)* I hate cookies! I hate coffee! I want to go home!

Arrende *(Catching and holding him with some force)* You are home.

Seth *I KNOW!!!*

Beat.

Arrende Cream?

Seth Nothing. Nothing. Nothing.

Arrende Nothing. Is not an option.

She forces him to sit. Beat.

Seth No cream.

Arrende *(Smiles)*

Seth Where are you really from?

Arrende *(Pompously)* I come from a long tradition…a long tradition of…

Seth Arrende. *Please.*

Beat.

Arrende I can't remember any more.

Scene 18

Horace has his checkbook out, but his pen hovers over it till the end of the scene.

Marion I've talked to her. —Make it out to cash. —I don't think it's just about you. The breasts aren't the problem.

Horace Really.

Marion It's lots of other stuff. But it will take a bit more research. —I've had a lot of expenses with Seth this month, too.

Horace Remember the goose that lays the golden egg. You want it to last.

Marion Actually, I think it's the Seth thing. It's stressing her out. You know her thing about disorder and all that.

Horace She is his mother.

Marion Makes it worse.

Horace I'm not leaving him in Rehab to get pecked to death by the bigger boys.

Marion There is a way. After the trial period I could…arrange a more permanent solution.

Horace Be very careful, Miss.

Marion What do you think I am? I'm a practical working girl—

Horace With a loaded syringe—

Marion —That you pay me to use.

Beat.

Horace So. Your practical idea.

Marion Seth and I rent an apartment. A nice little basement on the other end of the Island. Round the clock care. He could write his songs and I could go shopping. All it would take is a little plastic card.

Horace I see—

Marion With a $10,000 initial / limit.

Horace Let's get this straight, Miss. Your job is to care for Seth on the premises. Every three hours, *on* the hour. The whole point of Home Parole—

Marion —He's better at ground / level.

Horace —is to readjust to his family in a secure environment.

Marion He's fucking scared of heights!

Horace An elevated life has its challenges for all of us, Miss.

Marion I'm telling you, Seth / doesn't deal—

Horace The sooner everyone's…adjusted, the sooner we can all go Outside.

Beat.

Marion What?

Horace Lillian feels more secure in a hygienic setting.

Marion So she stays, we all stay? Is that the problem?

Horace I think it's better to say that the glass is half-full. We need to carefully add to it, drip by drip, until one day, it overflows down the elevator and we can return to normal life. As a family. Drip by drip.

Marion Horace!

Horace You don't smash all your eggs underfoot in one basket. You need to learn patience, Miss.

Marion All right. *(Beat)* Patience is expensive.

Horace writes the check.

Scene 19

Lillian and Marion lie in post-sex langor. A used latex glove lies on the floor.

Lillian Tell me your worst fantasy. Not the most pleasurable. The worst.

Marion I don't have them.

Lillian slaps her playfully.

Lillian Don't lie to Mama.

Marion I kind of *do* them instead. For other people.

Lillian Oh.

Marion *(Teasing)* Are we jea—lous?

Lillian No, of course not. *(Beat)* I think we're out of time. Horace will be / wondering where

Marion Horace is crying in the bathroom. There's a trail of wet feathers. Seth's doing the crossword, very very slowly. Arrende's working on her resume. We've got at least fifteen till any of that / changes.

Lillian Why is Horace crying? I don't like to think of him crying.

Marion He misses himself. —So, what about you?

Lillian I'm not missing anything.

Marion What about *your* fantasy? "The worst."

Lillian Oh. I, well. I don't really have them either.

Marion Bullshit.

Lillian Working with Arrende gives me a creative outlet.

Marion Yeah but that's work. What about play?

Lillian This is play.

Marion For you it is.

Lillian pulls back. Beat.

Lillian I told you. Arrende is my creative outlet.

Marion *(Teasing)* Same body, same room—you should get out more!

Lillian Artists can work for years on the same / theme—

Marion Right. We should probably get moving—

Lillian We do a lot of variations—

Marion *(As if leaving)* The others will be / wondering—

Lillian Well I do have…I really don't have fantasies. But I have my worst dream. A lot.

Marion Oh?

Lillian It's—Oh, it's nothing.

Marion We really are out of time.

Lillian Everything's gray in my dream. Steel gray. The operating table, the ceiling, the sky outside, the surgical gloves, the mirror—

Marion —Like always—

Lillian —But *in* the mirror too—I look away, and down at my hands—my skin's gray, like fine soft ash.

Marion This is erotic?

Lillian I touch my skin, this soft, soft, dead-color skin…and it starts to bump and wrinkle and these little lumps start forming—a dreadful pink color like Valentine's candy. I can't stop stroking my arms, my face, my neck…then lower…my decolletage—

Marion —Your what?

Lillian Shhh…and the little pink lumps start to get hard. My clothes sort of disappear and I'm naked inside this skin-sac, shriveled like…an elephant's scrotum.

Marion Ewwww—

Lillian But the bumps, the bumps just keep on pushing out rosebuds. And I shudder and rub and stroke and they stand up and erupt and I'm on fire, I just can't stop, they keep popping out like sexual measles, and I'm calling out for help, and *she* comes in like she always does "Yes, Madam" and then…this is terrible…

Marion What?

Lillian She *smiles*. And then she slowly, softly, with the purest cruelty, starts to rub me all over, knowing I'm out of control, that I'll burst if she…and she does…and I'm coming, not once, but all over, every bud bursting and hurting and oh, oh oh, my neck, my ears, my butt, my hips, inside my knees, between my *toes*…I'm dribbling and writhing, oh oh oh…so humiliating…Finally the last spasm is over and I, I, I curl up on the floor inside this deflated old skin and now the little buds are just dried-up sores.

"Help me Arrende" I say and she smiles wider and says "Shhhh" and then with her nails, slits open my gray elephant-scrotum skin, and it half-hurts and it's half-divine, and she peels it right off me and there I am, inside. Just…me.

I close my eyes and when I open them again, she's gone and everything is reborn. My new pink skin folding round me like a rose, all soft and new. Every cell, every breath is new, every old thing is gone, every memory, every scar, everything, everything, everyone. I will never need anything ever again.

Beat.

Marion Wow.

Lillian It's a bit cold in here.

Marion I never remember my dreams.

Lillian No?

Marion As a rule.

Lillian Rules are good. *(Beat)* Horace has nightmares.

Marion What about?

Lillian Oh, nothing. —Being trapped on the moon…I wonder what Seth's nightmares are.

Marion He doesn't need them. He *is* a nightmare.

Lillian —Person.

Marion Nightmare *person*.

Lillian He's my son.

Marion Just playing. *(Beat)* Joke. —Lillian? —Oh, lighten *up*.

Lillian Would you just. Hold me.

Marion I've got to see to Seth.

Lillian Please.

Marion No. Nothing personal. I just can't. Get your husband to do it.

Marion leaves.

Lillian *(Calling after Marion)* How is Seth, anyway?

Lillian straightens herself up. Checks her hair, her lipstick. Resets the trestle table for surgery.

Lillian Arrende! *Arrende!*

Scene 20

Seth and Horace.

Horace You should leave time to adjust.

Seth No, I'm adjusted.

Beat.

Horace Well, for all of us. Normal life… It can be. You know.

Seth Yeah.

Horace Hard.

Seth What.

Horace Freedom is a hard thing.

Beat.

Seth What has that got to do with normal life?

Horace I don't know.

Beat.

We should have some. I think.

Seth Some what?

Horace I can't remember. I'm itchy all over. A little dark corner, yes, that's it.

Beat.

Seth Is this a father and son talk?

Horace I wish I had a nice blanket.

Horace leaves.

Seth Well, Dad. I hope you find one.
(Sings) High high in the sky
In a little steel cage
The windows cracked
And the walls were dirty.
The canary died
Its feathers turned gray
And its toes turned up
So they stuffed it
And dyed it yellow
Now it sings
On cue
(Changing tune to Louis Armstrong song)
"And I think to myself
What a wonderful world."
Do you like my song, Dad?
Do you like that song, Dad? Dad? *Dad!*

Horace reappears.

I asked you: Do you like my song!
Do you like my fucking song!

Seth runs over to his father and starts waltzing him, but roughly.

(Singing) And I *think* to my*self*
What a *won*-derful *world*…
And I *think* to my*self*
What a *won*-derful *world*…

Seth violently whirls and lifts Horace around.

Horace *(Clucks)* Marion! Marion—Code four.

Marion runs in, half-undressed and injects Seth in the neck.

Seth Oooooh.

Horace What the cluck is going on. It's every three hours, *on* the hour—

Marion *(To Seth)* I'm so sorry sweetie.

Horace If you kept to the pills, every three hours, *on* the hour then this, this *(Clucks)* I hate it when you have to do— *(Clucks)* Look at him.

Marion I got caught up.

Horace So I see.

Seth Marion.

Marion *(To Horace, pushing her breasts toward him)* OK, have a good look—Want a feel?

Horace I'm a vegetarian now. *(Clucks)* Where are the blankets kept?

Horace exits.

Seth Marion? Why don't we fuck anymore?

Marion Life's like that, peaches. No middle ground.

Seth We shouldn't have come here. You don't love me anymore. I'd never strangle you again. You know I'll be good.

Marion When you're good, you're floppy. When you're bad, I'm dead.

Seth *(Giggles)* Yeah. I guess that's right. *(Beat)* Do you think Dad's all right?

Marion Relative to what.

Seth To normal.

Marion Huh. Hard to judge.

Seth He was talking about it.

Marion What?

Seth Normal life.

Marion Nostalgia. That's bad.

Seth Marion? Do you think I should get a cock ring?

Marion What for?

Seth What does Mom say about me?

Beat.

Marion Do the crossword, honey.

She pushes the paper at him and leaves.

Seth *(Singing a little)* High high in the sky,
Like an old glass eye
That couldn't cry—

Seth peers at the crossword.

One across. "High pitched lover, safe and courtly."
Hmm…."Cheerleader?" —Nope.

Beat.

I wonder what happens in the black spaces.

Beat.

The words are all surrounded.

Beat.

They're just little white bridges over the darkness.

Dad?
(Sings sotto voce) And I think to myself…
—Dad? Why wouldn't you dance with me?
(Calls to absent Horace) I like your feathers.

Scene 21

The latex glove lies incriminatingly on the floor. Marion rushes in to retrieve it, but Arrende has already seen it. Arrende walks deliberately over to the glove, picks it up with tongs.

Arrende You dropped something.

Marion snatches for the glove. Arrende keeps it out of reach. Marion gives her back her scroll. Arrende gives Marion the glove.

Scene 22

Horace, alone with his mirror. A fluffy, chicken-ish moment. Arrende enters. She politely clears her throat, waits.

Arrende Good morning.

Horace Is it? —Oh. Arrende?

Beat.

What is it?

Arrende It is our scheduled time, Sir.

Horace Oh—oh, so it is. I thought it was later.

Arrende Shall we begin?

Horace Of course.

Arrende "Ooh, I see you're a big man."

Beat.

Horace What?

Arrende I'm sorry. Shall we start again?

Horace Oh—yes, why not. —Do we have any blankets? I like the woolly ones. But not scratchy wool, soft wool.

Arrende I think so. Should I get you one?

Horace Later. Weren't we in the middle of something?

Arrende We can continue.

Horace Yes.

Arrende "Ooh, I see you're a big man."

Horace I don't feel big. I feel itchy.

Arrende "I bet you're even bigger…up close."

Arrende gets down on her knees, reaches for Horace's fly.

Horace Why are you down there?

Arrende This is what we always do, sir. But frankly, my knees are feeling it.

Horace Is it? —Are they? *(Beat)* Is that all?

Arrende No. Next is "I can give you what you need."

Horace I think I need a dark corner and some straw. Arrende, would you mind—Would you scratch the back of my neck? And the light's so bright. Bright white.

She scratches his neck. Feathers float out.

Horace Ooh, that's good. Cluck. Yes…A little corner. Cluck. A blanket. It's not hard to be happy—Why isn't Lillian happy?

Arrende ———

Horace Tuck me in Arrende.

Arrende helps Horace to settle in a nest-like corner. She goes to leave.

Horace Arrende?

Arrende Yes, sir.

Horace Thank you.

Arrende *(Beams)* It's a pleasure. Horace.

Arrende leaves. Horace nests. Marion enters.

Marion Horace. This isn't going to work. You should talk to her. It's like—there are limits.

Horace *(Blinks, flaps)*

Marion I've done all the research I can, and I just / don't feel—

Horace I'm all scratchy. Scratchety-scratch.

Marion Please. Focus. She needs you. Or someone. But not me, it's not about breasts even if they are kind of an added extra, like a design feature you know, it's optional, not the basic engine. Which needs more than a tune-up. Which is like out of my skill-base. Seth's my limit there anyway, you know what I mean, they get under your skin. And fuck that for a joke. I'm starting to have dreams. And that's not good. It fucks up your judgement.

But you, Horace. You have to let her under your skin. So that's it. My last paid advice. Get in there and hold her and try not to cut yourself. Cash will be fine. Me and Seth will leave tomorrow.

Horace *(Petulant)* Seth-to-death. Scratchy / up to here.

Marion Bottom line, this situation is not working for your son. He really doesn't have a head for heights.

Horace Light too bright. Nighty-night. My neck? Scratchy my neck?

Beat.

Marion Horace—what did you just say?

Horace *(Offering his neck)* Just a little one.

Marion thinks. Then takes the wallet from Horace's back pocket.

Marion There, that's better now. More comfy.

Horace squats clucking, presenting his neck for a scratch. Marion takes a credit card from the wallet. Then scratches his neck.

Marion Let's feather your nest.

She pulls all the bills from the wallet and tucks them in around him.

Horace Good girl. Good girl. Lighty-night.

Scene 23

Seth, center stage, is puzzling over the crossword. Arrende is on the balcony above him. She is crouched, hunting with a butterfly net at the window. She lunges forward a couple of times, trying but failing to catch something.

Arrende *(Lunges)* Haha!

She pulls a dead pigeon from the net.

Huh. Heart attack.

She holds it by a wingtip and drops it from the window.

Seth Arrende? What are you—?

Arrende As you see. Catching pigeons.

Seth Oh. *(Beat)* Why?

Arrende I am sending out my resume.

Seth Cool. *(Beat)* What's wrong with email?

Arrende There is a magnetic field distortion in the building. Electronic communication is no longer possible. And as I am no longer able to use the elevators—Hah!

Arrende swoops and catches another pigeon. She ties an envelope to its foot and throws it out the window. It plummets.

Arrende Work in progress, as your mother might say. Lighter paper next time.

Seth Isn't that like, cruel?

Arrende It could have flapped harder. We all could.

Seth Maybe it was already dead.

Arrende In that case, the question of cruelty is redundant.

Lillian *(Offstage)* Arrende!

Arrende Shoot!

She runs off.

Seth I didn't know you could run! That's awesome.

Seth starts playing air guitar to the music in his head.

Seth *(Sing-song)* Na na—na na na—
High high in the sky
Like a dirty sigh
My girl is coming by
Sooooon…

(Speaking) Not bad—

(Sing-song) Stuck up in the stars
Like a…
Like a…na na na

Marion enters, waving Horace's credit card excitedly.

Marion Guess what, sweet pea—

Seth *(Absorbed in song)* Na na na na…like a…um…guitar

Marion Wake up! Good news—

Seth I'm *writing* a *song*.

Marion Fuck you, I'm *writing* the checks

Seth It's for you.

Marion Oh.

Seth *(Sings)* High high in the sky
Like a Lemon Pie
My girl is coming by
Real soon…
Stuck up in the stars
Playin' air guitar
My girl and I are dancing
In the Moon…
(Speaks) light

Marion That's—that's very nice.

Seth *(Smiles)*

Marion Don't look at me like that.

Seth Like what?

Marion You're creeping me out.

Seth What?

Marion Like a sick puppy.

Seth *(Hurt)* You're fucking sick.

Marion Yeah, that's right. Now. *Look. (Shows credit card)* From Daddy.

Seth He gave you that?

Marion Sort of.

Seth Fucking great! We're out of / here!

Marion Wo—wo, not so fast. I have to deal with *her*.

Seth Fuck her.

Marion You want her to call Parole?

Seth No.

Marion Patience, angel dung. *(Refers to crossword)* Look, you've still got one to go. When you're done, we'll be out of here.

Seth Marion? Did you like my song?

Beat.

Marion It was all right.

Scene 24

Lillian waits in her studio. Arrende rushes in, trailing a few pigeon feathers.

Lillian You're late. You're *never* late.

Arrende *(Rushed)* Madam I have no choice but to terminate my employment with you.

Lillian Arrende, please. We've barely started.

Arrende But it is time.

Lillian I have to ask you something.

Arrende All right. But then I must terminate…

Lillian Yes. Yes. —Arrende, have you noticed anything…odd about Horace lately?

Arrende In what respect?

Lillian In a, um, a kind of species orientation kind of way.

Arrende No.

Lillian Does he seem distracted?

Arrende At times. At times, not.

Lillian I know we agreed not / to talk—

Arrende I cannot discuss my private sessions with him. Nor can I discuss with him my private sessions with you. It is a condition of my employment and your marriage contract.

Lillian What is wrong with you lately, Arrende? You're talking like a robot.

Arrende I am a foreigner. We are unpredictable when we are not robotic.

Beat.

Lillian You're really pissed about the female parts thing aren't you.

Arrende It makes it harder to function. Especially in gravitationally challenged / environments.

Lillian We're not going to get any work done today, that's obvious.

They glare at each other, then begin The Game.

Arrende In that case ma'am I'm afraid I must terminate my employment with you.

Lillian Oh no! Please do not terminate your employment with us.

Arrende I'm afraid I must terminate my employment with you.

Lillian Oh no! Please do not make me beg.

Arrende I'm afraid I must make you beg.

Arrende forces Lillian to her knees, and traces the pathway that she narrates along Lillian's body.

If you cut down the center line of the body
Every organ is available to your outstretched hand.
Each in its nest.
The kidneys—home of fear.
The liver—seat of the soul.
The lungs—home of grief.
Every time you lie, the lungs harden a little.
How about you, ma'am? Are your lungs moist
And soft…and pink…?
Or are they old and hard and blackened—

Lillian What? This is not / part of…

Arrende *—Keep your eyes down—*
If you cut down the center line of the body…
past the belly…
You reach the sweet cage of the hips.
A woman walks from her hips
but where do I walk?

Lillian Arrende!!

Arrende *(With building urgency)* My head just floats, tied by the neck, this long head-strong head-string string-me-along we made beautiful together—

Lillian Please. Stop.

Arrende —Ma'am…Lillian—
We're so close…to just floating away.
And smells, the well's—
all dried up—gone.
Smell of children—Do I have…?
Smell of fear: nothing
No bleeding even when you cut me…
with your…not just the hair—fine scare—shine blades
but no more touch—fever or red—spilling rage—

Lillian *(Really scared)* Please Arrende. Stop.

Arrende Please—Lily. I'm begging.
Cut—cut, cut—cut me up and open
This broken—Let it hurt
A wound that keeps on wounding
A female wound to let the world in
Just *something* to let the world in
and give me some sobbing weight
I beg beg beg beg beg / beg beg beg…

Lillian Arrende—I *can't*. I can't cut people up.
There are procedures. There are rules. This is America.

Beat.

Arrende If you cut down the center line of the body
Every organ is available to your outstretched hand.
Shrunken inside its chrysalis:
This body, house of fear.
This well of gray hours.
This preserve of dried time.
And you are a fool who courts the dust.

Lillian looks up.

Arrende Keep your fucking eyes down.

Scene 25

Seth alone.

Seth Mar—i—on! —I'm writing you a song.

He riffs on air guitar, gives up.

Ma—ri—on! — *(Listens to the silence)*

My head feels like it's inside a condom.

(Sings) High high in the sky
Like a dirty sigh
My girl is coming by
Soon—
Stuck up in the stars
No air to feed my air guitar—
(Half-hearted air guitar riff) Na na na na na nah
—It sounds fake.

He gives up, mimes smashing guitar.

Actually we're fucked, Marion, 'cause songs can't get up this high. You gotta catch them like 'flu. Jammed up close with other sick people breathing out their morning coffee half-dead dreams.

Here it's just me and the furniture.
Swa-a-a-ying in the wind.
It's a long way down

To splatter like trash all over the road.
"Oh, he died of building fatigue"
Or metal fatigue or flesh fatigue
and fucking guys in army fatigues all over town guarding the bridges
—do you think they know something we don't?

Whoa steady. Don't get paranoid. That's *stress*.
Low stress in a dress, think about that
skirts lifting up over subway grills,
that's what my songs are
dirty air rising out of a subway
like fingers up a white skirt…mmmm…
Marion! Come here!…
This was a crappy plan. Worse than Rehab.
—Marion!

Seth sizes up the window.

Look, the sun's a big yellow pill.
I could just swallow *that*.
Wash it down with mother's milk—
(Roaring) Aaaaaaaaooooooooooooowwwwww

Seth runs, flat out, toward the audience as if preparing to dive into the sun / out the window. Marion runs on, tackles him to the floor.

Marion You little bullshit artist.

Seth You don't love me anymore. You love that fucking ice cube on legs—

Marion She's your mother.

Seth Not my fault.

Marion It's just homework. So get over it.

Seth Yeah, on what? Carpet burns?

Marion You are fucking high maintenance, Seth. I should have asked for a raise.

Seth I can help you with that.

He stands, puts her hand on his crotch

Marion Oooh this is new

Seth kisses her gently. Strokes her hair.

Seth You're my girl. *(Beat)* I hate heights. I get seasick.

Marion Just one more day / baby face.

Seth I'll be all right / on the ground.

Marion It's gonna happen real soon. I've found us a basement under a traffic jam. With hot running water and guitars in every room.

Seth All right! You're beautiful. —If you touch *her* again, I will kill you. You hear me?

Marion Yes, angel dung.

Seth I love your hair.

Marion I love you too.

They kiss, begin to make out.

Seth I love your breasts. I love your neck. It's so white…and soft…like a little mushroom…

He clasps his hands round her neck.

Marion No, Seth.

Seth Please…Just this once…I'll stop in time, promise…

Marion No.

Seth *(Tightening hands quickly)* But I *want* to.

Marion whips out her syringe and injects him. This time he falls straight to the ground, unconscious.

Marion Strike three.

She stands looking at him, as sad as Marion can ever get.

Oh well. Nice dream.

Beat. She plays with Horace's credit card.

I guess it's just me, then.

Marion exits. Arrende enters, sees Seth sprawled on the floor.

Arrende Seth.

Seth Mmmrrrggghh

Arrende Wake up Seth. It is time for coffee. *(Beat)* It is time for lunch. *(Beat)* It is time for the crossword. *(Beat)* It is time to wake up, Seth.

Marion *(From offstage)* Arrende!!

Marion runs in wearing lipstick and coat and carrying a suitcase.

The fucking elevator's not working! Fix it!!

Arrende looks at her.

What?

Arrende *(Indicating Seth)* You dropped something.

Marion What's it to you?

Arrende Pick it up.

Marion Go to hell. Get me / out of here.

Arrende Did you want to use the elevator?

Marion helps Arrende drag Seth into a sitting slump on his beanbag.

Marion The elevator?

Arrende Is out of order. As you observed.

Marion Don't fuck with me, you bionic bitch!

Seth *(Still mostly asleep)* Marion?

Marion Shhh, sweetie. *(To Arrende)* Get me the fuck out. Now.

Arrende Are you terminating your employment?

Marion What's it / to you?

Seth Don't leave me.

Marion Seth, I'm just, um. Going to the store. For milk.

Seth OK.

Marion *(To Arrende)* Happy now? Let's go!

Marion pulls out Arrende's resume (the one she took from the fallen pigeon).

Is this in your fucking contract? Seeking other employment? *PRIVATE* surgical records?

Arrende Of my body—

Marion Of her patented creative property.

They glare at each other. Deadlock. Then Arrende points to the exit sign she showed the audience at the start of the show.

Arrende The stairs.

Marion You're kidding! / Seven miles—

Arrende Seven miles of stairs. —It's better with surgically-enhanced thighs.

Marion What!!! But—the oxygen—is it pressurized? How long / since anyone's—

Arrende I'm sure you'll find out.

Marion Arrende. Please.

Arrende Take it. Or leave it.

Marion goes to leave. Arrende blocks her, holds out her hand for her resume. Marion hands it over and storms toward the exit.

Seth Marion?

He tries to stand. Marion stops, but can't turn to look at him.

Marion I loved your song, Seth.

She rushes out. Seth falls forward into Arrende's arms.

Seth *(To where Marion was)* I love you too.

Arrende carries him out.

Scene 26

Lillian is at the breakfast table. She is dressed up and has the nervous energy of someone preparing for her first parachute jump.

The building creaks and groans intermittently through this scene.

Lillian Where is everybody? Horace? Time to rise and shine! *(To her reflection in window)* You know, I think I'm done with the Arrende thing. It's gotten old. Time for a fresh start. And what a beautiful day for it… The sky is this brilliant color, even though it's freezing outside. You'd never know it's winter. —Arrende! Can you get the coats out? They're behind the gas masks. Arrende? —Where *is* everyone?

Arrende shepherds Seth in.

Lillian Go and get Horace. Tell him we're having a Going Out Rehearsal.

Arrende *(Looks at Lillian)*

Lillian Please.

Arrende leaves.

Lillian Why is Seth on his own? Where's Marion?—

Seth She's gone.

Lillian What? What do you mean?

Seth She got sick of your bullshit. She quit.

Lillian But she can't have. We haven't paid her yet.

Seth Yeah well she's gone.

Lillian But I wanted to show her the / art galleries and…

Seth She's not *your* nurse, Mother.

Lillian It's Lillian.

Seth Yeah right.

The building groans. We hear chicken clucks.

Lillian What's that noise?

Seth Thunder and lightning.

Lillian It can't be. Seth, look at the sky. It's perfect.

Seth Yeah, it's all perfect.

Beat.

Lillian How's the crossword going? —Oh, you've nearly finished it. Last clue—

The offstage sounds grow louder.

Seth "A ruptured moment." Starts with H.

Lillian Membrane, surely. / A ruptured membrane.

Seth *(Singing to himself)* Give me water water water when I'm thirsty
Water's a / mighty good drink when you're dry—

Lillian "Hymen" most likely.

Seth *(Singing)* Give me kindness when I'm / sickly
Cause I want to go to Heaven…

Creaking, groaning and clucking sounds.

Lillian What's that noise?

Seth *I GOT IT! I GOT IT!*

Lillian Arrende!

Seth That's it! "A ruptured moment—" Heaven!
(Singing) Cause I want to go to Heaven

Lillian This is not an opera, Seth.

Seth I'm good at crosswords. You're useless.

Lillian Seth. Heaven is a perfect state. What is perfect cannot rupture or it would no longer be perfect. Horace!!

Seth See what I mean? You've got the wrong mentality.

Sound of scuffling and agitated chicken clucks.

Lillian Horace!

Arrende shepherds in Horace.

Hi sweetie. We need to expand our horizons. And so, we are having a Going Out Rehearsal. We'll do it in stages. Today we will descend to the garage and next week—we will open the garage doors.

Horace *(Clucks)*

Lillian I know, but you can read it in the car. Remember?

Horace *(Clucks)*

Lillian People did that all the time. I'm sure they still do.

Horace *(Clucks)*

Lillian Well, you'll have to take a bagel—

Horace *(Clucks)*

Lillian No, we're out of low fat.

Thunder. Building cracking sounds. The crack in the floor widens and dust spurts from it.

Seth *(To Lillian)* "A Ruptured Moment."

Arrende *(Looks at crossword)* "Hiatus."

Seth "Heaven."

Thunder. Cracking and groaning.

Lillian *(To Arrende)* Did you hear that?

Arrende I hear things when they are there—

Seth She hears everything. It's just static through her wings though—

Lillian Arrende doesn't have wings.

Horace *(Clucks)*

Seth I like your hair like that Dad.

Thunder. Horace crawls under the table, clucking and shaking.

Dad's scared, Lillian.

Lillian No he's not. He's not.

Thunder. The crack in the floor opens wider. Horace runs away.

Horace? Horace?

Lillian runs off in pursuit.

Seth Now everything's fucked—

Arrende True—

Seth —It's not just me.

Arrende But without gravity, nowhere to fall. That is the silver cloud.

Seth "Silver lining."

Arrende My English.

Seth I like your English.

Lillian returns.

Lillian Where's Horace? I've lost my Horace.

Arrende There he goes.

Horace dives into the crack in the floor and disappears.

Lillian Horace!!!

Lillian dives after him. They disappear. Dust, feathers, silence.

Seth I finished the crossword.

Arrende Good.

Seth All that blue sky. It's beautiful.

Arrende Yes. It is.

The building cracks apart and dies, howling and groaning.

A flash of light shoots from the crack in the floor. Then darkness. Silence.

When the light returns, the entire building has collapsed.

Everyone is gone except Arrende, who is suspended,
weightless,
mid-air,
in a luminous blue light.
Black out.

End of play.

The Vigil or
The Guided Cradle
Crystal Skillman

Yesterday's Future:
Crystal Skillman's *The Vigil or The Guided Cradle*

Interview with Chris Mills

I remember, very clearly, meeting Crystal Skillman.

I had heard great things about her from the fantastic women of 24seven Lab; we were having our first meeting, so I was eager. I remember that she was young-looking—fresh-faced and pig-tailed—with endearing enthusiasm. I thought: I wonder what this sweet young miss has written a play about. From the first scene, I was taken by the sophisticated craft; the play seemed wise beyond her years. With clear characters, a sense of urgency, and a strong pull toward a direction, toward desire—and dialogue that sounded like people talking—the play's dark subject continued to be beautifully presented and shrewdly interrogated. Turned out that the writing was *exactly* the wisdom of Crystal's years.

Brecht tells us to give our dramas a bit of historical distance. He holds a canny belief that we learn from watching the predicament of others, taking lessons from those like ourselves, though not us; easier to see the speck in our brother's eye than the log in our own. Crystal's method in *The Vigil* satisfies Brecht's agenda even as she incorporates her own. *The Vigil* considers the question of torture; it's outlined early as a central focus, a settled problem set in a deep (and notorious) historical moment. As such, the contours of pain's infliction are easy to parse and reject: hooded, be-robed persecutors, by candlelight, are easy to hate. It's not until we've developed our readerly antipathies and alliances that the slowly unfolding question of our own culture's—and possible contemporaries'—complicity comes to the fore. As the Foreigner abandons her dying mother's bedside and seems to follow in her father's sadistic footsteps, we understand the full weight of torture through an ever-widening set of perspectives. In this way, we have the opportunity to examine the problem at a distance, noting its dents and scratches, before we are forced to see our own reflection in the surface. Readers move through the cathartic story of one character's tragic arc, even as another's won't let us off of the emotional hook. We are simultaneously satisfied and agitated, creating a process of theatricality that lingers long after the text is back on the shelf.

What you will read here is surely the leanest, most muscular version of the play. I observed the process of honing and buffing, now you, lucky reader, have the many-faceted outcome to enjoy.

Chris Mills First question, of course: Why torture?

Crystal Skillman In 2004, a play of mine was produced at a festival in Prague by Drama of Works, a NYC theater company. We all got off the plane, freshly arrived in this magical city, and the first place we naively entered was the Torture Museum. As the museum went on and on, we came to realize these were all the actual instruments of torture used. When I turned one corner I saw a full display of how The Vigil (or the Guided Cradle) torture device was the origin of Sleep Deprivation torture, and the Abu Ghraib photos, which had been exposed only a day earlier, popped into my mind. This was the same thing, and I understood it immediately. I knew I wanted to write a play about that. I'm lucky that Impetuous Theater Group and the Brick Theater both loved the play so much they jumped on the opportunity to produce it together in Spring 2010.

CM How did you research/prepare for writing the play's sixteenth century section? Is it an Inquisition reference?

CS At the Torture Museum only The Vigil mentioned the name of an inventor. I still have my original ticket from the Torture Museum where on the back I had written his name: Ippolito Marsili. But I knew that I wasn't interested in writing a history play—I wanted to make a point about today. So I consciously chose not to research the period while writing. That's why I think the play is so imaginative. In working on the play in production we dove into the research and found there's great power in associating Ippolito with the start of the Renaissance (so more fifteenth century) and a more modern way of thinking, which of course instantly sets him apart from these torturers still "stuck in the dark" so to speak.

CM The stories you tell from Prague give a lovely sense of place and folklore to the play. Were the stories fundamental to the play's formulation?

CS Yes! I think writing Foreigner as a tourist there was my own personal way of entering the play. A lot of these local stories that worked their way into the play are the ones that grabbed my attention. The clock. The apostles. Golem. They were like little secrets that drove me through the challenges of writing the play.

CM I'm interested in your use of a split stage, which you introduce very early, and work with well. Could you speak to how it affects your working process?

CS I knew I wanted each period to affect each other in subtle ways—like a tennis match. So in this case I didn't plot any of the play at all. I titled each scene before I wrote it and then wove in that detail. In a similar way, the visual world of the play and its split stage has this sense of discovery. We start the play feeling that our twenty-first century scenes are simply in conversation with the medieval period, but also are somewhat removed, until—for one moment—we are in the same place, same time.

CM The specter of bad American behavior hangs over this play, feeling like the consequence of the text's early torturers. How does this function for you as a political (or non-political) statement?

CS As horrible as it may seem, we all have that possibility to be either torturer or prisoner. In this play we watch characters from rich upbringings, religious, poor, those with an ignorant political life, those very aware—all who at some point perceive that they are in situations that call for these choices. Why? And what is our responsibility within that question? How we enable torture can be subtle. Looking away does just as much damage as planting a bomb. The play finds that the key is in whose face you see in front of you when faced with these choices. The minute it is familiar, everything changes. How do we find a way to see ourselves, our family, in the faces of strangers? If we can do that, we take a step closer to being able to change.

Chris Mills teaches in the drama department at Tisch School of the Arts, and Playwrights Horizons Theater School, and is a dramaturg with Theater Mitu, 24seven Lab and Young Playwrights, Inc. She's made theater with groups such as Philadelphia Alliance for Performance Alternatives, Walnut Street Theater, Chicago Shakespeare Company, Stage Left, Lucky Pierre and Goat Island Performance Group (among others). Her work has been published in *[1968]: Moments of Culture in Context*, *TDR*, *Art Journal*, *Theater Journal* and *The Village Voice*.

Characters

Foreigner/Girl, mid-20s.
Translator, 30.
Ippolito Marsili, early 30s.
Aldo, early 20s.
Balto, late 20s
Prime, early 30s
Jan, mid-20s.

Place

Summer, Prague.

Time

Between now (21st century) and then (15th century).

Playwright's Note

The set should be minimal and not "realistic."

Production History

The Vigil or The Guided Cradle was first presented by Impetuous Theater Group (John Hurley, Artistic Director) in a co-production with the Brick Theater, Inc. (Michael Gardner, Robert Honeywell, Artistic Directors) on April 22, 2010 at the Brick Theater in Williamsburg, NYC, with the following cast and credits:

The cast and creative contributors were:
Foreigner - Susan Louise O'Connor
Translator - Dion Mucciacito
Ippolito - Christian Rummel
Aldo - Travis York
Balto - Vinnie Penna
Prime - Alex Pappas
Jan - Joseph Mathers

Director - John Hurley
Set Designer - Sylviane Jacobsen
Lighting Designer - Olivia Harris
Costume Designer - Meryl Pressman & Holly Rihn
Sound Designer - Anthony Mattana

To Obtain Rights To Produce This Play

Please contact: Crystal Skillman at crystalskillman@gmail.com.

The Vigil or The Guided Cradle

Scene 1. What They Are Saying

Now, early summer morning on a street in Prague. A distracted American—the Foreigner—sees several men, women, children eating and singing in Russian at an outdoor café. She stops and listens. A shadow looms on the wall—the Translator. He goes up to her.

Foreigner It sounds lovely.

Translator Not if you knew.

Foreigner You understand…

Translator It's Russian.

Foreigner Oh, yes.

Translator Prague invites many nationalities.

Foreigner You live here? Well, I'd love to know. To know what they're saying. Do you speak Russian?

Translator Yes, well I translate many languages and—

Foreigner Do you? Then what are they saying?

Translator It's not important.

Foreigner I'll pay you—if you tell me.

Translator Alright, "okay"? You say that in your country.

Foreigner Yeah, okay.

Translator Okay.

He translates the song as they listen.

The doors break
Soldiers come
Take you
Search your women
Row by row

But shame is a stain
That will grow and grow
Until, until you know
You must not sleep in shame

Foreigner Oh. It's not that lovely, is it?

Translator It's an old song.

The Russians seem to be arguing. Foreigner listens.

Foreigner What they're saying now—I feel I understand what they're—

Translator They say they are content.

Foreigner It's luck we met.

Translator Yes.

Foreigner Could you show me things around?

Translator If you like.

Foreigner Really? Because there is more I'd like to see, to know.

Translator Then shall we move on?

They do.

Scene 2. The Devil's Throat

Then, early sixteenth century. Large dining table in a castle fortress. Afternoon. Gleaming chicken, shiny apples and bread—a luncheon of torturers. Aldo twists his knife into a piece of chicken, turning the blade back and forth, showing Balto. They ignore the stranger who is there, silent, eating.

Aldo Hah! Is *this* the way?

Balto A stuffed pig would have been better—more like the man!

Aldo Tied for how long?

Balto Two to three months in my iron hold, then their bodies do all the work—back spasms and convulsions.

Aldo A stuffed pig would have been better, the anus better too. Wider. I've got a hook that goes right through—

Balto A *hook?*

Aldo What?

Balto Old school.

Aldo I've been assisting here for almost a year and you still act like—

Balto Until you do it yourself—it's all—

Aldo All…?

Balto Talk.

Aldo Not for me. I've got tons of ideas. (If anyone would listen!) The way I wanted to design it—

Balto *(Rolling his eyes)* The "hook?"

Aldo Yeah, I came up with an idea to put a release on the handle that would push out three fingers of new spikes inside. See! Hah!

Balto Too quick.

Aldo Not the way the spikes are positioned. It would bleed them slow. Mostly. *(Eyes the silent stranger, whispers to Balto)* Who's the new guy?

Balto I don't know.

Aldo Why doesn't he talk?

Balto Ask him yourself.

Aldo *(To stranger)* Excuse me—you're to be here with us? *(Stranger stares blankly at him)* He doesn't speak the language that's for sure. He's Italian, I bet. Where-have-you-come-from?

Balto It doesn't help.

Aldo What?

Balto It doesn't help to ask him in your language if he doesn't know it, you rank turd.

Aldo Talk to me like that again and I'll rip your eyes out, feed them to the dogs!

Beat.

Balto So you think he's Italian?

Aldo I don't know. Could be Italian.

Balto Then talk to him in Italian. Go on—

Aldo Didn't learn it.

Balto Oh you didn't? You are one stupid bitch aren't you?

Aldo I told you!

Balto Settle down. Italian—there isn't anything to it—devil's language if you ask me—comes out all raspy, not defined, animal-like. Coming out of a throat like his.

Aldo So no need to know it.

Balto There's a need to know everything, Aldo. To know how to deal with it. *(To stranger)* Parli italiano? He's dumb. Or god forbid Spanish. *(Stranger cuts into his food and eats)* But he has the right idea. *(Balto takes a bite)* Mm! Tender, alright—but now I want pig.

Aldo You shouldn't be eating that—without Prime being here. You should wait. We should wait.

Balto I'm just picking—he won't know the difference.

Aldo He will. Like when they were working on that crippled boy but they switched from using the knives to the hot pokers and forgot to ask permission—Prime knew the minute he came in.

Balto He should.

Aldo *(Imitating Balto)* "He should."

Balto Shut up! Prime told me about the whole operation. Each country getting rid of their worst cases while the church gets their confessions and we get time to perfect our methods. And if Prime happens to like a great invention (such as my thrilling new and improved iron hold)—he'll make sure those white hats use it everywhere.

Aldo I know how it works.

Balto Then you better get it through your thick skull—if you want to progress around here you have to start thinking like the man in charge. Only better. I tell you—I wouldn't be as controlling as Prime.

Aldo You just said he should know everything.

Balto I'm just saying things could be more efficient under different leadership. There could be a time when those who do the work have complete control.

Aldo While Prime's watching.

Balto Someone's always watching, Aldo. The trick is to make sure it's *you*.

Prime appears in the doorway.

We'll speak later.

Prime Gentlemen.

Aldo Good day, my lord.

Balto Great day to you, sire.

Aldo and Balto kiss Prime's ring.

Prime A good day's work, I trust.

Aldo Most excellent sire. With my team, we had a real break through with our subject.

Balto He died.

Aldo But not without a confession! I helped write it myself—the devil was in every inch of him but we pulled it out—with my hook!

Prime And I was not notified.

Aldo I ran to inform you but you weren't in your chamber and it was all working so well and—

Prime Maybe too well.

Aldo We can be blamed for losing him while you were out riding?

Prime You can be blamed for anything, my dear Aldo.

Aldo and Balto cower—until Prime laughs. They join in with overly hearty laughter.

Balto A great wit, my sire.

Prime And you my Balto?

Balto In my room I'm on the verge of a spontaneous confession with that blasphemous witch. The hag will do anything to save her daughter. Taking them both in was genius.

Prime Where is the daughter?

Balto The girl? Haven't started with her, she's hanging in the lock.

Prime The dark lord is deep in that one. I must continue to conduct my investigation for the marks upon her flesh.

Balto and Aldo give each other knowing glances.

Balto *Of course*, I understand. You must inspect her again. I am having quite a time getting her mother to confess. But I should break that hag tomorrow.

Prime Impressive—around what time would you say?

Balto About noon, then about four to five hours further with the pokers for confirming the confession, if you'd like to stay.

Prime You are exact, Balto. Always on time, like perfection. Speaking of perfection, have you met the latest of our experts, gentlemen? May I introduce Ippolito of Sicily. *(Gesturing to the stranger)* He comes from a most noble line of Generals—

Ippolito Interrogators, if you please.

Balto And he speaks our native language so—

Aldo Perfectly.

Ippolito And I assure you, I do have impeccable hearing—as I assume you do as well, gentlemen, even though I speak through such a raspy throat.

Prime *(Introducing them)* Balto, my right hand man, and Aldo, well…he's learning. Ippolito wrote to me about the new method he's working on and I knew I had to bring him here. I have no doubt you'll have all sorts of questions for him.

Balto What do you use?

Ippolito Nothing.

Balto I'm sorry—perhaps my hearing *is* a little daft—

Ippolito I said nothing.

Balto I don't understand. Then what do you do?

Ippolito I keep them awake.

Prime A completely new concept. Scientific, as he says. You deprive them of sleep and…how did you put it?

Ippolito The prisoner's mind becomes my own. As I take from his mind everything he knows.

Prime And what is truly remarkable is that there is no physical damage done to the body.

Aldo But a method like that would make ours—

Ippolito Obsolete.

Prime Yes, you have much to discuss over lunch, I'm sure.

Prime turns to go. Aldo, Balto rise.

Aldo We—we waited for *you*, my lord.

Prime Oh. I've already eaten. Pig. Good day, gentlemen.

Prime leaves. Ippolito smiles at them, keeps eating. Aldo and Balto sit.

Balto *(To Ippolito)* You are a smart bastard, aren't you—

Ippolito raises his fork and impales Balto's hand to the table.

Ippolito So you hear it now from your devil's throat—tell anyone of this and you will never sleep again, I assure you.

Ippolito pulls out the fork from Balto's hand and uses it to eat his meat. Balto holds his bleeding hand. A clock begins to chime.

Aldo How's that for perfection, Balto? Ha, ha—

Ippolito looks up—Aldo shuts up. Ippolito continues to eat. Aldo starts to eat, watching Ippolito. The clock continues to chime.

Scene 3. Time As We Know It

The Old Town Square in Prague. A few hours later. Translator and Foreigner stare up at a huge clock which chimes.

Foreigner Everyone gathering here, around—does that mean it will happen soon? So many people. Does this happen every time?

Translator Every time.

Foreigner *(Laughing)* It's just funny—talking about time—and we're waiting for the clock to—

Translator Three minutes.

Foreigner It is so hot, man. *(She drinks from a bottle of water)* Thank you for getting this for me—I was getting so thirsty.

Translator Do you want to know what it means before you listen?

Foreigner Yes, oh yes. Please.

Translator shows her on a postcard, while referring to the looming clock in front of them.

Translator It was built in the 1490s by a master clockmaker. It imitates the supposed orbits of the sun and moon around the Earth—

Foreigner So many hands.

Translator That hand with the sun shows three different types of time. Old Bohemian time (24 hours from the sun setting), Babylonian time (when the period of daylight was 12 hours) and—

Foreigner And the middle?

Translator That is time as we know it.

Foreigner Now.

Translator Now.

Foreigner With us looking at the clock.

Translator You'll see Twelve Apostles appear in the windows there. Perfectly carved. Each of them will be holding an object, a symbol.

Foreigner Like what?

Translator It's been so long since—

Foreigner I'm sorry I keep thinking—

Translator What?

Foreigner That you know everything.

Translator No. Well, yes.

He smiles.

Foreigner Is that a joke? Were you joking? Oh! I didn't think...

Translator Yes?

Foreigner Funny.

Translator *(Out of nowhere)* What kind of "Miss" should never attempt to translate?

Foreigner Ah...what?

Translator It is a joke.

Foreigner "Miss?"...oh, like a girl? What kind of "Miss" should never try to...

Translator Translate.

Foreigner Um, I don't...

Translator "Miss"-Interpret.

Foreigner Ah—hah, hah.

Translator Since you like jokes.

Foreigner It's a local one.

Translator It's actually from your country. From around the American Revolution.

Foreigner Maybe you do know everything. Me, I'm all over the place. Supposed to go to grad school but I mean I still don't even know what to major in. Maybe I won't even go. I can just learn—just go to places and... *(Notices she's going on, embarrassed, points to picture)* I would like to hear more about the clock if you still want to...

Translator It was built not only to keep time but house the offices of the King. Years after it was finished, the clockmaker's son tried to destroy the clock. *(Pointing)* You can still see the damage.

Foreigner Why would he...?

Translator Because after it was built the King blinded his father, the clockmaker.

Foreigner God—why?

Translator is looking right at her.

Translator So only here would remain such beauty and perfection.

Beat.

Foreigner This whole city, it's beautiful.

My mom. She's, sick. In a hospital back home but uh, my dad said there was no use to me just waiting, being there. Asked me where I wanted to go and I decided I wanted to go to someplace considered magical. My father said he knew the perfect place. Here. Her cancer keeps getting worse since we came, they said they would call if—

I shouldn't have come.

I shouldn't be here.

Translator I'm glad you are.

They are very close now.

Foreigner *(Looking at clock)* Look! Something's happening—It's starting! Right—it's—there are figures on the outside that are moving. Right—look—the Skeleton—

Translator Death. He pulls the rope with his right hand. In his left hand he holds—

Foreigner An hourglass.

Translator He turns it over.

Foreigner Time passing.

The clock chimes, they look up, watching.

I've been having the most terrible dreams.

Translator Yes?

Foreigner *(Puts hand to head, sweating)* God.

Translator Are you…?

Foreigner I just—I feel…hot. Dizzy.

Translator Let's get you back—

Foreigner No. No. I don't want to go back there…not yet. Okay?

Translator Okay. Let's find you a place to rest.

Scene 4. The Weight Inside

Interrogation Room. Later that afternoon. Jan is bound. Ippolito goes to him.

Jan I know what you're going to do. Going to touch it. My cock.

Ippolito That's what they do here? I tell you what—you stop this little game and I'll let you sleep.

Jan That's your game. Sleep. The guards were laughing. What you want them to do. Keeping me up for what? Pouring water down my throat, leaving me in darkness, hanging me up by my wrists. Not what they're used to. They think it's shit.

Ippolito It takes time to make others.

Jan Make them…

Ippolito Understand what you intend to do. It builds in you. Patience.

Jan And you're a patient man.

Ippolito I know the importance of waiting.

Jan It's a part of the game then.

Ippolito It's no game. Not for you, the way *you* look.

Jan I look. I look fine.

Ippolito Your eyes blinking. How do they feel Jan? Your eyes.

Jan Swollen. Purple.

Ippolito From keeping them open. Not like that clockmaker—they took his *eyes out* I hear. They took a spike I think. Two spikes while he slept. One for each—

Jan Is that what you'll do?

Ippolito It doesn't happen like that.

Jan Not with you.

Ippolito No.

Jan Then what? Going to carve me up?

Ippolito You're in the wrong room for that. Try down the hall.

Jan It doesn't matter what you do. I won't—

Ippolito After he was blinded, the clockmaker couldn't even see his own work anymore.

All those Apostles he carefully carved. It must have been difficult for you to watch the clock strike the hour, knowing what your father had been through.

Jan Fuck you.

Ippolito Stood in the Old Town Square once myself. Can't imagine why anyone would want to destroy such beauty.

Jan There was no beauty in it. Not for me.

Ippolito No. What mattered to you was inside. But it didn't work. Did enough damage, killed tourists in the street, men, women, some children if that concerns you. But for all that—the King's men they live and you, you're here with me. As for your friends that helped you—

Jan You think I'll confess? Give you their names?

Ippolito I'm not even certain you had anything to do with it. Doubt you had the brains to even try. Burning those Apostles as you say you did. Bet you can't even name them.

Jan Pig slop.

Ippolito Peter.

Jan Puke.

Ippolito Paul.

Aldo peeks in.

Jan Shit.

Ippolito Simon.

Jan Tongue.

Ippolito Thomas.

Jan Blood tits.

Aldo You speak Czech to him?

Jan Blood. Tits.

Aldo What's he saying?

Jan Tits.

Ippolito We're talking about the Twelfth Apostle. "Blood tits."

Aldo *(Totally not understanding)* Right.

Ippolito What do you want?

Aldo I just wanted to see how you do it Ippolit—

Ippolito draws a curtain separating Jan from them.

Ippolito Never speak my name in the room! *(Ippolito grabs Aldo, takes him aside)* You want to talk to me, talk to me.

Aldo Prime—he's taken me off. Punishing me—says I should have run and got him before we finished the last one. I can't just sit around. I'm getting stupid.

Ippolito *(Still pissed)* Getting?

Two screams are heard offstage.

Aldo It's that witch mother and that daughter of hers—that girl down the hall. Balto's got two at once. Bastard.

Ippolito Then bother *him*.

Aldo Prime said he'd allow me to assist. Assist you.

Ippolito No.

Aldo spots a crudely-made sketch on Ippolto's work table. It depicts a naked man strapped in a corner, beneath him a sharp pedestal, just like what Ippolito is carving now.

Aldo *(Reading title on sketch)* "The Vigil or the Guided Cradle." I see he's and this is going to go...he's going to go down on that. He's strapped into that like a spider. And if he slumps, closes his eyes. Down he goes right onto it. His...I thought you didn't use anything.

Ippolito Nothing that marks.

Aldo His insides will be torn up.

Ippolito No.

Aldo No?

Ippolito Just enough.

Aldo You don't start him out like this, with that under him?

Ippolito Introductions are important.

Aldo Not with him. No one can get him to confess.

Ippolito I'm not after confessions.

Aldo Then what? *(Ippolito ignores him, keeps working)* Prime's family all served the church. He was piss-poor until he worked his way up, found this place. Balto—his family's well off if you can believe it. And for him, I think he just likes doing it. But me? I like, I like seeing how it all works. Understanding. Do you know what I mean?

Ippolito When you haven't slept. You hear things, see things that aren't there. What secrets you know, how you guard them…it changes. Being awake, one hour turns into two, seven, endless. He'll tell us who helped him and we'll stop them from doing it again.

Aldo This can save people.

Ippolito That's my hope.

Aldo *(Looking at Vigil sketch)* This sketch it's all dark, the lines are muddy. No composition to it. Amateur, if you don't mind me.

Ippolito *(Sarcastically)* No, do go on.

Aldo When I was little, at the church, down in the village, I worked on the windows for the doors. I can do better. Mind if I...? *(Aldo "fixes" the sketch with a charcoal stick)* My father did it, so I gave it a try. I liked coming up with new ideas for things to make.

I designed the windows. White Hats put them in. *(Standing aside so Ippolito can see the difference)* Now you see?

Ippolito It serves the purpose. Good.

Aldo My windows weren't good. Told them not to put them up, not ready. So I smashed them with my fists. My hands bleeding. *(Looks down at his clenched hands)* Balto—he's crazy mad you know. About his hand and all. What he says. I'd watch myself—guard myself sleeping.

Ippolito I *don't*.

Aldo What?

Ippolito I don't sleep.

Ippolito opens curtain. Jan spits on him.

Aldo You let him do that?

Ippolito You said you wanted me to teach you.

Aldo Yes.

Ippolito hands Aldo the cradle, turns to Jan.

Ippolito *(To Jan)* You have a choice—what will be done to you. You stay awake, confess, give me names, that's my vigil. *(Gestures to the cradle Aldo holds)* You sleep, then this will be your cradle.

Jan It will be yours too before your job is done—Ipp-o-lito.

This startles Ippolito. Aldo looks at him. Together they begin to assemble the Vigil.

Balto approaches Prime at his desk. Prime inspects the sketch of Ippolito's procedure.

Prime Ippolito is a soulful man. Passionate.

Balto Have you seen his eyes?

Prime I have seen his eyes, they are like yours, like any others.

Balto His eyes look down upon how *we* do things. You don't find such a man dangerous?

Prime I have taken my precautions. Aldo's been sent to put a gaze on him.

Balto *(Growing heated)* But what do you really know about him?

Prime I know we're lucky to have him. Things are changing Balto. How the church supports us. We're under more scrutiny than ever. We have to be more…inventive about our methods.

Balto I don't trust him.

Prime I see. *(Looking at Balto's bandaged hand)* Your hand…looks nasty. Hurts?

Balto It'll pass.

Prime What is it you say happened again?

Balto Got a little excited is all. Using the poker to burn that witch mother's ear, but she'll be done soon enough.

Prime Her daughter, the girl. I went to investigate her after lunch but her lock was empty.

Balto I decided to move her.

Prime Why?

Balto She's getting heavier. Needed to be laid on a rack. Mine are full so I'm having her put into Chamber A.

Prime Ippolito's station.

Balto Well, yes I suppose it is.

Prime She's gotten heavier?

Balto Odd, isn't it? Usually they lose weight. But to gain after a few months and with the church asking so many questions.

Prime looks at him, knowing what he means.

Prime How heavy is she?

Balto Like there's a weight inside her.

Prime She must be examined.

Scene 5. The Glass Eye

A room in an older, run down hotel. Foreigner enters, looking around, as Translator follows through the open door with beer and food.

Foreigner And those people in the lobby. Where I was—was like Mickey D's and Wendy's. But here—authentic. Dumplings. Cabbage. Beer!

Translator looks for bottle opener. Foreigner offers him a swiss army knife.

My father gave it to me. Don't even know why I still—

He takes it, looks at it, puts it on table. Twists off beer top, she smiles awkwardly. Takes the beer, drinks a little.

Translator You're feeling better?

Foreigner *(Eating, drinking)* A little. It's like I'm starting to feel like a human being again. A person. Being here.

Translator Most people think this hotel's a dump.

Foreigner It could be poetic. All sorts of places are inspiring to people. Mansions, shit-holes. It all depends, right?

Translator Perspective?

Foreigner You boil everything down to the essence, you know. You're full of clarity.

Translator I keep focused.

Foreigner What keeps you so focused?

Translator It's the love of something.

Foreigner You don't hear people talk about that anymore. Love.

Translator It's how you love. What you would do for the thing you love.

Foreigner Yeah.

Translator You know what I mean?

Foreigner I haven't really been in love like that.

Translator It can happen very quickly.

Foreigner All the way here, I was thinking—what if I just didn't go back? What if you and I—I don't know, what if we stayed here. *(Gets embarrassed)* It's stupid.

Translator No. But—wouldn't your father miss you?

Foreigner is silent.

You don't get along with him.

Why?

Foreigner When I was a kid, just a kid, he gave me a stuffed animal.

Translator Stuffed?

Foreigner Not real. A bear. We call them Teddies over there. When you're little you're supposed to hold something stuffed, usually shaped like an animal for security. And you tell it things you'd never tell anyone else. Because you think no one else is watching I guess, maybe like a *confession*—Not that I'm religious—I was dragged to church but...what about you?

Translator My faith is strong.

Foreigner That's great! I don't have anything like that. Most of us don't in America—we say we do but—it's like accepted bullshit. But we're really into confessing, I think. Or I was. So I told this bear everything. Even when I had gone through my father's dresser drawers. I found a tin can in the back of one of the drawers with a lot of war stuff from the 70s—old medals, buttons, but then I found a photograph of him, looking so young, smiling. In his uniform. He looked really happy, but in a way that scared me because it was a kind of happiness I hadn't seen in people. And he was holding something up in his hand that seemed red, his whole hand seemed red. And it was clear that it was someone's ear. That night I told my bear what I saw. The next day my father was waiting for me at the bottom of the stairs. He asked me what I thought it was he was holding in the photograph and I said I didn't know. He told me it was a bird. A little bird that had fallen from the sky, splattered. He had picked it up. I asked him why he was smiling in the picture and he said he was smiling because the bird was smiling. Then he asked me to put out my hands, palms up. He hit them.

He said, "Keep it to yourself."

I was convinced it was the bear. That his glass eyes had told on me.

That night I took the bear. I ripped out his glass eyes. And I put them in a tin box I found in the darkness of my drawer.

Translator And then. Did you feel safe?

Foreigner *(Unsaid: Yes)* I should go back. I should be getting—*(Foreigner's feels dizzy again—her head hurts)* God.

Translator You feel bad.

Foreigner Worse since I—

Foreigner looks to food, drink.

Translator I had an animal too—one for holding. A monkey, I think. My brother shot it up. He was training to shoot, if needed. We'd use things around the house.

Foreigner *(Unsteady but concerned)* Training for what?

Translator You can barely keep your eyes open. You should go to sleep.

Foreigner No. The things I see—when I dream.

Translator Yes, but you should go to sleep.

Foreigner I don't want to sleep.

Translator Then keep your eyes open.

Foreigner tries to get up but can't. Translator rips open her dress, takes it off violently. Underneath is a medieval slip. She struggles, fights him, but he holds her down. Takes a photo out of his pocket, shows it to her.

I also have a photograph I keep. The one your father is holding down. That's my brother. Number 3306. He's the red in the photograph.

He binds her to the bed. Takes her phone, things, exits as Prime slowly comes into the room. Prime goes to the Foreigner—who is the Girl to him. He avoids looking at her face, just takes in her body. Puts his hand on her stomach, feels the child inside her. Reacts. Thinks. Takes out a knife, holds it over her stomach, about to strike. Jan, now in the Vigil, sees, speaks urgently to distract him.

Jan My father. He taught me, what we do, what we choose to do never dies. They blinded him. Two spikes. When I saw—I became a made thing like my father told me Golem was—made from clay, sent out to kill his enemies—went out to kill like you now, but like Golem, you caught me, strung me up, tried to burn every part of me, but you couldn't burn my heart because it *is a clock*. *(Prime goes to Jan, the knife still in his hands)* A made thing and made things like her and I cannot be stopped even if we want to stop. We hurt those who hurt us.

Prime You really think you could hurt me.

Jan No.

Prime smiles, pats him on the head, turns back to girl.

But *her* heart is the heart of a clock and when it strikes it will strike you. Hard.

Prime can't help it—he looks at Foreigner's face. Tries to raise knife again but has lost his nerve. Ippolito enters, Aldo following. They see Prime over the girl. Prime quickly pockets knife, acknowledges them, defensive as if "caught."

Prime She had to be examined. Balto didn't tell you?

Ippolito looks at the girl, then at Prime knowing what he means.

I've discovered a matter I'd like to discuss.

Ippolito In a minute.

Prime's anger flickers for a second.

Prime Don't be late for dinner. You wouldn't want the meat getting cold.

Prime leaves. They all look at the girl.

Jan What will happen to her?

Ippolito You shouldn't think of others. You should think of yourself.

Jan That's all I've ever done. And look where I am.

Jan closes his eyes.

Aldo He's asleep.

Ippolito Let him—a few minutes. He was getting used to it anyway. Now he'll feel it even more when he wakes up.

Ippolito takes off his work apron, readies himself to meet Prime.

Aldo She's pregnant isn't she?

Ippolito There are things you learn to keep to yourself Aldo.

Ippolito leaves. Aldo looks to Jan sleeping. Then to the girl sleeping. He looks at Ippolito's apron. Puts it on. Walks around imitating Ippolito's walk. Says a few of Ippolito's phrases, like:

Aldo *(Softly imitating)* There are things you learn to keep to yourself Aldo.

Stops in front of the Vigil. Steps up into it, with Jan still in it, binds himself into the ropes around him, the cradle underneath. He imagines what it's like.

(As victim) No…stop… *(Then as torturer)* You fucking tell me *(As victim)* I don't know—I don't know what you want me to say *(As torturer)* you know you fucking know *(As victim)* No! *(As torturer)* tell me or I'll do something to your eyes *(As victim)* please don't—oh god—I'll do whatever you say *(As torturer)* then tell me *(As victim)* what? *(As torturer)* tell me what I fucking want to hear *(As victim)* I don't know what you want to hear *(As torturer)* What? *(As victim)* I'll fucking tell you *(As torturer)* so tell me, so fucking tell me what it is *(As victim)* what is it? *(As torturer)* don't mock me, you pig shit! *(As victim)* I'm not—I swear to you. *(As torturer)* Tell me or I'll tear out your eyes with my hook. *(As victim)* I don't, I can't. *(As torturer)* Tell me. *(As victim)* Please! *(As torturer)* Tell me or I'll never let you sleep. I'll make you bleed from your eyes, your hands, your knees until you spill out from today until tomorrow. Until you tell me— *(As victim)* Yes—I confess—I confess I worshipped the devil, I betrayed my neighbors. I denied God, my king, my land! *(As torturer)* Yes—you did! *(As victim)* Yes—I did! Yessssssssss. *(As torturer)* Yes.

Jan Then?

Aldo *(Startled by Jan)* Huh?

Jan You think it's so different up there? It doesn't matter how it's done with one day bleeding into the next—it's the same because you're always waiting for it to happen, being left in the darkness, feeling it around you.

Aldo I don't get that.

Jan What?

Aldo Poetry.

Jan It's simple.

Aldo Then say it like that.

Jan It's when it gets dark. When you're alone in the dark. When you close your eyes and that's it, you're…

Aldo Thought you wanted to sleep.

Jan Not just sleep.

A scream is heard offstage.

Aldo The witch mother. She's still—

Screaming turns into a wailing, then stops. Silence.

Jan Is she?

Aldo I won't scream. Not at the end. Never.

Jan Whatever happens, I don't think you can control what you…God… here I am telling you…

Aldo Stop laughing. *(Grabs his neck)* Or I'll take care of you with my—

Jan *(Through being choked)* Hook? Go ahead. I'll tell you something—every time I hear Ippolito—his voice—I imagine he's in it—up there—screaming, and it's like my heart moves again, like I'm alive. Like there's a sweetness to it.

Aldo backs away from him.

Aldo You're a sick fuck. *(Jan laughs at him)* I'm not. I have a purpose. That's not sick. Not like you.

Jan You want to be like him.

Aldo You want to be like her sleeping.

They both look to the girl.

But she looks dead.

She looks dead already.

Scene 6. The Red In The Photograph

A few hours later. Hotel Room. Translator plays with Foreigner's knife, opening and closing. The phone is in front of him. He realizes Foreigner is awake, watching him, closes knife, puts it in his pocket.

Translator I don't want you to die.

Foreigner But you will kill me if my dad doesn't free your brother.

Translator I have no choice. My family—if there is a shame like this, it must be taken care of. I must—

Foreigner You did. You— *(Unsaid: Raped me)*

My father tells me lots of things.
Shows me lots of things.
I might know.
Where your brother is.

Translator turns to her.

Show me again. Your photo.

The Translator goes to her with the picture.

Can I have one hand free to…

Beat, then the Translator unties one of her hands, and gives her the photo. She holds it. Closes her eyes. Chimes from the clock are heard in the distance.

Prime addresses Ippolito from his desk, on which a large case sits. Balto stands at attention. Aldo slips in, late, but not unnoticed.

Prime Nights I hear everything. The breathing in each room, candles flickering in the hall, the chiming of the clock. When I found this place I told the church what I could make it. My hand rested on the gate and it opened on its own. I was led here. Found my way home, as I hope you have, Ippolito. *(Prime opens the case, shows Ippolito)* They call it the Smiling Dog on account of the teeth on the blade.

Ippolito You want me to butcher her.

Prime I want you to take the thing out.

Ippolito And kill her in the process.

Prime If you don't, I would hate to see what would happen to you. But if you do what I ask with this, I will make sure the Order will do everything within its power to bring your Vigil method to any country you wish.

Balto Such promises! *(To Prime)* Serving you should be enough.

Ippolito *(To Balto)* As it is for you?

Aldo It would be an honor to assist you.

Ippolito I work alone.

Aldo But I really want to—

Prime As you wish. Rest tonight. You can begin tomorrow. Won't you, Ippolito?

Balto Dear Ippolito, Prime has asked you a question.

Beat.

Ippolito I have no need to rest. I work tonight.

Ippolito takes the case.

Prime I would like to see the progress for myself. Within the hour Ippolito.

Ippolito leaves them and walks into the Interrogation room, the case still in his hands. Looks up at his creation—Jan in the Vigil. Walks over to the girl.

Jan What does she look like?

Ippolito *(Soft—a realization to himself)* Familiar.

Jan She reminds you of someone. I only ask what you ask yourself—what does it feel like within her?

Ippolito It is none of your concern, none of mine.

He puts the case on his worktable.

Jan But still—she's there.

Ippolito Yes.

Ippolito opens the case about to take out the knife but as he does the Foreigner, now the Girl in her dream, has already opened her eyes. Breathes. Speaks.

Girl Hello.

Scene 7. The Violets on the Hill

Ippolito turns, startled. She goes on.

Girl Did you see the violets coming up here? We have violets where I come from. And birds…they swoop over the lake. Swoop. Swoop. Swoop and then—do you know this?

They change.

We learned that in church. They change into something else. Like magic, though you're not supposed to say that. They told me I shouldn't say things like that but that's what it is because the birds are swooping then they become—bats!

It's quiet then. In the trees. In the dark.

What's in the case?

Ippolito Can you tell me where you came from? Your name?

Girl I hope it's not a surprise. I hate surprises.

She sings.

There was, there was a girl
With a smile in her eye and a lonesome curl,
She had a way with singing and sing all day
Or so her momma'd say—

I know my mother's there—just through the wall. I'd hear her all the time. Each time I'd hear her… *(Unsaid: scream)* I try to think she's singing. All the songs she's sung to me. I haven't heard her in—She's been quiet. And then they moved me. When they brought me here they said I was a present. And then…

Let's play a game. "What were you before?"

Okay, I'll go first.

Before I was a girl, I was an eagle and I'd swoop down on anything that didn't behave, teach them some manners. Your turn.

Ippolito I can't—

Girl Just close your eyes and think.

Ippolito I don't let my mind wander.

Girl Why?

Ippolito You can't understand.

Girl I understand there's something inside me. And it moves even though it shouldn't. I know it was put there and it grows. Where's my mother? Why don't I hear her?

Ippolito She's gone.

Girl She's hiding. She's making herself very small so no one can see. Not even the wolves. Like my father. Mother said he was a wolf.

Ippolito Do you think I'm a wolf?

Girl I won't tell you unless you play. "What were you before." It's a game.

Ippolito A game.

Girl It's easy, like this, "Before I was here…"

Ippolito I don't—

Girl Try.

Ippolito I don't know how.

Girl You just…start. You think back about being in the woods, when it's dark, and it's quiet. And you hear the wind, the trees. You think back to things that were, what was, before you were here. Before you were alone.

Ippolito Before I was here, I had a house.

Girl Made of sticks!

Ippolito No, there were walls and rooms and—

Girl It was pretty.

Ippolito Yes.

Girl Were there fields and hills?

Ippolito There were grapevines and lakes.

Girl With birds that turned into bats!

Ippolito I guess so.

Girl And what were you?

Ippolito I was a man.

Girl Nooo—you were a boy.

Ippolito Yes.

Girl And there was a girl. A *lady*.

Ippolito Yes.

Girl My mother told me there is always a lady. She told me—What does your lady look like?

Ippolito She looks like. The sun.

Girl Not like here.

Ippolito No.

Girl Not like this place. In the dark. Did she have something growing inside her?

Ippolito A daughter.

Girl Like me?

Ippolito Yes.

Girl And she was a baby. You held her.

Ippolito Yes.

Girl And she grew up. Like me!

Ippolito Yes.

Girl She's my age?

Ippolito Yes, almost.

Girl I could be older. I forget sometimes. She's pretty?

Ippolito Oh, yes.

Girl And I am.

Ippolito You are the only thing of life I have seen in so long. You are beautiful.

Girl Like the violets.

Ippolito Yes. Yes.

Girl Why don't you show me what's inside?

Ippolito Soon.

Girl My name is Esmerelda. You can call me Essie. What's your name?

Ippolito Ippolito.

Girl What kind of a name is that?

Ippolito It's Italian, Sicilian and a little Greek. But don't tell anyone. It means—horse of rock!

Girl That's...that's crazy.

Ippolito It's what my mother told me.

Girl You have a mother?

Ippoltio Yes.

Girl What does she look like?

Ippolito Big and fat and always cooking. I'm sorry you're—you're hungry, aren't you?

Girl The man who came, he fed me before he—

Beat, she gets quiet.

What do you dream about?

Ippolito I don't dream.

Girl Everyone does.

Ippolito I don't.

Girl Did you dream when you were a handsome boy?

Ippolito I was never—

Girl You are handsome now.

Ippolito You think so.

Girl You are. You are very handsome. And you don't look like a wolf.

Ippolito No?

Girl But you could.

The man in the corner. Does he have a face?

Ippolito Yes.

Girl I want to see. Please.

Ippolito holds up Jan's head.

Girl Hello.

Jan Hello.

Girl Why is he like that?

Ippolito It's something I made.

Girl Is he in a house?

Ippolito It's a Vigil.

Girl What's that?

Ippolito It's when you can't sleep.

Girl Why can't he sleep?

Ippolito He's done something bad. He has to tell me things.

Ippolito pulls curtain so Jan is unseen.

Girl Tell you what?

Ippolito What I need to know.

Girl Will you put me in a house like that?

Ippolito Why?

Girl Because I lied to you. My name isn't Essie. Because I don't, and this will be funny to you, I don't remember my own—

Ippolito I'm sorry.

Ippolito looks at the case.

Girl I'm not. I don't want to remember. I want to be something else. To change. Don't you?

Why won't you show me what's in there? What's inside?

Ippolito No—please.

Girl Why? Where are they? The lady, your daughter?

Why aren't they here?

Where are they?

Ippolito They've gone.

Girl Where?

Ippolito Please just—I want to remember.

Girl What?

Ippolito How she was. Alive. I see my daughter when I see your face.

Girl You do. You dream. Of your lady, your daughter, your house and what you were before.

Ippolito No.

Ippolito crosses quickly to the case.

Girl You dream so you can change. It's a game. "What were you before?"

Ippolito opens the case, takes out a large knife that gleams.

Ippolito I can't change.

Girl I don't believe you.

Ippolito I was a wolf.

He crosses to her with the knife.

I built many houses, I would give them to others to use on others who had done bad, bad things. I had everything, the house with grapevines and a lake. A wife like the sun and a daughter. Until some of these bad men—they—They found out where I lived. Found my wife like the sun and my daughter... And when I came home, my wife, my child was... They were lying there. It took time, but I found one of the men. I took him back. Put him in a house. Until he told me where the other bad men were. I found them too. And I—

Until I felt nothing.

Until I couldn't feel—anything.

Ippolito is right over her. A beat, then he undoes her ties with the knife. She sits up.

I did see the violets when I came up the hill to this place. Tiny footprints. A child's. Yours.

Girl What was her name? Your daughter?

Ippolito *(A name he hasn't said in a long time)* Elizabeth.

Girl Then I am Elizabeth. And I am beautiful.

Ippolito You must not stop, you must not think. You must not question. You can only know what you are.

He holds out the knife to her.

You must be stronger than you think to find your way. You must be a wolf. Do you understand?

She takes the knife. Lights change as Ippolito goes to Jan in the Vigil.

The Translator's shadow looms on the wall. He is on the cell phone. He ends the call, enters the hotel room. Foreigner turns to Translator.

Foreigner You know those dreams I was having? I think I'm enjoying them. Maybe it's the drugs, huh? And I'm not thinking of my mother and if she's…or my father and what he's done. I'm thinking about you and I want to sleep, not to be alone, to be…I don't blame you for what you've done so, maybe…ok?

Translator I consider what I have done as enough. Unless your father—

Foreigner Doesn't keep his end of the bargain, free your brother, of course.

But while we are waiting, I would like to…again.

Translator starts to go to her.

This time—without the lights.

Translator In the dark?

Foreigner All I ask.

Translator turns off the lights. It's very dark. Lights rise on Jan and Ippolito, for a moment, left alone in the Interrogation room.

Jan You know what they'll do to you when they find out you let her go.

Ippolito Yes.

Jan But you choose to stay here.

Those that helped me with the clock, my friends, they all died that night.

Ippolito Why would you tell me now—like this?

Jan I choose to give you my confession.

Ippolito Why?

Jan Because we're the same. We've lost the same things.

Ippolito I don't—

Jan It's not something you can understand even though you know.

When they come back. I don't want to be in their hands.

Ippolito.

Beat.

Ippolito Close your eyes.

Ippolito suffocates Jan as the lights come on in the Hotel room. Translator's throat has been cut. Foreigner holds the bloody army knife, untying herself furiously.

Foreigner You wanted to—fuck me, kill me—just because of what my father did to your brother? He didn't do shit! You liar! You shit fucker!

Fuck you!

Fuck your brother—

Fuck! Oh god, oh god—

Translator touches his neck, looks at the blood on his hand.

Fuck! Fuck!

Translator is shaking, reaching for her.

Fuck. Are you? Fuck. Fuck.

She tries to stop the bleeding but he slumps on the table.

He's not moving.

In the Interrogation room, Jan lies motionless on the ground. Ippolito faces the Vigil, starts taking it down. Aldo rushes in.

Aldo Prime's dead. His throat's cut like a pig. Where's—Where's the girl? Ippolito? You let her go? You actually let her—

Balto enters holding the bloodied smiling dog knife.

Balto Have pity Aldo—Ippolito's a man, like any other. No. Worse than that. Much worse. Turns out he's got principles. Even though he lets a girl do his dirty work for him, not that I mind how the right man's been put in charge. And by the right man I mean me.

Do you hear me Aldo?

Aldo!

Aldo *(Hurt)* Yes. You were right.

The Vigil or The Guided Cradle   225

Balto *(To Ippolito)* This will hurt. But don't worry. It will be just enough.

The town clock begins to chime loudly, louder and louder as Balto approaches Ippolito.

The Foreigner goes to Translator, touches his dead body, his ear.

Scene 8. The Gift

The interrogation room. A hooded Prisoner sits. A shadow looms—about to enter. It's the Foreigner.

Foreigner I'm sorry about the hood.

They've hurt you?

Prisoner They pissed on me.

Foreigner The bruises on your back. The bites.

Prisoner Dogs.

Foreigner Like wolves.

Prisoner I did nothing wrong. My brother, he said he knows people, that he'd make things right.

Foreigner It didn't work out like that.

Prisoner You spoke with him. You know him?

Foreigner When I woke up after—

I asked my father to take me here. This place. I open the doors, walk down the hall and I can hear what they're doing.

Prisoner You've made a mistake. Look at my face, I'll show you.

Foreigner It doesn't happen like that. Not with me.

Prisoner What happens with you?

Foreigner takes the chair Ippolito once used, sits in it facing Prisoner.

Aldo and Balto walk down the Hall. Balto wears Prime's robes.

Balto Aldo, I thought you understood. Ippolito is in your care. This is your first. This is where I started. And now look. Look what you can become.

Balto sits at his desk.

Aldo Me? Of course, I want to, I will but I never…Not to someone I knew…I know him. I thought you'd…it's your right.

Balto I trust you Aldo.

Aldo You don't even want to watch?

Balto And you must trust what I ask of you.

Aldo But I don't—

Balto Shut up. There is much I must do. Understand Aldo?

He hands him the smiling dog knife. Aldo is still upset, but nods, exits. Balto goes off.

Prisoner *(Beginning to realize)* Last night when the guards—when they hit me—they said something about my brother—and a girl—

Foreigner There was a girl. I was the girl. And I brought you a gift.

Foreigner takes out a card, puts it in his hands.

Prisoner The hood.

Foreigner No.

Prisoner Then how am I supposed to…

Foreigner I'll tell you. It's a postcard. It's of the clock in the town square.

Prisoner My brother—

Foreigner Yes, he was there too.

Prisoner Whatever my brother has done to you, he is not me.

Foreigner No.

Prisoner I have not done this to you.

Foreigner He's dead. They won't tell you. So I came to…

Prisoner How did he die?

Foreigner He died for you. It happened very quickly.

He told me the clock.

It shows three types of time: And this here, the middle ring, is time as we know it.

What we choose now.

A beat. Foreigner looks at the tied Prisoner for what is very short, but might seem like a very long time.

She takes off the hood to see Ippolito's face.

She frees him. He holds up his free hands.

Ippolito Why would you…

Foreigner Because you did it for me.

Foreigner takes back the postcard, still looking at Ippolito. She backs away.

Aldo appears, he sits where Foreigner once was interrogating Ippolito.

Aldo There are only two choices we have: to dream or not. Awake or asleep. Vigil or Cradle.

Foreigner leaves. Aldo grabs Ippolito's free hands, starts to string him up in the Vigil but Ippolito stays focused on where the Foreigner has gone, looking after her.

You taught me so you tell me, you fucking tell me why you let her go!

Ippolito I believe we can change Aldo.

Aldo I believe in torture and I will torture you. And I believe that after, after I do, others will torture you.

Ippolito I believe she saved me.

Aldo brings down the smiling dog on him.

Abrupt blackout.

End of play.

Rewind
Laura Eason

Laura Eason: My Chameleon Collaborator

Jessica Thebus

Laura Eason—writer, adaptor, director, actress—is a chameleon of sorts as a playwright. Her work has a great diversity in terms of style and aesthetic. Her plays can range from a tightly focused two-character play to a transformational ensemble piece to an epic adaptation of a literary work. One cannot read a play of Laura's and identify the voice or style immediately, and when you read many of her works side by side, what you notice is her uncanny ability to shape-shift—to become the voice that the particular play and its characters require. She then lets the play find the aesthetic and form that suits it. As a frequent collaborator of Laura's and a great fan of her work, I am amazed by her protean quality as a writer and her ability to pry open each moment of theatrical transformation, give it all the space around it that it needs, and let it unfold with both clarity of idea and beauty of form.

When adapting Charles Dickens or Edith Wharton, for example, she sinks into the voice of the author, while keeping her own sense of humor. When writing a more realistic play, she has access to the voice and experience of a vast number of highly-charged and specific characters. Each play is a unique and surprising journey. What they have in common is deep and detailed love of what happens in the theater. Laura gives us vivid relationships, a driving idea behind the drama, elegance of construction, precision of execution, and a skilled sense of the potential of theatrical space and transformation.

When I direct a Laura Eason play, both her adaptations and original work, I find myself thinking a whole lot about space and transformation.

Because Laura is a wonderful collaborator, the project of staging a new play of hers is rich with dialogue and tireless examination. As she pursues idea and character, I look for the moments of transformation that burn right in the heart of the play. The play might be funny, lyrical, beautiful, moving, intellectually potent and surprising. It is full of people we love and want to follow. But as a director, I need to identify the significant moments of transformation, and determine what kind of theatrical space Laura is imagining. Sometimes it is visual, metaphorical. Sometimes it is language-based, emotional, almost invisible. Regardless, during the course of the story, there is irrevocable change, and that change happens in theatrical space.

In *40 Days* a key transformation happens offstage, and we experience it through its aftermath. A man spends the night trapped on his roof by a flood, and he emerges into a beautiful speech about letting go of the things he is waiting for. His lost love will never call. His mother will never change. The life he thought he would have will never come to pass. The flood waters have broken him open, and we see this as he emerges from the image of the storm, and speaks to us.

In Laura's adaptation of Jules Verne's *Around The World In 80 Days*, a key moment is purely visual and aural. Phileas Fogg and the lovely Auoda are drinking tea on the deck of a ship, and the tea cups slide back and forth on a gracefully tipping table. They rescue the cups as they slide, drink, replace, and the slide continues. In silence and to music. A mundane, daily, routine act that doesn't have any real intimacy becomes a moment of falling in love, sensual and magical. It is not spoken, but yet is an essential turning point in the story and in Fogg, and the dimensional nature of the theatrical language is perfect for the play.

And in *Rewind*, with its themes of success and destiny, the key moment is late in the play but early in the chronology of the characters—Elisha and Jim have just met. They are talking, roasting marshmallows, and she asks him about what it's like to play music. As he describes it, articulating it for the first time to her and probably to anybody, we see him coming to realize why he needs to play music and what it does for him. At that moment, the part of you in the audience that has been wishing for him to just give up music and get on with his life is suddenly daunted. We see this young, hopeful, innocent man and, even though we know it will lead to his death, we can't help but want him to pursue his dream. And we are forced to examine what it means that we suddenly want this so badly, although we have none of his innocence. It is a moment of distinct transformation both for the character and the audience.

As a director, I live for these moments where things change, subtly, drastically, irrevocably. A lamp is lit in the story, and by its light we see the people clearly, where we have been with them, where the story will take them next. We also see the big passionate idea at the heart of the drama and start to feel the theatrical space it takes up. In this space, Laura takes us close to territory that is important to us, perhaps challenging or difficult, perhaps both disturbing and inspiring. We walk thorough it with the help of her humor and love of language, and the characters we have come to know so well make their way alongside us.

The great excitement of Laura's work is that she will write characters with the detail of an actress and craft the flow of story with the all-encompassing vision of a director, all the while deftly exploring a central human idea with the skill of a poet.

It is a great joy to follow her into the theater, and see what happens next.

Jessica Thebus is an Associate Artist with Steppenwolf Theatre Company. At Steppenwolf, she has directed *Intimate Apparel*, *Dead Man's Cell Phone*, *No Place Like Home*, *When the Messenger is Hot* (also at 59E59, NYC) and *Sonia Flew*. Jessica has worked with The Huntington Theater, The Goodman Theater, The Oregon Shakespeare Festival, The Kennedy Center, Lookingglass Theater Company, Northlight Theater, Victory Gardens Theater, Remy Bumppo, Writer's Theater, Redmoon Theater and The Piven Theater Workshop. Favorite projects include *Pulp* at About Face Theatre (Jeff nomination—Best Director, After Dark Award—Best

Production); *Winesburg, Ohio* also at About Face (Jeff nomination—Best Director, After Dark Award—Best Director); She holds a doctorate in Performance Studies from Northwestern University, and is currently a faculty member in the MFA Directing Program.

Characters
Jim
Noah
Elisha
Scaff
Ray

Place/Time
Scene 17. Jim's House - 1998.
Scene 16. Anton's Guitar Shop - Earlier.
Scene 15. Dressing Room - Arena Amphitheater - Earlier.
Scene 14. Hospital Waiting Room - Earlier.
Scene 13. The Marine Lounge Bar - Earlier.
Scene 12. Zero's Bar - Earlier.
Scene 11. Noah's Apartment - Earlier.
Scene 10. Jim and Elisha's House - Earlier.
Scene 9. Dressing Room - On the Road - Earlier.
Scene 8. A Recording Studio - Earlier.
Scene 7. A House in the Hollywood Hills - Earlier.
Scene 6. Noah's Apartment - Earlier.
Scene 5. On the Road - Earlier.
Scene 4. Jim's Apartment - Earlier.
Scene 3. Noah's Dorm Room - Earlier.
Scene 2. A Backyard in Lafayette, Indiana - Earlier.
Scene 1/Scene 17. Jim's House - 1981/1998.

Scenic Design
The set should be spare and transformational as it needs to span seventeen years and as many locations; which should be established as minimally as possible to assure fluid transitions.

Music/Sound Design
The sound design and/or music used in the world premiere consisted of music of the era by bands in the indie rock scene in Chicago. This idea is encouraged. However, if original music is used instead, the instrumentation should stay away from a standard rock/pop sound—namely drums, guitar and bass—and be of a different quality. The goal is to avoid giving the audience the impression that they have heard Jim's music, and, therefore, judge his talent instead of focusing on the larger issues of the play.

Production History

The world premiere of *Rewind* opened on November 20, 2009 at the Side Project, Chicago, IL (Adam Webster, Artistic Director; Dan Granata, Managing Director).

The cast and creative contributors were:
Jim - Chip Davis
Noah - Zack Buell
Elisha - Cyd Blakewell
Scaff - Shane Kenyon
Ray - Brett Schneider

Director - Anna C. Bahow
Scenic Designer - Annette Vargas
Lighting Designer - Diane Fairchild
Costume Designer - Stefin Steberl
Sound Designer - Misha Fiksel
Production Stage Manager - Tara Malpass

To Obtain Rights To Produce This Play

Please contact: Morgan Jenness, Abrams Artists Agency, 275 Seventh Avenue, 26th Floor, New York, NY 10001. Telephone: (646) 486-4600. Email: morgan.jenness@abramsartny.com.

Rewind

Scene 17. Ext./Int. Jim's House - 1998

Outside Jim's front door, afternoon. Noah, thirty-two, bangs on the door.

Noah *(Calling through the door as he knocks)* Jim? Jimmy? Jim? *(To himself)* Goddamn it. *(Calling through the door again, very frustrated now)* Jim!?!

From behind him Elisha, thirty-one, pretty and nine months pregnant, approaches. It is awkward between them.

Elisha *(Sarcastically)* I can't imagine why that's not working.

Noah Wow. Look at you.

Elisha Yeah.

Noah You, uh, you look good.

Elisha Thanks for saying so anyway.

Noah *(Trying to make small talk)* So...how's Gary?

Elisha He's good.

Noah Great.

Elisha *(Looking to the door)* Well...should we—

Noah Yeah. Thanks. Sorry to drag you out here like this.

Elisha It's OK.

Noah I didn't know who else to call.

Elisha reaches in her bag and brings out a ring of keys.

Elisha How is it possible he never gave anyone else a key?

Noah I wasn't sure you'd still have it.

Elisha *(Looking through the keys)* I don't remember which one it is. Man, I have to pee.

Noah I'm sure he's just passed out....

Elisha I'm sure. *(Accidentally dropping keys)* Shit.

She begins to bend down to get them, but can't. Noah grabs them and gives them to her.

Elisha Thanks. I think it's this one.

Elisha opens the door. As Noah and Elisha enter, they are hit with a strong smell. They both react to it, slowly venturing into the living room.

Elisha What is that?

Noah Probably garbage or something. You want to check the bedroom? Jimmy!?!

As Noah continues to look around, Elisha walks through a doorway into the bedroom.

Noah Jim?

Elisha *(With a small cry, gasping for air)* Noah! Noah!!

Noah El?

Noah *(Seeing what she sees)* Oh no. Oh no....Come on. Come on.

Noah pulls Elisha away.

Elisha We should call...we should call...

Noah Yeah. Yeah.

Noah picks up the phone and dials.

Yes, um, I'm calling because my friend, um, I'm sorry...you know, now that I'm actually on the phone, I, uh, I don't know if this should be a, a 9-1-1 call, if it's an actual emergency, because my friend, um, my friend is... is already dead. *(He listens)* OK. Yes. Thank you. Yes. It's uh, it's 1680—

Elisha 1860.

Noah 1860, sorry, 1860 North Charleston. A little yellow house. Yes, we'll be here. Thank you.

Noah hangs up the phone. Elisha rubs her hand on her stomach.

Elisha I have to go.

Noah Are you OK?

Elisha Yeah...I just...I have to go.

Elisha walks past him and steps outside. Noah is left standing in the living room. We hear a siren in the distance.

Scene 16. Int. Anton's Guitar Shop - Earlier

Jim, thirty-two, sits in the workroom of the guitar shop, drinking a beer and restringing a guitar. A small bell sounds as the unseen shop door opens and closes in the next room.

Noah (*Offstage*) Hello?

Jim keeps working and doesn't answer.

Anton? Anton?

Noah enters. He is very surprised to see Jim.

Hey, Jim.

Jim (*Not looking up*) Hey.

Beat.

He's at lunch.

Noah Oh. OK.

Jim (*Working, not looking at Noah*) What do you need?

Noah Nothing, really.

Beat.

He just….he had the name of this guy. I don't know if you'd remember them—Bulldozer?—but he used to play with them…

Jim Yeah.

Noah Well, the guitar player, the really tall guy? He's starting this little, you know, side project thing, not even a side project actually, because, of course, Bulldozer's not even together anymore, but he's looking for a drummer, you know, just to shit around, nothing major, but I—

Jim That guy still play?

Noah Yeah, but not for a while, I guess. He's been working. He had a kid and stuff. But…

Jim Wasn't he like a mechanic or something?

Noah Plummer.

Jim Right. Terrible fucking job.

Noah I guess he makes really good money.

Jim Still a terrible fucking job.

Noah I don't know.

Jim Sticking your hands down people's toilets, pulling hair and crap out of people's sinks…

Noah I think he likes it alright.

Jim *(Going back to work, in disbelief)* Alright.

Noah *(Looking around the shop)* So, how long you been working here?

Jim A while.

Noah *(Re: guitar in front of Jim)* Nice Danelectro. Reissue?

Jim Original.

Noah It's cool. I loved your silver one. You still have it?

Jim Pawned it.

Noah *(Big news)* Shit.

Beat.

Well, I'll just give Anton a call later.

Noah looks at a Rolling Stone Magazine *lying on the counter.*

Saw the article, huh?

Jim Yeah.

Noah Our friend Ray comes off a little stupid, but it's good. For him.

Jim Um-hmm.

Noah He gives you credit for the single. That was nice.

Jim *(Wanting Noah to leave)* Do you want me to tell Anton to call you or…

Noah No. I'll, uh, I'll just talk to him later.

Jim OK.

Noah You know, if you're interested, there's this kid, he's playing Tuesday nights at Zero's. He's like eighteen, and he rocks—

Jim You going out on school nights now?

Noah So, I'll be there if you feel like coming by.

Jim *(No way in hell)* OK.

Beat.

Noah *(Never mind)* OK.

Noah goes. Beat. He comes back.

It's not like anyone expected you to be this, person, you know, any more than what you already were.

Jim *(Dismissing him)* Great. Thanks.

Noah I mean that, it's not like anyone's, you know, disappointed in you or anything. I know you're disappointed. We all are. Because it so easily could've…been different…

Jim What are you…?

Noah Jesus. All I'm trying to say is that everyone loves the record. Everyone I talked to who bought it thinks it's fucking great.

Jim All twelve of them.

Noah People really want to see you play again.

Jim Where? At fucking Zero's?

Noah We had some great shows there. It could be good just to play again.

Jim I can't just play anymore. Why is it so hard for you to understand that? You were supposed to be the smart one. But I forget that you're a big disappointment, too.

Noah OK. Whatever. See you.

Noah leaves. He comes back.

Look, I know you want me to get really pissed at you and—

Jim Why do you always just take it? You come back, like such a pussy, and take it and take it. I mean, what the fuck do I have to do to get you to leave me alone?

Noah OK. Alright then.

Noah exits. Jim roughly puts the guitar on the counter. He sits staring at it, then slowly starts to pulls the strings out of it.

Scene 15. Int. Dressing Room
Arena Amphitheater - Earlier

Interior of a dressing room backstage at a huge concert venue. There is a tub-full of beer and water. Through the wall the muffled sound of a rock band playing can be heard.

Jim sits on a couch, alone, staring intensely at the wall. He holds a half-full beer, which he chugs in one quick tilt. Next to the couch sits a newspaper. Jim looks at it for a moment and smiles.

He crosses to the table. He has a noticeable limp in his right leg. He chucks the empty bottle of beer into the garbage, the glass landing on several other glass bottles. He grabs another beer from the tub and opens it by banging the cap against the edge of the table. The cap flies across the room. He watches it go.

Noah appears in the doorway, dressed in suit-pants and a dress shirt, both look naked without the matching tie and jacket.

Noah Hey.

Jim You dressed up. I'm flattered.

Noah My office hours ran late. You guys sounded great.

Jim Thanks. Yeah. It was a good set.

Noah steps in.

Noah *(Re: the dressing room)* Nice digs here at the… *(Monster-truck voice)* ARENA, ARena, arena…

Jim Yeah. Beer?

Noah No, thanks.

Jim Come on, for old time's sake.

Noah Oh, well, if it's for old time's sake.

Jim reaches for a bottle of beer for him.

Where are the other guys?

Jim Watching Ray's set.

Noah That crowd is unbelievable.

Jim I know.

Noah Can you imagine it being like that all the time?

Jim Yeah, I can.

Jim opens the bottle but spills a bunch of the beer.

Shit!

Noah Don't worry about it.

Noah takes the beer and sits on the couch, tapping his feet in rhythm to the music coming through the wall. Jim stands, unconsciously rubbing his right thigh. Noah looks down at the open newspaper sitting next to the couch.

This review about last night?

Jim Yeah.

Noah *(Skimming the article)* Even when this guy's saying something good, he's a dick. Remember when his band opened for us? What were they called? Like "The Fountainheads" or some pretentious bullshit.

Jim *(Laughing)* Yeah.

Noah But it's exciting.

Jim It is.

Noah Already getting press and attention. And you were right. You sound great with those guys. That drummer, he kicks ass.

Jim This isn't the guy I told you about. He got way too fucked up on the road, so I had to replace him.

Noah Yeah?

Jim These guys are twenty-one, twenty-two years old. You remember.

Noah I do.

Jim They ride around in the van with these huge grins on their faces, like they're on their way to get the best blow job of their lives. They don't even care that they're hardly making shit. They just love to fucking play.

Jim gestures to the wall.

Ray sounds good, huh?

Noah Play that much and you're bound to. But it's cool he brought you on the tour, opening for him in all these cities…it's big.

Jim Well, I did write his hit, even though no one knows it.

Noah Except losers like me who read the liner notes.

Jim Right.

Noah You're getting some good money, though, right? You'll be able to just play for a while.

Jim I'm using the money to buy back the master tapes from the label. The tapes for the last record.

Noah (*Shocked*) But…that's, like, eighty thousand dollars or something, right? That'll eat up all your money.

Jim When I put it out, I'll make money from the record.

Noah You have someone to put it out yet?

Jim Not yet.

Noah Even with the song being a hit?

Jim Even with the fucking song.

Noah Well, the tour'll do a lot.

Jim *(Bitterly)* Yeah, I'll ride Ray's wave to the top.

Noah A lot of people would feel lucky for the chance.

Beat. Chris Scaff, thirty, stocky, almost over-dressed, leans his head in the door. Noah nods cursorily but does not get up.

Scaff *(Overly casual)* Hey, Man! Jimmy said you might be coming by.

Noah Yep.

Scaff Ray and the guys will be really happy to see you.

Noah I'm sure they'll be thrilled.

Jim Hey, Scaff, any of those label guys show up yet?

Scaff I didn't see them.

Jim You left passes for them, right?

Scaff Of course. They're probably still up there. It's early yet.

The music from above comes to an end. The sound of a roaring crowd can be heard.

I'll be back.

Scaff leaves.

Noah That was mighty cordial.

Jim Yeah. Well…

Elisha, regular size, stumbles into the dressing room.

Elisha Oh. Hey. I was headed to the…sorry. Hi.

Jim Hi. I didn't know you were here.

Elisha I was just getting my coat.

Jim You sick?

Elisha I keep feeling like I have to throw up.

Noah OK, bye.

Elisha You sounded great.

Jim You saw my set?

Noah What were you looking for again?

Elisha I put my coat in Ray's dressing room, and I…

Jim Back down the hall, on the left.

Noah Can't imagine how you missed it.

Elisha Well…nice to see you.

Jim You, too.

Elisha I'm really glad things are turning around for you.

Jim Well, I don't know if I'd say turning around, but it's going good.

Elisha It was great Ray brought you on the tour.

Jim Yeah... everyone seems to think so.

Elisha Well...

Noah See you later!

She leaves.

How can you even talk to her?

The sound of talking and laughing is heard outside the dressing room. Ray, twenty-six, sweet faced and dressed in casual rock musician duds, ducks his head in the door.

Ray Jim told me you might show up.

Noah Hey Ray!

Ray *(Taking a rumpled pack of cigarettes out of his back pocket)* It's been too long, man.

Noah Are you going to...   **Ray** So, how have you...

Ray Go ahead.

Noah *(Re: the crowd still roaring)* Are you going to play some more?

Ray Yeah, just gotta have a quick smoke. By the end of the set, I'm dying. And, they'll wait. You see Elisha?

Noah Yep.

Jim chugs the rest of his beer and throws his empty bottle into the garbage. The glass shatters as it hits other bottles in the garbage can. Ray jumps at the sound, then laughs at himself.

Ray Shit! I'm getting a little paranoid.

Noah I read about the show in Seattle.

Ray It was scary man! You know, it's great, all the attention and everything, but then, when you're in front of a couple thousand people, your mind just starts to wander, like, if someone really wanted to fuck me up, what could I do?

Noah Yeah. But it's unbelievable, everything that's been happening for you guys, in less than a year.

Ray Not totally unbelievable, but I'm happy about it, you know. I guess I owe a lot to you guys, huh?

Noah looks at the floor. Jim opens another beer.

Well, Jim's been kicking ass with these new guys.

Scaff (*Offstage*) Ray.

Ray (*Looking out the door*) Hang on one second. Elisha and Gary are leaving.

Jim turns and watches the figures offstage. Suddenly, he charges out the door. Offstage a struggle ensues, Noah and Ray drag Jim back into the dressing room.

Noah Stop it! Stop it!

Jim still flails and hits Ray in the jaw. Ray falls back. Noah tries to calm Jim down.

Come on! Jimmy!! Stop it!

Jim charges at Noah, punching him in the stomach. Noah crumples to the floor. Jim backs away. Scaff rushes in and goes to Ray.

Scaff You OK?

Scaff helps Ray to his feet.

Ray Un-fucking-believable. We're doing you a big favor here, you know?

Jim You're doing me a favor?

Ray I'm done with you, man. Whatever I owed you…we're even. Good luck, good fucking luck. *(To Scaff)* Get him out of here.

Ray exits.

Scaff I'm sorry, Jimmy, but I think you'd better grab your stuff and go.

Jim Look, Scaff, I'm sorry. You know I didn't mean to…

Scaff You need to get out of here. Sorry, Jim. But you should go.

Jim Come on…

Scaff Now.

Scaff exits. Elisha leans in.

Elisha Jimmy? Are you OK?

Jim doesn't look up. Noah looks at her. She looks to Jim, then to Noah, and exits. Noah stands. Jim remains still.

Noah I'll leave you to it then.

Noah exits. Jim sits on the floor, head in his hands. He slowly lifts his eyes to the wall as the sound of the crowd swells.

Scene 14. Int. Hospital Waiting Room - Earlier

Noah, wearing rumpled clothes, paces in a hospital waiting room. Ray, equally disheveled, is seated, staring at the floor.

Noah You should go home Ray.

Ray No, I'm alright. I'll have a smoke and get some more coffee. Do you want some?

Noah Yeah, thanks.

Ray Black?

Noah Yeah.

Ray goes. Elisha rushes in.

Elisha I just got your messages. We were traveling for like twenty-six hours.

Noah It's OK. He opened his eyes.

Elisha Is he going to be OK?

Noah They think so.

Elisha Son of a bitch! What the hell was he thinking!?

Noah It's alright.

Elisha No! What a fucking asshole!

Noah He was taking the pain pills for his leg and he just drank too much.

Elisha Why was he drinking at all? What an asshole!

Noah It was an accident.

Elisha Sure.

Noah Things have been better lately.

Elisha Please! He had a total meltdown when he lost his Mom. And having to deal with his Dad all alone? And that whole thing with the actress!

Noah He said he was doing better about that.

Beat.

He's written some good new songs.

Elisha Writing a good song was never the problem! I mean, he was still leaving little riffs on my answering machine, asking for my opinion, like, two weeks before the wedding! What was he thinking?!

Noah Maybe he thought that'd be alright with you.

Elisha Are you kidding!?

Noah I shouldn't have called you.

Elisha He did this to himself. What did you expect me to say?

Noah I just thought you'd…I don't know.

Elisha I can't believe we're here again. Have you been here all night?

Noah Yeah. Ray's here too. He found him.

Elisha Poor kid. Is Jim's Dad here?

Noah He said he didn't see the point in coming up if he was unconscious. So, I called when Jim woke up and he said he'd try and come up tomorrow.

Elisha He was probably terrified. How ever would he ever explain Jim killing himself in the annual Christmas letter?

Noah He wasn't trying to kill himself. He just thinks he's indestructible.

Elisha He's proving his point. I know he's feeling trapped. God, I wish he had more options.

Noah He can always get a job like a regular person.

Elisha It's not what he wants.

Ray enters behind them carrying two cups of coffee. He freezes as Noah and Elisha's conversation gets more heated.

Noah *(Angry)* Not everyone gets to do what they want.

Elisha He barely has a high school diploma. He has no other skills. What do you expect him to do? String guitars for five bucks an hour? Move back to Lafayette and live in his Dad's basement?

Noah *(Raising his voice)* Why is it always extremes with you two?

Elisha You don't have to raise your voice, Noah, I'm not trying to say anything upsetting.

Ray *(Announcing his presence)* Hey…hey you guys.

Elisha Hey Ray.

Ray hands the coffee off to Noah.

Noah Thanks, man.

Ray *(To Elisha)* You just got back, huh?

Elisha We came straight from the airport. Gary's parking. I heard you found him.

Ray Yeah. We kind of had an argument…about some music stuff on the phone.

Elisha I'm sorry.

Ray He was pretty mad, so I went over to talk to him. And he'd left the door open, like actually a little bit open. It hadn't been very long.

Elisha You saved him.

Ray I kept thinking though, it was my fault, you know. Getting him so mad.

Elisha He's upset about a lot of things, Ray.

Ray *(To Noah)* I just feel like I should have asked him about the song, you know?

Elisha What song?

Ray One of Jim's songs is on my CD. That's what I called to tell him.

Elisha He didn't know?

Ray No.

Elisha You didn't ask him? Scaff didn't ask him?

Ray We recorded it, just, you know, to see. We didn't even know if we'd use it. But when it turned out great, we put it on the record.

Elisha Why didn't you ask him?

Ray Scaff said that the record company still owned the rights. So, we didn't technically need to tell him or anything—

Elisha Didn't technically need to tell him? Is that what Scaff said?

Ray I thought Jim'd be happy. It'd be this great surprise.

Elisha I guess you were right about that.

Beat.

Noah So, you're leaving on tour soon, aren't you?

Ray We play a warm-up gig here in Chicago on Thursday then go to New York on Friday.

Noah Cool.

Ray Of course, the record comes out Tuesday so we're doing a bunch of promotional stuff there, playing at Tower, stuff like that.

Noah That's great.

Ray Then we start the huge tour.

Noah I'm sure it'll be cool.

Ray I wish you guys were still together. I'd try and get you on some of the local dates.

Elisha Some local dates? That'd be mighty generous, Ray.

Ray *(Backpedaling)* Well, you know, the label controls the out of town booking…

Beat. No one speaks, everyone waiting for someone else to say something.

Well, you know, I think I'm starting to crash. So, since you guys are together, maybe it'd be alright if I took off?

Noah Yeah, we're OK. Thanks Ray.

Ray I'll check in later.

Noah OK.

Ray And congratulations Elisha. Say hey to Gary.

Elisha I will.

Ray raises his hand to Noah. Noah does the same. Elisha watches Ray go.

Did you know about the song?

Noah *(Too quickly)* No.

Elisha Did you?

Noah No. I didn't. Did you?

Elisha *(Too quickly)* Of course not.

Beat.

Why would Ray not have asked Jim's permission?

Noah I don't know.

Noah offers her some coffee.

Want some?

Elisha You like it too strong.

Beat.

Last time I saw Jim was just after the car accident. Out of the blue, he called and asked if I could take him to the grocery store. His leg was still pretty bad, and he had no license, DUI, suspended, whatever it was, and of course, no car. Sitting there in the passenger seat, he looked so…small, you know? So…regular. Not this…

Noah What?

Elisha Well, you always did admire him.

Noah I admired him? And stop talking about him like he's dead.

Elisha Coming over here, I was so sure he was. I was so sure he'd done that.

Noah Disappointed?

Elisha Not funny.

Noah But didn't you feel just a little relieved? Just a little bit?

Elisha No!

Noah After everything?

Elisha No, of course not.

Noah No matter how much he drives me absolutely crazy, I can't stop worrying about him. Thinking about him. When Ray called me, I actually felt…relieved. Like, finally, the end of the story. We could move on.

Elisha But…we have moved on.

As they sit together in silence, not looking at each other, the noise of the hospital becomes more present.

Scene 13. The Marine Lounge Bar - Earlier

Noah and Jim drink at the bar.

Jim I keep thinking, maybe I'm totally wrong and all of my songs suck. Maybe they've always sucked.

Noah That's not true.

Jim But how do we really know?

Noah What?

Jim How do we know if something is good or not?

Noah You just know what you like, I guess.

Jim But is there, is there some kind of like, internal, you know, what's the word?

Noah Instinctual?

Jim Instinctual, you know, response to stuff that's genuinely good? Like, why are the Beatles considered good? Forget the fact that some assholes say they suck. They're fucked. I mean, The Beatles are good, right?

Noah The Beatles are good.

Jim OK, but forget what we think. Are they considered good because a lot of people like them? Or is there some, some, you know…

Noah Intrinsic?

Jim Yeah, intrinsic. Wait, what does that mean?

Noah Fundamental, essential, like it's inherent in the thing.

Jim OK, yeah, is there some intrinsic goodness to the work that people just have to see? Or is it just time and place and popularity? Because when we recorded that record, I thought it was good. You thought it was good. Elisha thought it was good. The guys at the label thought it was good. Even fucking Scaff thought it was good. But, now, after all that shit, I don't know how to know if anything is good anymore. Because the cream separates, don't you think?

Noah What?

Jim I mean, has there ever been a guy you thought was fucking genius who didn't amount to something?

Noah Plenty of geniuses died penniless, in obscurity and all of that.

Jim But maybe in their time, maybe they did suck. But time passed and people starting liking different stuff and, just like that, they were good.

Noah I think you're spinning your wheels here.

Jim OK, well, maybe all we really want is people we think are cool to like it.

Noah What about just having faith in yourself, in whatever it is, that it's good, no matter what anyone says.

Jim But any idiot can convince himself he's a genius. Isn't convincing everyone else you're a genius what it's all about?

Noah I don't know. But plenty of people who are really well known and sell tons of records totally suck!

Jim Do they suck!? Or do we just not know what we're talking about!?

Noah Well, I certainly don't know what we're talking about!

Jim Well, we never got that far out there, so we'll never know what people would have thought. Or maybe the fact that we didn't get out there is the answer, you know?

Noah Whatever.

Jim Why do you do that?

Noah Because it's pointless to talk about this.

Jim But you see what I'm getting at.

Noah It's late. I have to get some sleep.

Jim Oh man! I had the weirdest dream last night.

Noah takes a long drink of beer.

My Dad and I were in this plane and it crashed. And my Dad is running all over, helping people with their injuries and stuff. And somehow everyone knows his name, "Over here Dr. Ward, over here…"

Noah Uh-huh.

Jim So, the great Dr. Ward is tending to the wounded, and all I can do is stand there with my guitar asking everyone for requests. "Can I play something for you?" Then this pretty brown-haired girl, she asks me to play "Pale Blue Eyes." So, I do but the guitar is out of tune and it just sounds terrible and they start booing, these people that are lying there, bleeding, dying, they start booing me.

Noah Did you stop?

Jim My Dad turns around and says, "Stop fooling around and make yourself useful." So, I start running. And I am fucking lost in the forest. Just running around, trying to find something else I can do. But there's nothing. Finally, I end up smashing my guitar and burning it for firewood. Then the brown-haired girl and I were at some campfire, doing it under the stars.

Noah You always were in it to get laid. Come on, I'll drive you home.

Jim I'm fine.

Noah Yeah. OK. Well, I'm going to piss and then we'll go. Give me your keys.

Jim *(Setting keys on the bar)* I'll leave them on the bar, OK. Don't make me look like an asshole.

Noah OK. OK.

Noah takes out a few dollars and puts them on the bar.

Jim Are you tipping for me too?

Noah Why?

Jim *(Throwing two dollars on the bar)* I am not so fucking broke that I can't leave two dollars on the bar. Here.

Noah OK. *(Noah pockets his money)* I'll be right back.

Noah goes off. Jim grabs his keys and the two dollars off the bar and rushes to the door. He is noticeably without his limp but very drunk. At the door, he stops, turns around and puts the money back on the bar. He rushes out the door. Beat. Noah returns. He looks around for Jim but sees that he has gone.

Shit. Shit!!

Scene 12. Int./Ext. Zero's Bar - Earlier

Noah and Ray sit in a shabby dressing room talking. Ray is strumming a '68 SG.

Ray You think you'll play with another band?

Noah Sad to say, but the late nights are kind of tough for me now.

Ray Well, I was talking with this guy, Seth, cool guy, younger guy, but he's putting together a new band, they're looking for a drummer, I thought of you...

Noah Thanks but I don't think I can swing it right now. I'm really out of practice anyway. New SG?

Ray I've been feeling so optimistic lately, I couldn't help myself.

Noah It's nice. Who always played a '68 SG? Marc Bolan?

Ray No, he played a Les Paul.

Noah Of course. Angus Young.

Ray Right. I've actually been listening to a lot of T. Rex lately. I never get sick of it.

Noah You know what old stuff I never get sick of? Thin Lizzy. I think I'll have them play "Jailbreak" at my funeral.

Ray How is it though, that the "Running Back to You" song has the exact same riff as the chorus of "The Boys are Back in Town?" Did they think no one would notice? It's just a little slower, but it's the same riff. And it's on the album before "The Boys Are Back…" so people would notice it right away if they knew the hit. I never understood what they were thinking.

Noah I think they just didn't give a shit.

Ray Which is exactly the way to be. You want to try?

Noah takes the guitar and begins to play a few awkward chords.

Noah My guitar playing is still terrible.

Ray I hope Jim plays again.

Noah It'd be a waste not to. He's still got a good shot.

Ray You know, we've starting working with Scaff…

Noah Really?

Ray He's still in good with the label, and with the take over, the label's huge.

Noah I'm sure.

Ray I feel kinda weird about it, because, I mean, I wouldn't have even met him without you guys. But, we're probably going to put out a CD with them…

Noah Really?

Ray And Scaff was talking about some of Jim's songs.

Noah Jim's songs?

Ray The label, they still own them, you know, so Scaff was saying, maybe we could do one of those songs.

Noah Cover one of Jim's songs?

Ray Yeah. And I think it'd be cool. I mean, I love those songs. I think they're genius. So, what do you think he'd say? I don't want him to take it the wrong way.

Noah *(Slowly)* Huh. Well…if the label still owns the songs, you don't have to ask for his permission, you know. You could just do it.

Ray Yeah, but you know how much those songs mean to him.

Noah But even if you record it, who knows if it'll end up on the record.

Ray Right.

Noah Well, I'd say, record the song and see what happens. If it works out, it'll be a good surprise. If not, then he won't be disappointed.

Ray You don't think I should ask him for his permission or anything? I know he's really protective of his stuff.

Noah It's business now, Ray. It's business now.

Outside the club, Jim and Elisha stand in front of the bar's run-down exterior.

Elisha I really need to get back in, I don't want Gary to be alone too long.

Jim He's a little out of his element, huh?

Elisha Not really. He represents a lot of these guys.

Jim I just meant that he's so much older than—

Elisha I get it.

Jim So, how is it?

Elisha What?

Jim Him.

Elisha What do you want me to say? That it's great?

Jim At least then I'd understand.

Elisha Well, he's great.

Jim Uh-huh.

Elisha Don't act like you know better.

Jim Well, he's loaded.

Elisha It's not about the money.

Jim It was always about the money.

Elisha I'm going in.

Jim Does he inspire you?

Elisha He's together for one thing…

Jim "Together?"

Elisha He doesn't lose his shit every time things don't happen the way he wants them to…

Jim Does he make you feel like a rock star?

Elisha Stop it.

Jim Why do you keep showing up everywhere?

Noah sticks his head out the door and sees Elisha and Jim talking.

Elisha Ray is Gary's client.

Jim I don't remember him supporting us so much…

Noah Please shut up and come in. You guys are killing me with this shit.

Elisha We'll be right there.

Scaff approaches.

Noah Hey, Scaff.

Scaff Hey kids.

Noah What are you doing here?

Scaff You know, just checking things out.

Noah Ray said you've been coming to a lot of their shows.

Scaff They're a great band.

Noah We wouldn't disagree with you. He said you've been rustling up some major label interest.

Jim I'll be sure to tell them how great you worked out for us.

Scaff Look Jimmy, in my book, you're really talented, regardless of the bad blood or whatever. But, there is only so far that takes you. You need to take responsibility for your part, you know?

Jim Whatever you say.

Scaff goes in. Jim looks at Elisha, then Noah, turns, and goes.

Noah Jim? Jimmy?

Jim is gone.

Elisha When is this going to get easier?

Noah You tell me.

Beat.

You should have told him about Gary, you know.

Elisha When Ray found out he said he wouldn't say anything.

Noah How do you think that felt?

Elisha Don't act like you're looking out for his best interest. You're just trying to make me feel bad and I won't.

Scaff comes out.

Scaff Gary's looking for you, El.

Noah See you.

Noah goes back into the club.

Elisha I don't understand why they're so mad at me! What did I do that was so wrong?

Scaff They're just disappointed at the way things turned out. We all are. But, you're still doing what you can for them. In fact, I talked to Ray about your idea, having him cover one of Jim's songs.

Elisha Yeah?

Scaff Yeah. He's into it.

Elisha I don't know if Jim'll go for it or not…

Scaff Neither do I.

Elisha But I'd like to see him get something out of it, after all this time. Those songs are…the best.

Scaff nods and starts to head into the club.

Scene 11. Int. Noah's Apartment - Earlier

Noah sits at a table grading papers. There is a knock on the door. Noah looks through the peep-hole and opens the door. Jim is revealed in the doorway. Noah doesn't let him in but talks to him in the hallway through the door-jam.

Jim Hey. Thought I'd come by and see if you wanted to go get something to eat.

Noah It's one o'clock in the morning. I should have been asleep, like, three hours ago.

Jim I had to get out of the house. Sitting around watching the clock tick is driving me out of my fucking mind.

Noah Sorry, but I have to finish grading these tests.

Jim Come on.

Noah I can't. I told them I'd hand them back tomorrow.

Jim They're fifteen. They won't care.

Noah It's not good to tell them a deadline and not meet it. Then they don't respect you when you give them one.

Jim They're fifteen. They don't respect you anyway.

Noah While that might be true, I'm still trying to do what's right. Maybe this weekend?

Jim OK. Yeah. *(Starts to go but stops in the hallway)* Do you know what it was?

Noah What?

Jim Things were alright. Then the deal fell apart and she left.

Noah I don't know. Maybe it made her see some things? I'm not sure. Anyway, I'm happy to talk about this, really, I am, but, I really have to…

Jim Yeah. Yeah. OK.

A long beat.

OK. I'll see you.

Jim leaves. Elisha comes out from the bedroom, coughing.

Elisha He sounded awful.

Noah He looks awful. So do you actually. *(Touching her forehead with his palm)* You're pretty warm. You're sure you're doing the right thing?

Elisha Yeah.

Noah I can't believe how much I miss it.

Elisha What?

Noah The band. Don't you?

Elisha I miss the attention. But there's a lot I don't miss.

Noah Like?

Elisha The smell of those dressing rooms. Lugging equipment.

Noah You never lugged anything.

Elisha Yes, I did.

Noah *(No you didn't)* OK.

Elisha Most of all, I will not miss the stupid talk, talk, talk with the millions of loser bands we played with. If I never, ever hear another conversation about gear again I'll be happy.

Noah You talked your fair share of gear.

Elisha OK, maybe I did, but not nearly as bad as most of you guys. I mean every make and model and what did Paul McCartney play on "Revolver," and what did Pete Townshend play on "Who's Next." I mean, who the hell cares?

Noah A Rickenbocker and Telecaster but you're totally right, who cares?

Elisha It's a good thing bands never stay anywhere very long, because girls would realize what a bunch of boring, single minded morons you guys are and you'd never get any action.

Elisha coughs. Noah rubs her back and she leans into him.

Noah So, what now?

Elisha I don't know. I can't bring myself to think about it.

Noah That's healthy.

Elisha Well, Gary said he'd give me a filing job if I wanted one.

Noah Gary?

Elisha What?

Noah Why on earth would he think you'd be any good at anything that happens in an office.

Elisha Shut up. He's trying to help me out.

Noah Everyone wants to help you.

Elisha Why is that?

Noah Look in the mirror.

Elisha Is that the only reason?

Noah No. It's just you, you know?

Elisha Thank you for saving my life—letting me stay here and not telling him. What would I do without you?

Noah touches Elisha's head.

How long have we known each other now?

Noah Since ninth or tenth grade. Like ten years, I guess.

Elisha A long time.

Noah A long time.

She turns and looks at him. She slowly leans into Noah and kisses him on the lips. He slowly responds, then suddenly breaks forcefully away.

Stop it.

Elisha What?

Noah What are you doing?!

Elisha I just thought…

They look at each other for a beat.

Um…OK. Well. I guess I'll go.

Noah No, it's alright.

Elisha No, really, I'll go. It's OK.

Noah Look, I know this is a weird time for you. You're sick…

Elisha I'll be fine.

Noah It's OK. You can stay. Ellie…

He goes to her and stops her from picking up her stuff.

Stop. You can stay, alright. I just don't understand what that was about.

Elisha I'm going, so you can stop it.

Noah What?

Elisha The innocent bullshit. I understand your loyalty or whatever but don't act like you haven't been wanting that to happen for ten years.

Noah What is happening to you?

Elisha I'm a realist, OK? Here we are, you and me, we might as well make the best of it. But, I'm sorry if I was compromising your morals. I'll get out of here.

Noah Where?

Elisha Don't worry about me, believe it or not, I've got a lot of options.

Elisha holds her stuff in one arm and picks up the phone with the other. She dials.

Hey, Gary…it's El. I'm sorry that I'm calling you at such an insane hour. OK, good. Oh, no, it's just a little cold, thanks.

Unseen by Elisha, Noah rubs his mouth with his hand.

So, I'm calling…because…

Lights shift.

Scene 10. Int. Jim and Elisha's House - Earlier

Jim and Elisha's living room. Noah, Jim and Elisha listen to Scaff. It is late afternoon.

Scaff They are just on a different schedule in LA. I know it's hard to believe.

Jim You were in LA for five days and got nowhere?

Scaff They're still getting settled. It was a huge takeover.

Elisha It's been six months.

Noah And almost a year, a year since we were in the studio.

Scaff It's taking a long time for them to make decisions.

Jim What's so hard? They either like the record, or they don't.

Scaff I know, with it sitting on a shelf, it seems like forever, but they have hundreds of bands to sift through, lots of relationships to decide about.

Elisha What about the other executives, those younger guys we met with?

Scaff Some of them are still there, and a couple of them are still really behind us, which is good. But they're all vying for a position now. And, like I said, anything with Randy Craig's prints is tainted.

Elisha Tainted? It's that bad?

Jim How much longer?

Scaff I really don't know, could be two weeks, could be two years.

Jim Come on!

Scaff I am just trying to be realistic here. They have you under contact for two more years, OK? They paid you for that—

Noah With the promise of touring and shows…

Elisha And putting out the record—

Scaff The contract was standard and according to it, they have already fulfilled their obligation, right? So, they can keep you as long as they want.

Jim But why?! Why not just let us go!?

Scaff They like the record, Jimmy, they do. They just don't think it's the right sound right now. They don't think they hear a hit. They just need some more time. No one wants to make the wrong decision. It may be a good thing.

Jim So…we just have to wait?

Scaff Yeah. We just have to wait.

Elisha How is this happening?

Jim Fuck them! I'll go back and release something on Mansize.

Scaff Listen to me, Jim. Listen. Until they let you out of that contract, you can not record anywhere and you can't release any of the songs on the record.

Jim But they're my songs!

Scaff No, Jimmy, they're not. The label owns them. And you—for two more years.

A long beat.

Jim Then I'll buy back the masters.

Scaff's beeper goes off.

Scaff That would set you back about a hundred thousand.

Scaff checks his beeper.

Jim What?!

Elisha Is that what they said? It would be that much to buy them back?

Scaff It came up. I have to make a call, guys. 'Scuse me, OK?

Scaff goes to the other room to make a call.

Jim If I had a hundred thousand dollars I wouldn't have needed them in the first place!

Noah I know.

Elisha Can you believe this? What are we going to do? What are we going to do?

Jim I really thought the record was good.

Noah It is good.

Jim Then why are they undecided? If it was good, they wouldn't be undecided.

Noah Don't give them that much credit.

Beat.

I guess I'll take that teaching job.

Jim I guess you should.

Elisha Please stop talking like that.

Jim You'll love that job. All those smart math nerds looking up to you. You'll be their hero.

Elisha What'll we do for a drummer?

Noah Don't be so sentimental, El.

Elisha You're the one who's abandoning ship.

Scaff comes back.

Scaff Sorry, guys, but I have to go. I'll be in touch if I hear anything. Until then, just sit tight. And we'll stay positive, OK?

Elisha So, we're done talking about this?

Scaff No, but there isn't anything else we can do now. You're frozen. And I have to go deal with something, OK. We can talk more tonight, if you want to, but right now I have to go.

Jim Well, then go!

Scaff What?

Jim Get out of my house! Get out of my fucking house!!

Scaff I understand that you're upset!

Jim Get out!

Scaff I know you're upset but be careful what you're doing here. Ellie, will you talk some sense into him, please?

Elisha I think he's right.

Scaff Noah?

Noah *(Very pointedly)* You know, all this music business stuff is a little over my head.

Scaff You guys are really stupid if you think I'm trying to fuck you over. I have a huge stake in this, too! It's been years for me, too! It's my fucking life, too!!

Scaff's beeper goes off.

Jim Just go!! Just fucking go!!

Scaff leaves shaking his head. Jim slams the door behind him, then slams it five more times in a row.

He's sucking their dicks! He doesn't care which of his bands hits as long as one of them does! He doesn't give a shit if we're frozen forever!

Noah Looks like it.

Jim Aren't you upset? It's your record too!

Noah No, Jimmy, it's not.

Jim You think I wanted to do that?

Noah You did it.

Elisha It doesn't matter anymore.

Jim It does matter!

Elisha I'm calling the lawyer.

Elisha goes to her purse, rummages through it until she finds a business card and goes to the phone.

Jim What lawyer?

Elisha Gary Whatshisname. The guy who negotiated our contract. I'm going to call him and find out if there is some way out of this.

Noah That guy was so cheesy.

Elisha He's very successful. He knows what he's doing. He represents some very huge people. He can at least help us figure out our options.

Jim I gotta get out of here. I'm going to get a beer. I'll be back.

Noah We'll come with you.

Elisha hangs up.

Elisha He's not answering.

Jim I'll be back.

Jim goes.

Noah I know I should go after him, but I just can't tonight.

Elisha I can't believe this. I feel like I'm losing my mind. I mean, what are we going to do?

Noah Go on to the next thing, I guess. I don't want to anymore than you do, but, it was always a long shot, you know.

Elisha I didn't think so. Why the hell do you think I've been hanging in there for so long?

Noah The music?

Elisha *(Getting her coat)* I'm going over to Gary's office and see if there isn't some way to save us.

Noah What about Jim?

Elisha I'm doing this for Jim.

Noah I mean, should I go find him?

Elisha Sure. Whatever. I'll see you later.

Scene 9. Int. Dressing Room - On the Road - Earlier

Dressing room of an upscale music club. Ray, smoking a cigarette, and Jim talk as Jim puts his guitar in its case. Noah finishes packing up his gear.

Ray I actually have been following you for a while, even before that one single got commercial airplay.

Jim Yeah?

Ray Yeah, I work at my college radio station, and, of course we played a bunch of stuff off your record, but I was hooked as soon as I heard those first two seven inches.

Jim Those were good songs.

Ray Great songs. And I love the new songs, too.

Jim Yeah?

Ray Yeah! That last song you played—man!

Jim Really?

Ray Yeah!

Jim casually pops the top off a bottle of beer against the edge of the table.

Ray *(Impressed)* Sweet.

Jim takes a sip of his beer.

Your tour van is so kick-ass. I can't imagine having anything that nice.

Jim Having a cool van, someone else booking your shows, getting to sleep at a hotel! Motel 6 is like heaven in comparison to where we've slept! If it can always be like this, I'll do it forever.

Noah begins to head out, carrying his cymbal bag.

Ray Hey, great show, man.

Jim Yeah, Noh, you played great tonight.

Noah *(To Jim)* Thanks. I hear I'm really good live.

Ray It was so cool to open for you guys.

Jim I was saying, they need to come up north, get Scaff to book them a few shows.

Ray That would be unbelievable.

Noah If Scaff helps, that will be unbelievable.

Ray smiles. Noah exits.

Jim We used to be able to book whoever we wanted to open because our local draw is so good, but now we've signed to this major and we have to clear everything through our manager…

Ray Yeah, Elissa was telling me.

Jim Elisha?

Ray Elisha, yeah, sorry. She was telling me about the record…

Jim Yeah, the record's suppose to be coming out in, like, a month! And we were signed by Randy Craig, the head of the label, so I think we'll get a lot of support for it.

Ray Very cool.

Elisha, a little drunk, sticks her head in the dressing room.

Elisha Are you coming?

Ray I'm sure my guys are waiting for me. It's like three hours home for us. So, I'll see you later.

Jim shakes Ray's hand.

Jim OK man, I'll be in touch.

Ray Great. Great to meet you, Elisha.

Elisha You too, Jay.

Ray takes off.

Jim Jay?

Elisha What?

Jim Ray.

Elisha Whatever.

Beat.

There's a really pretty one waiting for you outside.

Jim Whatever.

Elisha I think she's the prettiest one this week.

Jim Well, what am I supposed to do? I don't ask them to wait. And you know I hardly say two words to them.

Elisha What is it?

Jim What?

Elisha The fantasy…the girl in the crowd.

Jim Come on.

Elisha Tell me.

Jim Stop it.

Elisha I mean, how would you choose?

Jim Don't.

Elisha Really, how would you choose the lucky winner? What would it be? The legs? The ass? The blind adoration??

Jim Come on…

Elisha The way they see you, in all your rock star glory?

Jim In all my rock star glory.

Elisha They don't see you. I see you.

Jim I know.

Elisha How long before it happens?

Jim It's not going to happen. And you're a rock star, too.

Elisha I'm just faking it. Everyone knows that, especially you. And soon, you'll have so many important people to give you their opinions…

Jim Yours is the only one I care about. Look at me. Come on. It's you, OK? It's just you.

She drops her head. Jim holds her and starts to kiss her. Slowly, she kisses back. The kiss grows in passion and they are quickly entwined.

Noah enters. He waits a beat, clearing his throat. Jim and Elisha don't acknowledge him.

Noah Hey! Your old buddy Noah's here, standing right here in the room.

Elisha and Jim turn to Noah.

Jim What?

Noah There's some guy from some local music something waiting by the van for an interview.

Jim Shit.

Noah He said you said you'd meet him after the show?

Jim Yeah. Shit.

Elisha It's OK. Go. We'll be right there.

Jim You're OK?

Elisha Yeah.

Jim leaves. Noah starts getting his cymbals bag.

I hate that.

Noah I'm sorry. The guy just said he couldn't wait.

Elisha I hate that he's everyone's now.

Noah Isn't it what you wanted?

Elisha looks after Jim.

Scene 8. Int./Ext. A Recording Studio - Earlier

Jim, Elisha and Scaff sit in the control room of a well-appointed recording studio.

Scaff The label doesn't know shit. They wouldn't be able to tell a good drummer from a monkey. So it's up to you. Whatever you want to do, they don't care.

Jim How am I supposed to tell him?

Elisha We had the same problem with the first record.

Jim I know, but—

Elisha And I still don't think you're over it—how it sounded, that it could have been so much better. He knows he hasn't improved as much as he should have.

Scaff Live, the inconsistencies are easier to overlook.

Elisha He isn't up to speed. He can't handle the pressure of the studio.

Jim He gets nervous, blows his concentration.

Elisha We only have two weeks to finish this, Jimmy. We don't have time for these kind of mistakes.

Jim I know. I know.

Scaff The label has a lot of pro guys, studio guys.

Jim I don't want some studio guy.

Scaff Then we'll get a name, someone from a band you'll feel good about.

Jim How am I going to tell him?

Scaff It's business now, Jimmy. It's business now.

Elisha You don't owe him anything.

Jim I don't?

Scaff Look, ultimately, it's up to you. You can forge ahead and see what happens, but if the record isn't as good as it could have been, you're going to have to live with that.

Jim That's why I brought this up in the first place. But I don't see how I can do this. He's like my brother. More than my brother.

Elisha This is your moment, Jimmy. Don't underestimate how important this is.

Jim I know.

Elisha He'll understand eventually, he will. He knows he isn't the talent that you are. He knows that.

Jim But he's worked so fucking hard.

Elisha It's not your fault that he's not as talented as you are. It's not your fault. And you can't support him at your expense.

Jim I want to keep him in the band though. I want him on tour. He is still in the band. We got to this point together, you know. It's just that this record is so important to me.

Elisha We understand.

Scaff It's really important to us, too.

Jim I've got to have a smoke.

Jim leaves.

Scaff I'm shocked. I didn't think he'd want to do it.

Elisha For once, he's got to make decisions based on what's going to take him the furthest, not on how he feels.

Noah enters.

Noah Hey. *(An awkward beat)* I'm not late, am I?

Scaff No. We all just got here a little early. I'll get Jim.

Scaff leaves.

Noah Where's the engineer?

Elisha I don't know.

Noah What?

Elisha What?

Noah What's happening?

Elisha What do you mean?

Noah He was weird yesterday, and now you seem weird. Did he say anything at home last night?

Elisha He was on the phone with Randy Craig for a while, but he didn't tell me what it was about.

Noah He's being so uptight. It's fucking me up, him being such a hard-ass.

Elisha It's just really important to him, you know.

Noah It's important to all of us, but it's our record, too. I can't believe you're letting him play most of your bass parts again.

Elisha He can nail them faster than me.

Noah It doesn't bother you? You're good enough now that you should be playing.

Elisha It's not important to me. If he thinks it'll help the record, then...

Scaff enters with Jim.

Noah What's the story?

Jim looks helplessly at Scaff. Scaff nods encouragingly.

Jim Noh, you know, you know I love playing with you, right? Having you in the band.

Noah OK?

Jim But, we've, we've, uh... You remember last time we were in the studio, we had trouble, just the time it took to get good takes, really nailing the basic tracks?

Noah That was a long time ago, Jimmy.

Jim Well, there have been some concerns, from the label…

Noah From the label?

Jim From the label, that we are not moving fast enough. It's taking too long to nail things and they're worried we're going to run out of time…

Jim looks to Scaff who nods.

So, they have some ideas about what we can do about it.

Noah I'm sure they do.

Jim And one of those ideas is bringing in…bringing in another drummer…just to see if that might not be, if that might not be something we can, we can…

Noah You want to bring in another drummer?

Jim The label thinks it might be…

Noah Fuck the label. I'm asking you, Jim. You want to bring in another drummer?

Jim I think, this time, that we should listen to what they want, just to see what happens…

Noah Are you firing me?

Jim Look, Noh…

Noah Are you firing me?

Scaff We talked about this when you signed the contract…

Noah Of course, it's in the contract! What am I getting so upset about!?

Jim The label wants to do this…

Noah They're your songs…

Jim Not me…

Noah But you're letting them. You're fucking letting them.

Jim I'm sorry, but it's business now, Noah. It's business now.

Noah OK.

Jim But it'll be your name on the record. We're still a band. You'll be on the tour. No one will know.

Noah Have someone drop my kit off. I've got to go.

Noah leaves.

Jim Fuck!

Scaff When the record's done and you guys are on tour, the money will be coming in, it'll all be forgotten.

Elisha It was the right thing to do. We'll work it out.

Elisha rushes away. Jim bangs his head in his hands. Outside, Elisha stops Noah.

Hey, hey.

Noah Did you know?

Elisha No.

Noah Did you know?!

Elisha No! I didn't know. How could he tell me?

Noah How many years have we been waiting for this? How many years?

Elisha Maybe we can talk him out of it?

Noah They're not giving me a fair chance. I can do this. I've just been trying too hard or something. You know it's not even his opinion anymore.

Elisha You know he didn't want to do this.

Noah But he still did it.

Elisha This is his chance.

Noah It was mine, too.

Noah leaves. Elisha looks after him. Then she looks back toward the studio and Jim, wrapping her arms around herself.

Elisha Yeah.

Scene 7. Int./Ext. A House in the Hollywood Hills - Earlier

The din of a party in progress is heard. Jim and Scaff stand with drinks in hand next to a framed gold record hanging on a wall. Scaff nods his head to his right.

Scaff See him?

Jim With the hair?

Scaff He was the last next big thing.

Jim Who is he?

Scaff Steve Wolf.

Jim Never heard of him.

Scaff Exactly.

Jim What happened?

Scaff A lot of things that resulted in nothing.

Jim You're making me nervous.

Scaff Don't worry, the buzz is good.

Jim I don't know that that makes me feel better.

Scaff Why does anything positive freak you out, my man?

Jim It doesn't. It's just…these people suck.

Scaff They're the one's who'll get us where we want to be.

Jim I guess.

Beat.

Scaff So, do you think, I suck?

Jim What?

Scaff Do you think I'm, you know, like them?

Jim No, Scaff, you're alright.

Scaff *(Very sincerely)* You just can't depend on them. You have to listen to yourself. You know you're really, really talented.

Jim Thanks, man.

Scaff I mean, you know that, right?

Jim Sure. Yeah.

Scaff You just can't lose sight of that. Because, in the end, that's all there is.

Noah and Elisha stand out on the balcony, looking out at the city, drinks in hand.

Elisha They're all so pretty.

Noah Pretty? The coat-check girl is the most beautiful girl I've ever seen in my life, with the exception of the hors d'oeuvres girl, who is like a greek statue in her level of perfection.

Elisha Did you see the library?

Noah There's a library? This guy doesn't seem like the literary type.

Elisha And that antique cabinet in the entrance hallway…

Noah I guess your rebellious period is over.

Elisha What?

Noah The "antique cabinet?" Since when are you interested in all of that.

Elisha Since always, but we don't even have enough money to have a hallway in our apartment, so why talk about it.

Jim comes onto the balcony. He joins Noah and Elisha in looking out at the city.

Nice place, huh.

Jim I guess.

Noah It's the best food I've ever had. You know that tooth-picked stuff we filled up on?

Elisha That shrimp thing was so good.

Noah Well, that was just to kill time while they set up a buffet as big as a Cadillac in the living room.

Jim I saw it. I should have brought a suitcase. Here.

Jim reaches in his coat pocket and pulls out a huge handful of cheese cubes wrapped in a napkin.

Elisha Cheese cubes!

Jim sets the cheese cubes on the balcony railing. Noah and Elisha begin to eat them.

Noah Jimmy, when you said this trip was going to be first class, I never dreamed that we'd actually get to stand overlooking hideous, sprawling LA while eating cheese cubes from your pocket—memories that'll last a lifetime.

Elisha How's it going in there?

Jim I don't know. The Randy Craig guy seems genuine, but he just took off.

Elisha Isn't this his house?

Jim No, this is one of their "artist's" houses, some country singer.

Elisha This is a musician's house?

Noah Is that Capitol guy here?

Jim I haven't seen him. But there's one guy from one of the other labels we met with last time, that RCA asshole who talked so big and came up with nothing.

Noah Did you talk to him?

Jim Yeah, I went up to him and asked why it went down the way it did.

Noah You did?

Elisha Jim!

Jim I'm not going to kiss his ass. I know that record was great and should have gotten major distribution.

Noah What did Randy Craig say?

Jim Same as the rest. He loves the first record and wants to make another one with us. He's acting like it's a done deal. So is Scaff. But we've heard this so many times at this point, who knows.

Elisha But, it's looking good?

Jim We'll see.

Noah Worse comes to worst, we'll record for Mansize again.

Jim With what money? We need some money to make a great record.

Noah The first record is great.

Jim For a first record.

Scaff pokes his head out of the balcony door, smiling.

Scaff Nice view, huh? Wouldn't be too tough to get used to this lifestyle, huh?

Elisha Nope.

Scaff It's going well, guys. Really, it is.

They all look out at the lights below. Noah smiles and looks to Elisha. She smiles and looks to Jim. Jim smiles and puts his arms around her, kissing her cheek.

Jimmy, can you give me one more second? I have a couple more people for you to meet.

Jim You guys coming in?

Noah In a minute.

Jim and Scaff go. Beat. Elisha looks down below.

Elisha Man, it's nice up here.

Noah It's too high up for me, makes me nervous.

Elisha eats some more cheese.

Elisha This cheese is so good. Why is this cheese so good?

Scene 6. Int. Noah's Apartment - Earlier

Noah and Scaff look at artwork that is laid out on the kitchen table.

Noah I just don't exactly like it.

Scaff What don't you like?

Noah The color, the image, everything, pretty much.

Scaff Well, we have to get this to them today, so there's not much we can do.

Noah Why didn't we talk about this before?

Scaff I've been talking to Jim about it for weeks. I thought you all agreed on it.

Noah This is the first I've seen it. And, it's weird that Elisha is credited on the record.

Scaff No one knows she didn't play.

Noah I don't understand why she's still in the band. We need someone better than her. Did you try and talk to him about it?

Scaff I tried, but he won't listen.

Noah Why?

Scaff It's that thing he needs.

Noah Sex?

Scaff No, well, yes, but, it's the way she is with him.

Noah Harsh?

Scaff She doesn't just kiss his ass.

Noah And I do?

Scaff No, she just tells him things in a way that makes it seem like she's the only one he can trust.

Noah She's not getting any better.

Scaff Yes, she is. You're all getting better. Just give her some more time.

Noah Aren't you frustrated? Don't you want him to play with the best people?

Scaff Yeah, I do. Of course, I do. But he needs what he needs to do this.

Noah I mean, I know I'm getting better, but he's the star, I know that, and if I were him, I'd know I could play with anyone, that I didn't need anyone.

Scaff Well, right now, he needs you both.

A knock on the door.

Jim (*Offstage*) Hey! Rock star! Open up!

Noah opens the door. Elisha and Jim come flying in.

Did you hear it?!?!

Noah What?

Jim The song!!! Just now!

Jim takes his arm away from Elisha and rummages through his wallet, fishing out a worn slip of paper.

Elisha We were driving and some R.E.M. or something is on and then…

Noah They've been playing it for weeks.

Elisha Not the college station!

Jim Regular fucking radio!!

Jim picks up the phone and, looking at the paper, dials.

Scaff They played it?

Jim And the record's not even out yet. Scaff, you're a genius!

Scaff They played it!

Jim It was so great!!

Scaff I know the DJ. Occasionally, he'll play something that's not on their play-list, if he thinks it's really good.

Jim hangs up the phone, turns and looks at the artwork.

Jim It great! It's exactly what I imagined. It's fucking great!

Scaff I like it.

Noah Well, I kind of hate it.

Jim Of course you do. It's not your taste, Noh, but it's perfect for the record.

Noah How are you so sure?

Jim I just am. What do you want to change?

Noah I don't know. The color. The silver is too much I think.

Jim No. It's good. It's going to work.

Noah *(Giving in)* Alright.

Jim I know I'm right.

Jim claps Scaff on the back.

Scaff, take us out to dinner.

Scaff You take me out to dinner. I got the song on the radio.

Jim Come on. We're moving up in the world. Take us out, like a real manager.

Scaff Once I start making some real manager money, I'll be happy to.

Jim hugs Elisha as they look at the artwork.

Jim You like it, don't you El.

Elisha *(Pointing to the artwork)* I still think this should have been a little bigger.

Jim *(To Scaff)* Can we still do that?

Scaff I think it's too late.

Elisha It's OK.

Jim Really?

Elisha Really.

Noah I still hate it.

Noah's phone rings. Jim moves for it, but Noah gets it first.

(Into phone) Hello? This is Noah. Oh, hey, Doctor Ward. Yeah, well Jim's here, so I bet he did. Hang on. *(To Jim)* It's your Dad.

Elisha looks at Jim. Jim grabs the phone.

Jim *(Into phone)* Hey, Dad. Yeah. I wanted to tell you…No, no, I'm fine. I was…No, she's fine too. I actually had some good news that I wanted to…Yeah, I know it's just for emergencies but…OK. OK. Yep. OK. No. I'll just catch up with you later. OK. Yep. Bye.

Jim hangs up the phone. Beat. Elisha walks over to him, putting her hand on his back. Scaff gathers up the artwork as Noah grabs his coat off a kitchen chair.

Jim *(Quietly, almost to himself)* Fuck. *(Shaking it off)* OK. Come on! Chinese? How about Chinese? We are going to fucking celebrate!

The group exits happily.

Scene 5. On the Road - Earlier

Jim and Scaff stand outside trying to keep warm.

Scaff I loved the two seven inches, and I love the new songs. I think your songs are amazing.

Jim Thanks man. I'm glad. Because if it's not really great, why do it? I mean, a million bands are good, you know?

Scaff So, how close are you to recording?

Jim We've got all the material we need to go in the studio and record our first full length. It's just the money and the time.

Scaff I'd really love to work with you.

Jim Thanks, man. Honestly, we've had some other offers, but what we want is to work with someone that believes in us, you know?

Scaff I do.

Elisha and Noah sit in their tour van. Elisha is wrapped in a puffy sleeping bag. She takes a snack out of a brown paper bag.

Elisha Your Mom was so sweet, packing up little road goodie bags.

Noah She likes to think I'm still twelve.

Elisha So does mine, but for different reasons, I think.

Jim leans in the van, grabbing two beers.

Jim Is the heat working?

Elisha No!

Jim Shit. Well, I'm almost done.

Noah He seemed cool to me.

Elisha Who is he?

Noah Some super low-level A&R guy who wants to be a manager. He's very into us, though.

Jim He loved the show.

Noah How could he not have. It was great.

Jim Yeah. It was good.

Jim heads outside.

Noah You didn't even make your "I fucked up" face.

Elisha I don't make a face.

Noah You do.

Elisha Like what?

Noah imitates Elisha's "I fucked up" face.

I do not do that.

Noah Actually, you do.

Elisha *(Shivering)* It's too cold in here!!

Noah You're pretty ready to be home, aren't you?

Elisha I just wish we still had heat. And that we didn't have to sleep in the van or on some stranger's floor. And that it didn't smell so weird in here. And we could afford to eat somewhere else besides McDonald's.

Noah We get Arby's sometimes.

Elisha When? When do we ever get Arby's?

Outside, Jim and Scaff drink the new beers.

Jim So far? I think the best was when we were driving around in St. Paul. I was listening to the radio, whatever the college station is, and out of the blue, on came our single. Hearing my music for the first time, out in the world, suddenly, I felt like, I felt like I was finally alive.

Scene 4. Int. Jim's Apartment - Earlier

Late afternoon. Jim and Elisha lay in the rumpled sheets of Jim's bed. Jim looks at the clock.

Jim Shit! It's 3:45. I have to go.

Elisha *(Reaching for him, pulling him back)* No.

Jim I'm supposed to be at practice in fifteen minutes.

Elisha I need more of you.

Jim I have to go. We're auditioning a new bass player.

Elisha What happened to Elliot?

Jim Got some girlfriend he's worried about leaving, doesn't want to tour, so...

Elisha pulls Jim in and kisses him. He resists at first but starts to give in. Then pulls himself away, getting out of bed, putting on his clothes.

I have to go.

Elisha Can I audition?

Jim For the band?

Elisha Yes!

Jim You don't play.

Elisha You always said how easy the bass is—I've been teaching myself.

Jim No.

Elisha Come on! I'm totally musical. And every bass player you get is either irresponsible, uncommitted or crazy.

Jim *(Sarcastically)* That's a really, really good reason.

Elisha You can totally boss me around.

Jim Now that's a good reason.

Jim leans in and kisses her.

Elisha And I can be on the road with you.

Jim I have to go.

Elisha You need someone who will be totally committed to you and your music. You have that in Noah, and you have it in me.

Jim I have to go.

Elisha Can we talk about it later?

Jim OK.

Jim kisses her and leaves. She watches after him.

Elisha *(Confidently)* OK.

She picks up a guitar sitting by the bed and tentatively starts to play.

Scene 3. Int. Noah's Dorm Room - Earlier

Noah sits at a desk full of books. Jim leans over him.

Noah It sounds great but I'm already committed to the internship.

Jim Noah…

Noah Getting a research job is really competitive. Sometimes they recruit you when you are still in school. I have to have as much experience as possible.

Jim You don't even want a fucking research job.

Noah Those are really good jobs. It's research or teaching and research has a much better—

Jim Noh, you can be some great math guy…

Noah Mathematician.

Jim …because you feel like you're supposed to, sitting in a room with numbers for the rest of your life until you go crazy. But, you love being a drummer. Don't you want to be what you love? I'm not saying quit school, I'm just saying, this summer, this one summer, this one and only summer of your whole life when you will be nineteen years old, be a drummer.

Noah So, drop the internship—that was really hard to get—to play a bunch of gigs at some crappy clubs—

Jim We are playing real shows already, with real bands. I mean some of these guys we're playing with are like twenty-five.

Noah I know.

Jim Do you think you're going to look back when you're fifty and say, "Oh, how could I have spent that summer playing drums? If only I had been doing math-puzzle-equation things instead of meeting girls and playing music!"

Noah You paint a vivid picture my friend. But, this internship is really very—

Jim Look, after this summer, if you have a bad time, I will personally fire you from the band and lock you in a room with the periodic chart and you'll never have to play rock music again.

Noah Mathematicians don't really use the periodic chart.

Jim We have a show in Rockford in two weeks and I have two new songs to teach you. So, tomorrow. Around three.

Noah I didn't say yes.

Jim leaves. Noah watches him go. Smiling, he closes the book in front of him.

Scene 2. A Backyard in Lafayette, Indiana - Earlier

Jim sits next to Elisha on a log near a bonfire. They roast marshmallows.

Elisha This is like a fall thing. It's weird to be doing this in the spring.

Jim takes his marshmallow out of the fire and blows on it.

Jim I like it.

Beat.

Elisha I really like your band.

Jim You've seen us play?

Elisha Uh, yeah, a bunch of times. I'm in English with Noah and I'm friends with Rebecca, you know with the red hair, so I go to a lot of those parties with her, where you've played.

Beat.

So, are you going to keep playing, after school?

Jim Of course.

Elisha Because, I mean, you are totally good enough to keep playing…

Jim Thanks.

Elisha I mean, of course, you know that. But, it's just, a lot of people are, you know, nervous about that stuff, 'cause it's so risky and difficult and everything.

Jim But isn't everything really risky and difficult, in a way.

Elisha Yeah, I guess.

Jim I'm no good at anything else. And music is what I want, so I should be doing it one hundred percent.

Elisha I wish I could be like that.

Jim Like what?

Elisha Have one thing that I really want and just do that, stop worrying about back-up plans and options and what I should be doing. My father always says "everything in moderation." I used to think that was good advice...

Jim But it's not. It has to be all or nothing. At least for me. All or nothing.

They watch the fire for a moment.

Elisha What's it like?

Jim What?

Elisha Playing. You don't have to tell me, if you don't want to.

Jim What do you want to know?

Elisha I don't know. What you think about, I guess.

Jim It's hard to even say. I'm just in it, you know?

Elisha In it?

Jim In the song.

Elisha How?

Jim Well...

Elisha I want to know.

Jim The main thing is you don't think about your hands anymore. They just know where to go. You don't think about the song, it's moving forward without you even thinking about it. And you hear the music, but it's not like it's coming from you, you're just in the middle of it. And nothing, no other bullshit from your life or the world or anything touches you. You're just in it, and there's just the song.

Elisha Wow.

Jim Is that weird?

Elisha No.

Beat.

Well, you are super-talented, so I'm sure it'll workout. We'll all see you in *Rolling Stone* and be really excited.

Beat.

Jim There's nothing you want?

Elisha What?

Jim You said there's nothing that you want. Is that true?

Elisha Not one thing that I want, like, above all else. I mean not like for a career or whatever.

Jim There has to be something.

Elisha What do you mean?

Jim When you think about it, what do you want? I want to play music. When you think about it…

Elisha I don't know. I'm too on the spot.

Jim *(Smiling)* OK.

Beat.

Elisha Actually, I do.

Elisha leans into Jim. She touches her cheek to his, and slowly puts her hands in his hair. They kiss, a slow first kiss, pulling slowly closer and closer to each other.

Scene 1./17. Int./Ext. Jim's House - 1981/1998

Jim, dressed as his teenage self—like in the previous scene—plays a guitar plugged into a small amplifier. He might listen through headphones so no sound comes from the amp or we may hear him play for the first time. He plays awkwardly, still learning, repeating phrases, making mistakes but there is something beautiful about it. Noah, dressed as older Noah—from Scene 17—comes to his door and knocks. Jim can't hear him.

Noah *(Calling through the door as he knocks)* Jim? Jimmy? *(To himself)* Goddamn it. *(Calling through the door again)* Jim?

Elisha, pregnant and dressed the same as Scene 17, comes up behind Noah as he knocks and calls Jim's name.

Lights fade to a spotlight on Jim. He keeps playing, oblivious, lost in his music. Lights fade to black.

End of play.

The Quiver of Children
Charity Henson-Ballard

The Game Changer:
On Charity Henson-Ballard's *The Quiver of Children*

Louis Scheeder

The development process has been taking its lumps of late. I've heard artistic directors grumble that they never want to go to another reading, authors complain of being stuck in "development hell," and actors gripe that they feel that they are contributing to scripts by reading parts that will ultimately be played by "names." Well, *The Quiver of Children* might not have received a major production as yet, but its path through the play development process has been intriguing, fruitful, and edifying.

Any success that the process has delivered thus far must be credited to the tenacity of its author, Charity Henson-Ballard. When I was asked to write this introduction, I pondered over what I might say that was insightful or original. After all, the development process has been written about, dissected, and studied *ad nauseam*. Then I realized that Charity's commitment to the process was unique and all-consuming. She wasn't familiar with how one was supposed to comport oneself through the process. It wasn't that she didn't want to play by the rules; she just wasn't interested in how others played the game of play development. She was interested in her game. And she's got game! It just isn't other folks' game.

While I am primarily an acting teacher of undergrads at New York University, I also teach an ongoing scene study class for young professionals. Ms. Henson-Ballard enrolled in that class and we began, in the way that committed professionals do, to argue with each other. We probed and tested each other on our thoughts, experiences, and desires about acting—what we thought it should be, what the ideal way of representing behavior on stage might be, what one can do with words. She is herself a very well-trained actor, who earned her MFA at the Tisch School's graduate acting program. And, as we probed and fenced our way through various scenes, from Shakespeare to August Wilson, our mutual respect grew.

I was intrigued when Charity asked me to read a partial draft of a script she had written. If memory serves, she also asked me if I would be interested in directing *The Quiver of Children*. My immediate reaction was one of disbelief. Why would one entrust one's first play, an intense drama about an African American family set in Chattanooga during the pre-civil rights era to a middle-aged white guy, the product of a New York City parochial school system who went on to be educated by the Jesuits in both high school and college? What would I be able to bring to her play and whatever in the world did she expect me to bring? She then explained to me that the first test of the play would be at a women's theater retreat at Bard College, hosted by Voice and Vision, a theater company committed to developing not just plays by women, but their careers, dreams, and desires. The improbability of the project was just too good to pass up.

Our time at Bard College in the early summer of 2008 provided us with the most precious gift playwrights, directors, and actors can have: extended rehearsal time, unencumbered by the ongoing distractions of our urban lives. The process, though only lasting a few days, revealed another fantastic gift: as with all terrific writers, Charity knows how to write for actors. We plunged in, carrying rehearsal time over to lunches and dinner. At the heart of the process was a love and respect for the acting of the play. Somehow, we all instinctively knew that if we got the acting right, if we challenged each other with intention, emotional honesty, and clarity of action, we would reveal the play to each other. The actors didn't just "read" the play; they didn't settle for exploring the world of the play. The actors performed the text, they brought it to life in a forceful present. Rather than investigate what we had, the actors (assembled mostly by the playwright) infused the text with action, while presenting a rich emotional life that revealed layers of pain and joy.

By the fall of 2008, Charity had completed the play and we were asked to present a reading of the work for the Women's Project Lab members. Again, rather than "exploring" or "reading" the work, we dove in to a twelve hour rehearsal process that encouraged the actors to commit to choices, allow for human contradiction, and put themselves at risk. The actors once again revealed the strengths, problems, and risks that the play presented, and Ms. Henson-Ballard learned from the process and produced yet another draft of the script.

As a member of Women's Project Lab, Charity continued to hone her script and in the spring of 2009, once again under the aegis of Voice and Vision, a sturdy band of actors presented a revised, yet still monumental, version of *The Quiver of Children*. That performance (and I use the word advisedly) allowed Ms. Henson-Ballard to refine the script and cut it down to its present form.

In sum, I would argue that it is Charity's delight, belief, and commitment to the art of acting that has produced the play that is before you. Her sharpness, intelligence, and belief in the artist/actors that bring her words to life have produced this play. She is a brave soul, an innovative collaborator, and, to my mind, a gifted observer of the human condition.

Founder and director of The Classical Studio, Louis Scheeder has directed on, off, and off-off Broadway, and at regional theaters in the U.S. and Canada. He was Producer of Washington's Folger Theatre Group, is associated with the Manitoba Theatre Centre, and worked with the Royal Shakespeare Company in London. Louis has produced three off-Broadway shows, including Amlin Gray's Obie-winner *How I Got That Story*. Louis co-authored *All The Words on Stage: A Complete Pronunciation Dictionary for the Plays of William Shakespeare* and contributed chapters to *Training of the American Actor*. He is a member of The Factory Theatre (UK), has conducted numerous Shakespeare workshops at venues such as the Williamstown Theater Festival and the Public Theater, and serves as Associate Dean of Faculty for Tisch School of the Arts.

Characters
Rena, 54, the wise matriarch.
Ruby, 9 and 24, a good girl who likes to play house.
Edgene, 13 and 2, a boy who breaks his toys.
Asa, 59 and 3, a father and a son.
Thomas, 30 and 45, a father and a son.
Melody, 23, a protégé.
Peteman, 29, a prisoner, same actor as Asa.
Mona John, 28, a bride of Christ and a beauty.
Steven, 28, Melody's brother.

Place
Chattanooga, Tennessee.

Time
The past.

Playwright's Note
Abstraction is fine. Some things must exist, however (i.e. a piano). Although the landscape isn't literal, there must be a "feeling" that much energy has gone into making the house a home. There must be an experience of the color blue. There is a large willow decorated with random ornaments. The area beneath the shade tree is the home of everything dear: the Patterson Music Room, the desires of the players, etc. Another piano rests beneath the willow tree and is played by various characters, both in reality and fantasy. It is overgrown with flowers, sod, etc. The willow's roots embrace it. If we were to visit the Trenton home in the physical world, it would look like this: the back porch branches off from the kitchen and is bordered by a smal, lovely vegetable garden. The vegetable garden has a small pathway that leads into Edgene's paint studio: a rickety, blue storage garage filled with nude paintings. Crossing behind the house is a dirt road that wraps behind Edgene's paint studio. The living room and kitchen are adjoined by a narrow hallway that leads back to bedrooms, etc.

Production History
The Quiver of Children was originally developed in part with the support of Voice and Vision at the 2008 Envision Workshop Retreat for Women. *The Quiver of Children* was later selected for a staged reading at the Ohio Theatre in New York City in May 2009 and was directed by Louis Scheeder (New York University, Tisch School of the Arts). At the time of publication, this play is still under development.

To Obtain Rights to Produce This Play
Please contact: Charity Henson-Ballard via www.charityhensonballard.com, or via Rising Circle Theater Collective at info@risingcircle.org.

The Quiver of Children

Act One

Scene 1. The Law of Thy Mother[1]
Trenton Kitchen / Living Room - Evening

1941. A gramophone plays "Goodnight Irene" nearby. Lights up on Rena Trenton, fifty-four. She is in a dimly-lit kitchen. A strange auricular ringing is in the air. Lights up in the dimly-lit living room: a man sitting at the piano, his back to the audience. He "twinks" the keys, then begins to create a tune. He is Asa Trenton, fifty-nine.

Voice What you doin', Rena?

Rena Seein'.

Voice What you see?

Rena Him.

Voice Who he?

Rena Don't know no more.

Voice What you see?

Rena A tree.

Voice And?

Rena A body.

Voice What?

Rena A woman's body. Many women's bodies.

Voice And then?

Rena The twinkle. The shine. The dark.

Full lights up. The ringing ceases. Rena is handed a bowl by her granddaughter, Ruby, nine.

Ruby You the smartest woman ever, Grammy. I love you.

Rena Mutual, Ruby. But your GG could have been smarter. Love...

Rena shakes her head.

Ruby Is better?

Rena Hm?

Ruby Than bein' smart?

Rena gestures for the girl to turn up the volume on the gramophone. The child obeys. Ruby's brother, Edgene, thirteen, horses around with a wooden train car, getting in the way of dinner preparations. Ruby sets the table.

Rena *(To audience)* What do you see? A little black girl playin' house? A little black boy who breaks his toys?

Edgene drops his train.

There's so much more...

Thomas, thirty, enters.

Rena I was wonderin' where the world you was.

Ruby *(Proud of her napkin fan)* Daddy, look!

Thomas Lesson went late.

Rena Rich people the same all around: They think they own you.

Thomas They pay me to teach, so I teach. I like it.

He takes off his coat, then turns down the gramophone, noticing his father bowed over the piano. As he unwinds:

Rena *(To audience)* That Thomas: my son. The man in the dark: Thomas his boy, too… We raised him. And that—that vision—vexes me. *(Silence)* I can't control the feelin' to tuck my grandbabies in the bed, no dinner. Hug my Thomas so tight. As they pretend and play and work, my many visions keep me unsettled.

Thomas Smellin' good in here.

Rena *(Agitated)* You raisin' they kids. You got a family, too, and we waitin' on you when you work late away from your own. Listen to your mama, now. She know a few things.

Ruby Grammy smart.

Rena Listen to the baby, now.

Thomas The girl's got talent. She was playing me a song she taught herself.

Ruby I know a song, Daddy. You wanna hear my song?

Thomas Grown folk talking, Ruby. Hold on a bit.

Edgene races by. Thomas roughhouses him.

You gonna tear up this house, boy. What did y'all do today other than give Grammy a hard time?

Ruby Edgene got sent home from school.

The piano continues to play.

Rena He was flippin' skirts in recess.

Thomas Was he? *(To Edgene)* I know we know better how to treat women, Edgene.

Ruby It was some girl he liked.

Edgene Get outta my business!

Thomas All the more why you shouldn't be pulling up her skirt, embarrassing her on the play yard.

Ruby Oh no, Daddy. She liked it. Only thing was they got caught.

Rena That's enough, Cave Mouth. Y'all go wipe off your hands before you eat my food.

The children exit.

Thomas How's he today? Still not talking much?

Rena I can't do nuthin' else with that man. Ain't good for nuthin'. Might as well be a damned widow.

Thomas You bein' harsh, Mama.

Rena I've put up with these moods of his for years now. One minute he floatin' on a cloud, the next, you don't know what the hell wrong wit' 'em. And look what he did. *(She shows him a broken plate)* Broke my yellow dishes. All of 'em.

Thomas What'd he do that for?

Rena I don't know. I found 'em out under the tree. Could've been weeks ago, he took 'em out there and smashed 'em to bits. When my mama gave me these, she said they don't make 'em anymore.

Thomas I'll talk to him.

Rena Good luck.

The children re-enter and take their seats. Rena brings the plate of chicken.

Grace?

They all take hands.

Thomas Father, bless this food we 'bout to receive. May it nourish and strengthen our bodies and spirits. Forgive our iniquities. In Jesus' name, Amen.

Rena and Thomas dish food onto the plates. Edgene grabs a drumstick from the platter and chows down.

Rena *(Flattered)* Edgene! I oughta pop you for that one, boy. Asa, come in here and eat. Food's ready.

Asa plays. The children snicker.

Ruby I can go get him, Grammy.

Rena No, you eat, baby.

Thomas Give me a little more of them greens, Mama?

Ruby and Edgene show one another their chewed food.

Rena Y'all quit being fools and eat before I send you from the table.

They begin to eat and drink in a "civilized manner."

(Fed up) Asa, I ain't gonna tell you no more to get in here and eat!

Thomas Mama, it's alright.

The music stops in the next room.

Rena He drive me crazy.

Thomas *(To the children)* What y'all call yourselves doin'?

They all burst into laughter.

A loud bang shatters the spirit of the room. Rena falls backwards from the table. The air sustains a post-blast ringing. Thomas and the children look up at Asa, who stands zombie-like before the table holding the still-smoking pistol.

(Gently) Daddy. Gimme the gun.

Thomas removes the pistol from his father's hands and offers it to the children.

Edgene...Edgene—

Edgene crawls beneath the table. He covers his ears.

Ruby.

He sits Asa at the table, then hands the child the pistol. It rests flat on her palms. Lights fade to black on the Trenton House, with a special remaining on Ruby.

The willow tree illuminates. A lovely young white woman sings underneath, her voice gradually cancelling out the sound of the ringing. She is well-dressed, of some social-standing, pristine, etc. Her clothes are more "progressed" than that of the scene before: It is fifteen years later. Thomas steps from his house and enters the new 1956-world of the Patterson Music Room with young Melody, twenty-three. She cannot sing to save her life.

Scene 2. A Tree of Life[2]
Willow Tree / Patterson Music Room -
Day, Autumn, 1956

Thomas Listen to me...La.

Ruby Daddy?

Thomas Listen to my instructions. La.

Melody La.

Thomas La.   **Melody** La.

Lights down on Ruby. The tree dims.

Melody La. Oh, it's hopeless, Thomas. Let's go back to the piano again.

Thomas Your parents want you to be able to sing for their holiday party.

Melody I could play for them just as well and they'd be satisfied. It ain't no matter.

Thomas *Doesn't* matter.

Melody *Doesn't* matter. *(Beat)* Do you mean to tell me you speak properly at all times, even at home?

Thomas We've gone over this, Melody. How I am at home on my time is my business.

Melody Touchy, touchy. I don't mean anything by it. Just curious. *(Beat)* I like how you talk.

Thomas It speaks to you?

Melody Yes.

Thomas The language of the restless genius?

Melody Are we so transparent?

Thomas You mean do I know the meaning of the disaffected furrowed brow? And the hunkered slump? *(He taps her back, correcting her posture)* The bored huff of a musical protégé? Have we exhausted the infinite cosmos of music and magic, Melody? Heaven has depleted us already, has it?

Melody You're making fun of me.

Thomas My heart couldn't bear it. There is more for us, dear muse. Much, much more—

Thomas plays the song his father played many years ago. As he plays, Melody walks trance-like around the "room," which becomes all the more illuminated as little lights twinkle on (and in) the tree above. The sky becomes a heliotrope dreamscape. Thomas stops: an abrupt silence. It almost seems as if he has forgotten the music or made a mistake. During the next few lines, an empty silence crushes the air between them.

Melody This doesn't sound like Beethoven.

Thomas *(Distant)* I forgot to look into it: Who wrote it.

Melody No swells. No fussing. I like that. It plays you. You like this song.

Thomas No.

Melody No? But you just played it from memory! Can you remember the rest?

Thomas Hmm?

Melody The rest. A song without an ending? That simply can't be, Thomas.

Thomas I'm forgetful.

Melody I'm not. I am a genius, after all.

Thomas Thanks to me.

Melody All thanks to you, Mister Memory. Bring the rest, please. For next time? Pretty please?

He improvises a ditty signifying the end of a successful rehearsal. She applauds, simulating a devotee. He bows. Melody tosses her arms around his neck and plants a kiss on his cheek. Thomas carefully removes himself.

Thomas Until the next appointed time.

Melody Not until then?

Thomas You don't need extra help. You haven't for a while.

Thomas exits.

Scene 3. Lest I Be Full[3]
Trenton Kitchen - Afternoon

Grandmother Rena tutors Ruby, twenty-three, in the kitchen.

Rena You pinch the dough around your thumb with your other two fingers. Pinch, pinch, pinch...

Ruby Pinch, pinch, pinch...

Rena What a smart girl. Let me see? Oh, yes. A perfect cobbler.

Ruby Perfect.

Rena You gonna stare at it all day, or you gonna cook it?

Ruby Ooh, I forgot to heat the oven.

Ruby lights the stove. Lights up on Mona John pinning up her hair, her bare back to us. She hums beautifully.

Ruby Gracious me... *(She looks out the window)* Mona. Ain't you comin'? Cobbler best when it hot. I got the hot comb ready, too. Got the trimmin' scissors. You gotta bring your hair, though.

Mona John laughs.

Rena You make a lot of allowances for her. Why you let her treat you like this?

Ruby Pretty hair. Small feet.

Rena The girl selfish. Sittin' around to do her head. Don't make no sense.

Ruby This sash…Mona should have it. *(Ruby takes off her sash)* It'll be pretty in her hair.

Thomas enters. Lights down abruptly on Mona John.

Thomas Fix me some tea.

Ruby puts a kettle on the stove. Silence as Thomas takes off his shoes. Ruby picks up the shoes and puts them away.

Rena Work good today?

Thomas Those bushes out back are looking neglected, Ruby.

Ruby I got distracted. With the cobblers. I made leaves for the crust with the dough this time.

Thomas You know they think we're animals from the jungle.

Silence.

Ruby I baked a hen.

Thomas That's good.

Thomas exits.

Rena You ain't finished now. Brush your crust with egg and water so that it shine.

Ruby I'm forgettin' sumthin'.

Rena *(Insistent)* Your shine. Jesus.

Scene 4. Closer Than a Brother[4]
Trenton Kitchen / Living Room - Midnight

The back door knob jiggles, then gives as two black males, both in their mid-late twenties stealthily enter the kitchen. The two men are dressed quite well, although their style is somewhat "dated." They stop in their tracks when they hear a gramophone playing in the living room.

First man You hear that? Somebody awake.

Second Man Aw, c'mon, man. It just music.

He steps forward onto the first man's foot.

First Man You on my shoe, man.

Second Man Gee, I'm sorry. I can't see in all this pitch.

An eternal moment of silence.

Second Man So, we gonna just stand here all night?

First Man Shhh, I'm thinkin'. *(Beat)* You sure they ain't gonna mind us comin' here?

Second Man Nigga, this my family. Of course they ain't gonna mind seein' me.

The second man continues to creep around the kitchen. A light comes on as Thomas enters the living room holding a pistol.

First Man Oh damn! Somebody comin'! Somebody comin'!

The first man scrambles. The second man freezes.

Thomas I'm in the mood for shootin' tonight. Come on!

He aims. Ruby and Rena race into the living room.

Don't come out here, Ruby.

The first man finds refuge behind a chair as Ruby gets a better look at the second man.

Rena Edgene?

Second Man It's me, Pop!

Ruby runs over and embraces Edgene. Peteman, the first man, watches the reunion.

Ruby Edgene! Edgene! You back? I knew you was comin'!

Edgene What can I say? Good behavior.

Thomas They reward convicts these days?

Thomas approaches, but stays a healthy distance from the congregation.

Edgene Well, Pop, as a matter of fact, they do.

Thomas That's something to hear: Them rewarding Negroes for doing probably what you was supposed to be doin' in the first place.

Rena Thomas—

Thomas And I see you done brought another convict friend of yours to our doorstep. Thank you, Edgene, for doin' that. I 'spect you 'spect us to not only open our doors to you, but to him, too: some strange Negro.

Edgene Now it ain't like that, Pop. Done forgot my hometrainin'. This my boy, Peteman. Peteman: my family.

Silence.

Peteman *(Not a question)* How you all doin'?

Thomas Just fine, Peteman. Just fine. Pardon my suspicion right now, but surely you can understand as to why a man might wonder who you is, you bein' a strange Negro and all. And for all intents and purposes, to me, you are just that: a strange Negro. No offense.

Peteman None taken none dealt.

Thomas What was that?

Edgene How 'bout Ruby put on some tea for us to sit down and have some pie.

Ruby squirms.

Rena We ain't got no pie, Edgene.

Edgene No pie?

Ruby *(Painfully embarrassed)* Peach cobbler.

Peteman I ain't had no peach cobbler since my Mama died.

Ruby begins to dish out cobbler.

Edgene *(To Peteman)* Ruby makes the best cobbler in Chattanooga. She's a fine cook. *(To Ruby)* You still a fine cook, ain't ya?

Rena She's quite smart in the kitchen.

Ruby I do alright.

Edgene And make mine a coffee, Ruby, will ya? Next to Mona John, I'd say Ruby's cookin' is the thing I've missed most. *(Beat)* So, how y'all been?

Thomas You mean?

Edgene Well, I get Ruby's letters and—no offense, Ru—I don't really feel what I'm missin'.

Ruby I'm sorry, Edgene. I haven't had much to tell.

Rena I don't think he was sayin' nuthin' bad about you, baby.

Edgene I'm just tryin' to spark conversation.

Thomas The Pattersons have invited me to join them in Paris this summer.

Edgene See? Didn't know that.

Thomas Didn't tell you. Just asked a few days ago. Melody's been commissioned to do a concert and they said it would be their honor if I accompanied them overseas. I've always wondered what it was like over there in Europe. Paris is a glorious haven of culture, history and true art.

Edgene snorts.

Ruby I've read about Paris. They have fashions there. They say there ain't nowhere like Paris when it comes to fashion and livin' other than New York City. They say New York never sleeps.

Peteman I know I ain't ever slept while I was there.

Ruby You lived in New York?

Peteman Nearly nine years I was there. I got kinfolk who moved up there. Was in quite a bit of mischief while I was in New York…but I ain't ever been caught for nuthin' until I got to Chattanooga. Ain't that some shit!

Peteman laughs.

Ruby I'd love to live in New York. New York or Paris.

Thomas I don't know about you all, but I've had my fill of cobbler and conversation. Ruby?

Thomas exits.

Ruby Edgene, where you been at?

Edgene You'd rush back knowin' that waitin' on you?

Ruby I missed you.

Rena We all did, baby.

Edgene Well, I'm here now. And tired. So, this bein' a woman's house and all, I guess I'll go ahead and ask: Where can we sleep?

Peteman What you mean? *(To Ruby)* A woman's house?

Rena Better tell your friend, Ed, not to say that too loud around here.

Edgene Don't say that too loud around here.

Ruby Edgene, I kept your room nice for you. Mister Peteman, will the sofa make do?

Peteman It's more than plenty, Miss Ruby.

Rena She just Ruby.

Ruby You can wash up down the hall.

Peteman exits.

Rena Lord have mercy.

Rena follows him.

Ruby We should check on Daddy.

Edgene He alright. Listen, when did Mona get back?

Ruby I the one write, tearin' up my magazines and stuff sendin' you pictures and all you do is go on about Mona John—

Edgene Ruby—

Ruby I ain't goin' on about Mona John business, Edgene.

Edgene Why you fussin'?

Ruby I ain't—

Edgene I've longed for you, Sis. Thought about you every day.

Ruby No, you ain't.

Edgene I wanted nuthin' more than to wake up each mornin' here with you. Sunshine comin' in on me. House smellin' like bacon and spiced apples. It ate me up inside not havin' my Ruby girl.

Ruby True?

Edgene Yeah, true. And now just 'cause the topic Mona John you wanna clam up on me? Wow.

Ruby Course not, Edgene.

Edgene Chocked full of surprises here.

Ruby No, I—I ain't fussin'.

Edgene That's right. 'Cause my Ruby too good for that. I done had my share of worse, girl. Now I'm lookin' for some better.

Ruby Better go on in the shed?

Edgene What you know about the shed?

Ruby Daddy locked it up. Say you was nuthin' but foolin' around in there. Your paintin's in there, yeah? I ain't ever seen none. And Mona won't say.

Edgene Won't say?

Ruby 'Bout your paintin'. Can I see me some?

Edgene I don't think it quite right for you, Ru.

Silence.

Ruby Year ago.

Edgene What?

Ruby She been back about a year. Her daddy died. *(Beat)* And just so you know, Mona John done got some better.

Edgene She seein' someone?

Ruby Jesus.

Edgene Shoot, I mean someone real.

Ruby Edgene!

Edgene *(Laughing)* Well, at least I ain't gotta worry about him pluggin' her up.

Ruby It ain't funny. Don't laugh. Stop laughin'. Go to bed, Edgene.

Edgene What you gettin' so riled for?

Ruby You sick and disgusting and…and hateful. Shut your mouth.

Edgene Alright.

Ruby I mean it. I really mean it.

Ruby returns to her kitchen activities.

Edgene I ain't mean nuthin' by it.

Edgene leaves.

Act Two

Scene 1. Praise Her In the Gates[5]
Trenton Back Yard - Dawn

A car horn honks. After a seven second count, it honks again. A few beats later, rapping on the kitchen door. A voluptuous black woman enters, dressed in her Sunday best. Something about her is too magnificent, despite an unspoken desire to be tame.

Mona John Ruby! Come on! Come on!

Ruby rushes in, tying her bathrobe.

Ruby *(Whispering)* Shush! Mona John—

Ruby Daddy gonna hear you—

Mona John What's the matt—?

Mona John Ruby, why ain't you dressed?

Ruby I gotta tell you sumthin'. It was just last night—I ain't had time to warn you—

Mona John Warn me? Sister, you okay?

Peteman enters shirtless. He goes to the icebox, absolutely comfortable with his new surroundings. Ruby stares at Peteman. Mona stares at Peteman, then at Ruby.

Peteman *(Sipping from milk bottle)* Everything alright, Ruby?

Mona John Who are you?

Peteman Who are you?

Ruby Mona—

Mona John Ruby?

Ruby This here a friend—

Mona John I see how friendly he is. He so friendly, he bestowin' his naked chest!

Ruby No, he ain't my friend—

Peteman We just met last night.

Mona John Ruby!

Peteman Late, late last night. Almost killed me.

Mona John Ruby!

Peteman Wore me out, fed me, then put me to bed.

Mona John grabs a cup towel and swats at Peteman. She chases him around the kitchen as Ruby futilely tries to intercede.

Mona John You hush that filth. Hush your mouth!   **Peteman** What the——? Woman? You crazy?

Ruby Mona, no! You don't understand!

Mona John Don't talk to me like you know me, naked Negro. I ain't none your friend.

Edgene enters. Mona stops.

Ruby I tried to tell you, Mona John…This here…Peteman. He ain't my friend. He Edgene's…friend. They came home. Last night.

A long pause.

Edgene Mona. *(He hugs her)* It's good to see you. I wish I had known you was comin' over. I mean, I've been longin' to see you for, shit, forever, girl, but I wanted to make sure I did sumthin' to myself to look presentable to you. Not like this, with my mouth all stale. Can't kiss my woman for the first time with a yuck mouth and whiskers that prickle—

Mona John I don't really know what to say.

Edgene Girl, you ain't gotta say nuthin'. I can just look at you, see you doin' just fine and perfect. Let me get a good look at you. *(He turns her around. She is stiff)* That's my woman. Look just like a good dinner bird: plenty of meat on it.

Mona John That's enough, 'Gene.

Edgene Can't get enough of you, girl.

Mona John Well, you gonna. That's enough. I came here to take Ruby to my church. Ruby, you ready for church?

Ruby I just got up, Mona. I ain't get to bed 'til really late.

Mona John looks at Peteman.

Mona John I remember.

Ruby I'm so sorry. I know I been sayin' I'd go with you—	**Edgene** I'll go with you.
Ruby —for some time now, and each time, it seem like sumthin' always come up.	**Edgene** I'll go with you.
Ruby And it's not that I don't want to go. I just, well, have things that always come up.	**Edgene** Mona! I'll go withcha.

Long pause.

Mona John *(To Edgene)* Go get ready then.

Edgene Yeah? Alright. You don't go nowhere. I'll be right back. Peteman, you comin'?

Peteman Nigga, I'm likely to explode the moment I walk in there.

Edgene Well, I'm goin'. I'll be right back.

He leaves. Mona John walks over to the counter and pours a huge glass of water. She drinks all of it rapidly.

Peteman *(Aside, to Ruby)* Damn. She knows it's tap, not scotch?

Mona John *(Distant)* Really, Ruby. It's alright. Don't you worry about it, okay? I got—Um…waitin' for me. In the…Just go on to your church and let me know when you wanna come with me to mine. And Mister Pete, forgive the thing with the cup towel. Cold meat works wonders on welts.

She leaves. Ruby begins to prepare breakfast.

Peteman What time your church start?

Ruby Later. Scrambled okay?

Peteman On my plate, it don't stand a chance.

Ruby Mister Peteman?

Peteman Just Peteman's fine.

Ruby Would you mind putting on a shirt?

Peteman Ain't you seed a man's naked chest ever?

Ruby It caused a whole lot of mess this mornin': your man's naked chest.

Peteman takes the large cup towel just used as Mona's weapon and makes a bib out of it.

Peteman That Edgene woman? The way he talked about her nonstop back in lock, she don't seem nuthin' fun like what he say…other than she's built right and tight, that's for sure. Oh, and it's clear she can kick a nigga's ass. Said when he met her, she shook it on him 'til the moon give up and quit, and that was it. But she look like she'd burst into holy flames she go near a club.

Ruby Mona John done turned from all that. She got a job, take care of her nephew since her daddy died, and she workin' for Jesus now that she done found the church He built…or sumthin' like that.

Peteman That give a man the blues: to see a fine ass woman turn holy. Can't touch her. Can't even dance with her. What about you?

Ruby What about me? I believe in Jesus. I'm a Christian, but Mona say it ain't true because I say I'm Baptist. *(Invoking Mona John. Not mocking)* "Jesus wasn't Baptist, Ruby. Jesus was the Christ. Baptist sumthin' that came after Jesus, and only Christian is what people who follow Christ should be, and the Bible only say Christian and one church."

Peteman I mean about you and dance halls. You like to dance?

Ruby I don't know.

Peteman Well, why not? You work hard. It seem only Christian someone take you out and treat you to a good night of ballyhooin'.

She brings him a plate of food.

You gonna eat any?

Ruby Just wonderin' when you w'z gonna say grace.

He bows his head most reverently.

Peteman Grace.

He eats. She sips coffee and watches.

This a fine breakfast.

Ruby You go to them dance halls while in New York?

Peteman Eh?

Ruby I've seen pictures in magazines about that. Sammy Davis, Jr. with all them pretty dance girls. Fur coats and sparkles, men with cigars and a drink in they other hand——

Peteman Where that?

Ruby In New York! Where you from!

Peteman I know where I'm from. Just hearin' the way you talk about it, though, it sound much better. I'm like, shit, let me get in on some of that!

Ruby It special. The cab cars whizzin' and the subways rumblin'. Stars go to New York to be bigger stars. That where Marilyn Monroe go in the white dress and the hot air blow up her skirt. Things like that just happen on the street. The city makes what good even better.

Peteman Well, I like what you got goin' here. New York smell like hot trash. That air that blow up that white woman's skirt smelled like hot trash. Here smell like clean and the rottin' peach that done fell from the tree out back. That's what I like. Here a man take it easy. Here I see the sky nice and clear, nuthin' blockin' my way, no streets or walls blockin' me off——

Ruby We got train tracks. Train tracks tell you where you can't go. We close by the tracks, too. Our house right on the other side by Mitchelson's car yard. On the other side is where a lot of white people live in nice houses.

Peteman This a nice house.

Ruby Long time ago, it was a white man's house. Now it's mine.

Peteman It's yours.

Ruby Yes.

Peteman Not your Daddy's?

Ruby It's a Trenton woman's house. Always been a Trenton woman's house. Was my Grandmama Rena's.

Peteman And your Grandmama didn't have any girls?

Ruby Just my Daddy.

Peteman And, she went over him, your brother, to give it to you?

Ruby Yes.

Peteman And your granddaddy?

Ruby *(Less willing to share)* He didn't have a say.

Edgene enters, racing.

Edgene Where's Mona?

Peteman She left.

Edgene *(Upset)* What? But I'm ready now. I'm ready.

He races to the back door, unsure of which direction to run. Defeated, he sits. Peteman bursts into laughter.

Peteman Nigga, I ain't ever seed you whooped like this.

Ruby Edgene, you can go the church with me.

Edgene I ain't goin' nowhere.

Peteman Ain't that a kick in the dick!

Ruby We can eat together, you and me, and then we can go.

Edgene I done tole you, I ain't goin' withcha to that damned church!

He exits. Peteman roars. He walks over to Ruby, pouring himself another cup of coffee.

Ruby Trenton men always misplacin' they women.

Peteman I'll say!

Ruby My Grammy said that.

Peteman I ain't ever seed Ed take a kick in the dick so hard! Over a woman, too. Woo-wee! Hell, no!

Ruby You curse a lot.

Peteman Been cursed at a lot, so it's alright. What, it bother you?

Peteman taunts Ruby, bringing his face very close to hers. She recoils.

Ruby No! *(Beat)* Just noticed. That's all. *(Painfully embarrassed)* I do think I might be able to catch the early service at church.

She goes to leave.

Peteman Ruby.

Ruby *(Arrested)* Yes?

Peteman Let me take you out.

Ruby Okay.

She exits. Peteman sips his coffee.

Scene 2. Thy Father's Commandment[6]
Trenton Living Room / Patterson Music Room - Day

Rena dusts the living room. Thomas enters. He checks to see if anyone is around. Thomas goes to the piano. He plays his father's song. Lights in the willow tree twinkle. Rena stops cleaning and watches him. She approaches.

Rena What's that you playin', baby? I know this one? *(She hums)* Lord. It gonna keep me up all night.

Rena returns to cleaning. The music reaches silence and the tree lights begin to dissipate. Rena stops cleaning, sensing something.

Simultaneously, Melody enters into her music room. She sits down in front of the piano, plays a few Brahms measures, and soon loses interest. She begins to play the song Thomas taught her. The world beneath the tree begins to twinkle. Rena responds as if she hears.

Boy? What'd you do?

Melody plays the familiar measures and comes to a rest where the original music dissipates. Rena experiences a shortness of breath. She grabs her chest. The lights in the willow tree begin to fade. Melody begins again, adding more notes to complete a magnificent phrase. On and on she plays, creating a symphony. The willow tree shines. Struggling for air, Rena races to the back room.

Lights down on Thomas.

Melody stops playing.

Melody Oh, Thomas! Hurry and remember this song. I can't keep my hands from taking over!

There is a knock on the door. It is Melody's brother, Steven.

Steven Hi.

Melody Oh, hi.

Steven I'm sorry. Should I come back?

Melody No, it's okay.

Steven You can keep playing. I was just listening.

She plays again, then suddenly stops.

Keep going. I really like that. What is that?

Melody Was there something you wanted to ask me?

Steven I just wanted to know what that was. I'm not allowed to come hear you?

Melody Of course you are. It's just…you're not entering the room. You're just standing in the doorway.

Steven Oh. I guess you're right. May I enter?

Melody That's fine. *(Beat)* Dad sent you in here?

Steven I like it when you play. If you're not playing…well, there really isn't any other sound in our house. It's enough to drive you crazy. It's good what you're playing.

Melody Yeah?

Steven What composer? Did Thomas teach you that? *(Silence)* We need to talk about Thomas.

The willow tree fades. Lights down on the Patterson household.

Scene 3. He Correcteth In Whom He Delighteth[7]
Trenton Living Room - Day

Lights up on Thomas. Edgene pokes his head from around the corner. He backs up a few steps and makes noise with a can of brushes in his hand as he "approaches" the room. Thomas quickly composes himself. Edgene enters.

Edgene Oh, hey. I'm getting something to eat for breakfast. You know if Ruby made breakfast? I'm pretty hungry. *(Silence)* Then I'm gonna go finish me a masterpiece…Missed it some. So, if you need me—

Thomas Been doin' fine without you.

Edgene Have you seen ummm…Peteman?

Thomas Gave up on runnin' down bad luck Negroes.

Silence.

Edgene I see you workin', so…

Thomas Yeah. I'm workin'.

Edgene turns to leave.

Did I tell you—?

Edgene Yeah?

Thomas I started reading the Bible.

Edgene Nuh.

Thomas After Mama died. I had remembered someone saying that with wisdom comes understanding and with understanding comes peace. Something. I wanted me some of that so bad. Only thing was, we didn't have a Bible in the house. Mama said God gifted her to guide us, so I never knew to think that that was missing from our lives. I guess I could have bought y'all one, but I'm not smart enough to do what I've never been taught.

Edgene Ruby's got a Bible—

Thomas I'm talking about then. *Then.* The day I walked to Mitchelson's and bought it. My head was racing faster than my feet could walk. But I can't tell you one single thought. It was like all thoughts a person could ever have I was having right then. My breath was coming out like I was running. I was sweating. All I could think was that I was on my way to buy some. "Just hold on," I'd tell myself. "We about to get us some peace." I went down to Mitchelson's and bought me a nice King James with gold on the edging. You've seen the one.

Edgene Yes.

Thomas I didn't know where to start, let alone what to do with it. So, I said to God to come and show me something I hadn't learned yet, and I took the Bible and threw it up in the air so far, it hit the ceiling and landed on the bed open. "Give us some peace. Give me some peace." It kept playing in my head like some song that keeps coming. I stood over that Bible with my eyes closed and promised that I'd go to one verse and one verse only and that would be my lesson. That would be what I'd learn. "Happy is the man that hath his quiver full of them: They shall not be ashamed, but they shall speak with the enemies in the gate."

Edgene A quiver?

Thomas —of children. My children stand between me—

Edgene —and your enemies. *(Beat)* I'll be in my studio.

Thomas Your sister…She's weak-willed. Homely.

Edgene Pop—

Thomas Most women's garden's 'tween their legs, but Ruby keeps hers out back.

Edgene walks away.

She ain't got nuthin' nobody want. And you—

Edgene I paint. That's what I do. Don't have to start nuthin' with me, Pop—

Thomas Nuthin'?

Edgene You can have all the yesterday garbage. I'm home *now* and I'm stayin' home. I got brushes, good paint, and pieces in that shed waitin' three years for me to finish. And I'm gonna sell 'em. To people who want 'em—for hundreds of dollars. Shoot, thousands.

Thomas Hmm-hm.

Edgene Can't nuthin' make me think it isn't creation I'm makin' when I sit down with one of these brushes in my hand. Shoot, Edgene's creatin' everything all over, yes I am.

Thomas What'd you bring your boy for?

Silence.

Edgene Nobody's doin' anything…and we're family. We're supposed to be there for one another. That's what people do—

Thomas *(Overlapping on "be there for…")* What you bring your boy for? You our shame, Nigga. Our shame.

Edgene I'm shame? I'm shame? Outta my way.

Thomas Go hide. Go run, fool. That's what you best at.

Edgene What you best at? You done ate so much granddaddy's vomit, I smell it off your breath. Got your ticket to Paris yet?

Ruby enters from the hallway. Sensing the tension, she turns back around.

Thomas No, sister. We just finished. We done now.

Ruby I didn't mean to bust up your discussion.

Thomas No, we weren't talking much about anything. That right? *(Silence)* See. Weren't saying anything at all.

Thomas leaves.

Edgene I'm hungry.

Ruby C'mon in the kitchen.

They enter the kitchen.

I'll put some coffee on for you first so you don't have to have an empty stomach while I'm cookin'. I don't know what happened. I don't wake up late. When have you ever known me to wake up late?

Silence.

You and Daddy was at it. Was it about me?

Edgene Why would it be about you?

Ruby I've been slackin' on my duties around the house. *(She waits)* I've been up late these past few weeks. With Peteman. You ever ask him about the city, Edgene? We be lookin' at my New York picture books, listenin' to music and such, and he point to things and tell me, "I been there, and actually it's more like this or that."

Thomas enters, ready to eat. He sits at the table. Ruby turns to see him seated.

Edgene Go on.

Ruby That's all.

Edgene That ain't all. You was about to gush on and on about sumthin' and now you stopped it all up because folks come around. You're all closed up now cause eyes are on you!

Ruby Edgene—!

Edgene I done lost my appetite.

He races to his shed.

Thomas I'll eat whatever you was fixin' for him.

Scene 4. The Destruction of the Prince[8] Edgene's Paint Studio - Afternoon

Lights up on Edgene in darkness. He sits before an easel, his clothes spattered with red paint. He swigs from a flask.

Edgene Every night, I had this dream that seeped into another dream, then another. I'd be starin' at the bars in the window in bed, and before I knew it, I was paintin' a large picture, and it's my masterpiece. I can feel my arm making strange, new strokes, and my hand bendin' and twistin' with the directions of my wrist like there ain't no bone in me at all. But I can't see the picture I'm makin'. I can feel it magical, but can't see it. There's this huge shadow over me, and I realize that I'm under the kitchen table paintin' this picture, and the paint down my arm—it's Grammy's blood.

A knock. Lights up on Mona John. She is sexy and dressed for a good time. When he opens the door, she wraps her arms around him and plants a passionate kiss on his lips. We see nude paintings around the shed. This is a memory.

Mona John Baby be needin' that? Let me in, let me in. It's kinda brisk.

Edgene That warmed me up.

Mona John Ooh, you fresh. Feel good in here, though. Always feelin' good in here. Where you want me this time?

He points to the chaise lounge. She grabs his flask of whiskey.

Mona John Can I have some of this?

Edgene Sure thing.

She swigs and doffs her shawl and hat. He watches her.

Wait a second.

Mona John What?

Edgene Wait, wait, wait a second.

Mona John What? What is it?

Edgene You ain't ever this giggly and bright and stuff. What's going on?

Mona John Oh, c'mon, 'Gene. Leave me 'lone and let's do this.

Edgene You gonna tell me?

Mona John *(Cautiously, then building speed)* Well, I…went to my bank yesterday. And I've saved up. Enough.

Edgene That's good: to save.

Mona John Yes. I've been savin' so that I can…get out of dodge, baby. *(Beat)* For the past year, I been stoppin' on and off at the station to check the fares to Philadelphia, Baltimore, Boston, places like that. They been kinda steady for a while so that helped me gauge my spendin': tickets, a few months rent of a room, food, some clothes. And I'm there, now. I've saved enough.

Edgene Wow. So which one wins you?

Mona John Baltimore, I think.

Edgene Not New York?

Mona John Not sure if I'm ready for New York.

Edgene Shoot, girl. Not sure if New York ready for you.

Mona John I think I might try to model for photographs up there. Paintin's is nice and all, but I think I might want to do that now: take pictures. They get mass produced, they're easier to mail, you know? Printed in magazines and books. More people can see me.

Edgene Yeah. That's true.

Mona John So, today is my last stand, I guess you can say.

Edgene You doin' this when?

Mona John I bought my ticket today. Leavin' in a few weeks. Told daddy he can rent out my room. You should have seen his jaw hit the floor. Oh, 'Gene, the horror on his face was one of the prettiest things I done ever seen. "Kiss my ass, Daddy Briggs. Kiss my smooth, smooth ass!" *(Wrapping her arms around him)* You gonna miss me?

Edgene Aww, girl.

Mona John C'mon. Admit it.

Edgene I'm just gonna have to replace you, that's all. It's gonna take some work on my part. To find another model.

Mona John That's all you gotta say?

Edgene What?

Mona John "I'm gonna have to replace you?" That's it?

Edgene I've got a studio here, Mon, and life keeps on going even after you leave.

Mona John How did you just make this about you? I want you to be happy for me.

Edgene I am happy. I'm very happy for you.

Mona John Yeah?

Edgene Yes.

Mona John What you gonna give me?

Edgene What you talkin' about?

Mona John To remember you by. *(Re: paintings)* You got all these to remember me, but I ain't got nuthin'. I want one. Just a small one. *(She begins to kiss his neck)* A little sumthin'.

Edgene No.

Mona John stops, giggles and resumes her kissing.

No. They're mine. They're my work. You sat on your ass while I mixed the colors, selected the brushes, created texture with each layer of paint, and made your crooked tits into art. It's my work. And I don't just give it away like some pamphlet.

He walks over to his easel, takes a swig of his liquor, and lifts his brush, ready to work.

Mona John That's a shame to hear, Edgene. A real shame.

She walks to the chaise and begins to don her things.

Edgene Aww, c'mon! You kiddin' me? You kiddin' me, right? When you get all sensitive and stuff? Mona!

She heads to the door, Edgene following closely behind. Lights shift as Mona disappears into the blackness of memory.

I dream you turn around smilin' and kiss me. I ask you to marry me and you say, "Yes." You remove my shirt that's covered in paint. You strip me naked. You wash me clean. You use your fingernails to get the paint out the groove under my nails and I shine like new. You make love to me in the water. And I float like a deadman, not wantin' to come out afterwards. I float to the shore where you done gone on before me. And you done run off. With my clothes.

Act Three

Scene 1. A Slack Hand[9]
Trenton Kitchen / Willow Tree - Evening

Lights up on Rena beneath the willow tree. A strange ringing in the air.

Lights up in kitchen. Ruby puts her money into a teapot on top of the cabinets. She then empties a small bag of groceries, carefully removing her treasure: a glamour magazine. Peteman enters. He comes up behind her, peering over her shoulder.

Rena *(To audience)* I—I couldn't breathe. I tried, but—here: sumthin' rude. It pushed me. Tight: right here, see, here… *(She points to her chest)* A shaking. A—a quiv… *(Silence)* Trouble's comin', babies. It was buried deep down and some fool dig it up. *(Silence)* There was sound in the darkness. Then it stopped. In the quiet, there was a loudness. I can hear it comin'. What never shoulda been let out. *(Music. The tree twinkles. She studies the tree. She touches it)* A familiar vision. Tellin' me to get ready to… leave? I know this vision. *(Beat)* I gotta go. Edgene scream them pictures a' his get a good grand? Shoot. I say the wise thing to do is…love the children goodbye? No. Get me a grand. Travelin' shoes ain't cheap, babies. I'll miss you.

Lights down on Rena. The ringing subsides.

Peteman He's shorter than that.

He steals a kiss on the cheek.

Ruby Oh! My daddy gonna hear you laughin'. He don't like that sort of thing to go on here in the house.

Peteman Kissin' or laughin'? If you wanna spend time with Peteman, you gonna have to relax some… *(He positions his face in front of hers)* Let me kiss you.

Ruby My da—

She considers, then gives a quick peck on his nose.

Peteman Ooh. You a bad girl, Ruby.

Ruby No! Don't say that.

Peteman Bad fine with me. You got any ice? My hand hurtin'.

Ruby Yes. Did you see the new magazine I got? I been waitin' on this issue for a whole month. You see that Latin Quarter? Here, look at this. *(She finds a page and gives him the magazine)* Look at them dresses. They're mermaids! Oh, Peteman, they so beautiful. Look at the little glitter beads glued next to they eyes. And them's the Mills Brothers. See, right there? *(Peteman looks at the pictures)* Nobody here seem to like me talkin' about New York. Edgene usta listen to me talk, but he won't look through nuthin' with me no more. He get all mean if I want to do that. But I know sumthin'. Wanna know what I know?

Peteman smiles.

When I turn my back, Edgene be goin' through my magazines. He be lookin' all hungry, like he want to snatch the people from the pages. When I talk about it, though, he call me silly, like I'm pickin' at him. Sometimes, I wish that he and I both pack up and walk out of here. Leave the house and Daddy and everything. What's funny is that when I tell him that now, he curse at me.

Peteman Ruby?

Ruby Yeah?

Peteman Can I get that ice now?

Ruby Oh, yeah. Yeah.

She runs to the icebox, cracks a few cubes for him, and creates a makeshift compress with a cup towel.

It achin' you or sumthin'?

Peteman Yeah. I got a bad hand. See?

Ruby I've noticed the big ol' mark there. Never wanted to stare or anything.

Peteman Yeah.

Ruby It's rude to stare.

Peteman Yeah. *(Beat)* Makes it hard sometimes to work, too. Hold things. I need to get busy. But I don't think nobody want to hire a man with a bad hand.

Ruby Oh…

Peteman But I can do some things. I can make that car out back work for you again. I know car guts like second nature. I've rebuilt them from top to bottom and there ain't nuthin' like raisin' 'em up from the dead. That hum! Yeah, like a baby just born. Might take me a while, but I can do it. *(Beat)* That is your car, yeah? *(She nods)* Where'd you go if it worked? Take me with you? Maybe I fix it for you, you give me that kiss?

Ruby goes to the icebox.

I need sumthin' to do. *(Beat)* How you make your money?

Ruby Me? Well, my Granny left me some. Left all us some. Edgene spent his on canvas, booze and women, and owed a lot of people money, then got Daddy dragged into it. That was bad. I ain't have nuthin' to spend mine on, I guess. You lookin' for work?

Peteman I don't think it's worth the search much. When you got a bad hand, you got one all around.

Mona John enters.

Mona John Mister Peteman.

Peteman Ma'am.

Mona John *(To Ruby)* So, your brother's still here, then, yes?

Ruby He's paintin' right now, I think. Let me get you sumthin' to drink. Some lemonade.

Mona John No, Ruby. I—can't stay. Got a neighbor watchin' my nephew and he get loud when I'm gone too long. I just…really needed to speak to you.

Ruby You did? *(Silence)* Mona?

Mona John I know better how to treat somebody who's been so good to me, and I left you here with all this goin' on. No offense, Mister Peteman.

Peteman *(Shrugging)* Hey.

Mona John *(Weeping)* You the dearest friend to me ever, Miss Ruby. You comfort me when Daddy die. You the one I talk about the Lord with. Then Edgene come and I just…

Peteman Split.

Ruby Mona. I—I don't know what to say. You came here all the way for that?

Mona John Love me again.

Ruby I love you. I love you, Mona. Please, please. Eat sumthin' with us. I just came in from the shop and I got pie. Pecan. That sounds so nice, don't it?

Mona John I'm not interruptin' anything?

Peteman Nuthin' at all.

Mona takes a seat while Ruby prepares plates.

Scene 2. A Prince Persuaded[10]
Edgene's Paint Studio - Night

Rena creeps to the front of the shed and gently raps: no answer. She goes to a window, and lifts a broken tin pane to get a spare key. She enters, and after a brief moment, walks out studying a small painting. She bumps into Melody, who holds a few sheets of paper in her hands.

Rena Good Jesus!

Melody I'm so sorry. I don't mean to scare you—I just wanted to drop this by, to give him a gift. I like Thomas so much. He's so smart and is such a great man, and humble. His spirit is very much like yours, I can feel it. Please. Come where I can see you. This dark is a bit surreal and—I want to drop this by. Could you tell him for me?

Rena You lost?

Melody I'm sorry?

Rena I mean, Miss—

Melody I'm Melody.

Rena Miss Melody. You been playin' with Thomas.

Melody Have we met?

Rena No, I'm—a friend. And bless you for thinkin' I'm great spirit—

Melody *(Buttering)* I figure it takes one to know one.

Rena —but sumthin' tellin' me you oughta be over on the other side of them train tracks, Miss Melody, as I'm sure you got some good people worried about where you is.

Melody No.

Silence.

Rena You ain't meet no trouble comin' over here?

Melody The dark was amazing. Like the whole world was asleep and time stood still just for me. Not a soul was out. Except for you.

Rena *(Gentle)* You're a brave and different young woman, travelin' into new territory on your own.

Melody Some might think me foolish.

Rena No such thing. *(Beat)* I'm about to do some travelin' of my own, actually. Real soon.

Melody Isn't it wonderful and exciting? Knowing that you're going to a place where new people exist who will meet you for the first time? Who will see you? Speak to you? Grow to like you? And you're shaping it all on your own!

Rena I like you.

Melody It's like reading an extraordinary story, and you're the protagonist. The heroin. The goddess!

Rena Yes, I like you indeed! Listen, you didn't see me here, okay?

Melody I can barely see you as is.

Rena *(Urgent)* Truly, Miss. I ain't here now.

Melody You're not?

Rena In order for me to live the kind of story you talkin', I need to walk. Please Miss Melody: I can't tell you too much more than that. You said you could feel my spirit, how it's great?

Melody Certainly. That's real clear.

Rena Not here it isn't. For some reason, my spirit gets troubled here. It's like I hit my head on bein' regular and come back down to earth real slow, knowin' I'm not where I'm supposed to be. Everything here makes me know I ain't nuthin'. I pray all the time. I think I get through. I look for signs, like a bird or a funny-shaped cloud or sumthin', sumthin' to tell me which way to travel, which choices to make so that it comes clear why I'm here. And you wanna know what happened to me? I laid down a few nights ago after a dinner too heavy to hold. Early in the mornin', I woke up with a sensation on my breast. I couldn't tell if it was an itch or a pain, but it was sure 'nuf distinct. I touched my bosoms and felt a knot that vibrated at my touch like I put lightnin' in it. I had my mouth ready to spit out a curse when my eye caught a nice-sized brown spider goin' over the edge of the bed toward the ground. You know the kind: They sit in sheds and attics and barns. I can't quite remember, but I guess I had taken a blanket out of the back of the closet during the night 'cause of the chill of the air, and the window is broken and won't close. He must have held on as I flung the blanket in the air over and over again to spread it out. At least that's what I imagine. And I don't know if he was mad at me, but he knew where to go for me. As he crept over the edge of the bed, he smiled at me. Yes, he did. He had six or eight little eyeballs and they showed all black shiny, and half of 'em winked! That's when I knew he had just gotten even. Right in the center of my chest. Not my face, not my legs, but my breasts. He went for *me*. Have you ever seen what those spiders can do with a bite? First, you blister. A white pus bump or sumthin'. Looks like a salt water pearl. Feels like one, too, after while. You get hard in your flesh. That's because you're dyin'. You're dyin' around the pearl of it. Then your color fades away, the pearl fades away and you sink into yourself. Like a little grave pocket. If it opens, you have a hole in you, and sometimes they real big holes. And I was gonna have one right in the middle of my chest. When I saw him, I leapt up and grabbed a shoe ready to grind him into the floor for what he'd done...but he was long gone. I think he climbed through the broken window. *(Beat)* I know'd better. Layin' down in a worn-down room fallin' down around me. All these openings. Holes. Things not finished. *(Beat)* But I don't have a hole, Miss Melody. *(She touches her heart)* I deserve a scar in the middle of my chest, so stupid. Gapin'...but I wasn't given one. Can't see a trace of that bite. I've escaped it, and like that spider, I'm goin' to escape here, by a broken window.

Melody You're not frightened any?

Rena With everything I got.

Melody Of course, I won't say a word. It's just...I...don't want to walk up to that house. Just like you, I have something burning inside of me, but I can't just go and do it on my own like that.

Rena Somebody lied. Of course you can.

Melody Art doesn't work that way. There's always got to be someone else, even if they hate what you're doing. *(Beat)* Can you help me?

Rena You gonna get me caught, Miss Melody—

Melody I promise, I won't hold you up and it's easy.

Rena Alright. What is it?

Melody That key you took from over the window. May I have it?

Rena gives a Cheshire smile. She hands Melody the key:

Rena Don't be too brave, chile.

She leaves, never noticing Edgene standing beside the shed, drinking. Melody enters the shed. She combs through one nude painting after another, fascinated. Edgene stands just inside the doorway.

Edgene You're tresspassin'.

Melody Oh!

Edgene Who's you talkin' to? You brought folks with you here?

Melody No, no.

Edgene Hmm.

Melody What?

Edgene That ain't good: white woman out here by herself. *(Silence)* You really think that? Art always gotta have somebody else?

Melody I—I read about some cave paintings once. How thousands of years ago, some savaged caveman mixed blood and berries and painted how he saw the world. They found it far back in a cave, where it had been untouched for centuries, hidden. He did that so you and I would know he lived once.

Edgene You're one of my daddy's students.

Melody Melody.

Edgene Melody. I'm not a caveman.

Melody You painted all of these?

Edgene Yeah.

Melody They're naked.

Edgene Under our clothes, we're all naked.

She laughs.

So, we got to have somebody else.

Melody I can't take credit for it, actually. Your father said that to me: that artists' souls get sad without someone else. I didn't know what he was talking about until I realized how much of an artist Thomas was and how he craved the audience I wanted to throw away. I think I might have been just like him if…well. Many things.

Edgene You mean bein' black?

Melody I mean what happens. In life. There's got to be someone else. That's all I'm saying.

Edgene Someone to hear your playin'?

Melody Whether I'm perfect or not. Someone to see the play being performed, or read the poem. See the paintings. You're Edgene, right?

Edgene You've heard about me?

Melody Yes. Thomas never said you painted. I only knew about how you worked all the time and wasn't home much.

Edgene He told you that?

Melody He's very proud of you.

Edgene He's proud of *you*. Talk about you all the time. We grew up hearin' about you every week. Every concert you had. Every award you got. Every cold you had.

Melody I took up a lot of his time. Away from you.

Edgene It made him happy: to have somebody else. *(Beat)* You don't like my paintings, do you?

Melody What?

Edgene You seem a little nervous.

Melody I'm not.

Edgene You sure? I can cover them up. You're a proper lady.

Melody Don't do anything of the kind. Do you have buyers come to look at them?

Edgene Nobody looks at them.

Melody Well, that will never do. Someone has to see them. Otherwise you might as well have never painted an inch.

She examines the paintings.

Edgene How did you get in here, Miss Melody?

Melody I found this key here. On the ground. I'm so sorry. I—I came by because I wanted to give this to your father.

She offers him the sheet music.

He's been teaching me this song, and…I found the rest of it. I brought it here to give it to him. Aren't you going to take it?

Edgene grabs the music. Melody does not release it.

This is one of the most magnificent pieces I've ever played. I'm looking forward to playing it all the way through for him. I won't see your father until the end of the week, but will you tell him that for me?

Edgene I'll tell him. *(She lets go)* And…that key: It goes above that window outside, the one with the crooked pane. I always keep it in the same place.

Melody I'll replace it. Delighted to have met you, Mister Edgene Trenton.

Edgene watches her departure, then closes the door and secures the lock on the shed.

Scene 3. The Black and Dark Night[11]
Willow Tree - Night

Lights up on Thomas under the willow.

Thomas "Cherubim and Seraphim. That who do the music in God's universe, Son." My father, the greatest piano instructor to ever live, told me this, speaking passionately with very black and dry, cracked hands. He fixed transmissions. "The angels sing and toil: pushin', pullin' each star. You can hear 'em. I do," he said, "as I walk to work." And he taught me to believe I heard the swelling crescendoes of chords impossible to replicate with copper wire and sound holes. And in the night, we'd sit under the willow tree and listen to the stars play us a symphony. "Think back furtha, boy. Remember…Remember…" In my mother's womb, he told me, I kicked her extra hard when Uriel, the archangel of the sun, spun the sun on its axis. "Oh, yes, boy. The sun spin, just like the resta us. All that spinnin'. Ain't goin' nowheres." But I remember liking nighttime best. Tucked away snug in the blackness. Under the stars. Hearing God talk to us. And the sweat on Daddy's furrowed brow twinkled in the moonlight like the stars. His face: my black heaven. I heard God talk under the willow tree with Daddy. The stars hanging so low about us, they rested in the tree. "Can't nuthin' make the music of God, Son. No cat guts. Nowheres. Done tried." I didn't ask him what he meant, but after while, I didn't have to. I can tell you now, I don't hear stars any longer. I'm always hearin'…quiet.

Scene 4. Mercy About Thy Neck[12]
Trenton Kitchen - Night

Lights up in the kitchen. Ruby, Peteman and Mona John continue to eat and chat. Edgene enters.

Edgene Mona! Oh, Jesus, yes! All my people here! Everybody who helped me get on through. *(He sits)* Now, did we bless this holy pie before we broke bread? No, broke crust?

Ruby It's just pie, Edgene.

Edgene Well, I thought we might get book, chapter and verse on how to eat in a way pleasin' and acceptable in the eyes of the Lord.

Mona John Careful with your words, Edgene.

Edgene You worried? Don't forget, I'm the nigga who was askin' to go with you to the Lord's house.

Ruby Mona John came here already askin' forgiveness about that and we done made it right. Ain't no hard feelings about that forever-ago Sunday, Edgene.

Edgene How you forgive for me? I ain't talkin' about you. I'm talkin' 'bout *me*. That waddn't right, the way I see it: makin' plans with somebody then cuttin' out on 'em like that. I don't know me no Bible like y'all do, but I don't think you can forgive her for a bone I got. *(To Mona)* You care about my soul? *(Silence)* Y'all go. C'mon now. This a private conversation.

Peteman Man, I'm in the middle of my pie.

Ruby Your breath stink, Edgene.

Edgene *(Upset)* Get out!

Peteman and Ruby leave.

Mona John Been waitin' for your old self to show up.

Edgene Nah-nah-nah-nah-nah, girl. I seein' now. I see what gon' on here 'round this house. Everything.

Mona John Everything?

Edgene What is it? What this forgiveness thing? How it work?

Mona John Ed, you don't know what I carry—

Edgene Naw, dammit. You tell me, 'cause I want you to forgive me, and that be *it*. No more cold!

Mona John You want it!	**Edgene** Yeah, girl.
Mona John You want—	**Edgene** Yeah—
Mona John To be—	**Edgene** *(Hungrily)* Yeah—

Mona John —restored back. Released. Like it—never happened. Over and over again…Seventy times seven.

Silence.

Edgene Shit, that's hard. *(Beat)* Can you do that?

Long silence as she thinks.

Mona John Yeah. *(Beat)* Yeah. Yeah. *(She stands)* Bible study is at 9:45. I'll be by at 9.

She leaves. Edgene sits in contemplative silence. Peteman pops around the corner, checking to see if the coast is clear.

Peteman Where you been at? You pissy?

Edgene Hmnh?

Peteman Drunk, fool!

Edgene Hmnh…

Peteman *(Celebratory)* Ooh-wee, man! I smellin' it off your breath. What that? Come here. Come here.

He grabs Edgene's face and inhales his breath.

White lightnin'…

Edgene I ain't feelin' good—

Peteman I ain't had none of that in I don't know how long. Where you get that?

Edgene Thinkin' I'm gon' go lay down.

Peteman Nah, man. I ain't tryin' to hear all that. I'm itchin' to find some trouble to get into. Some place low down where nobody'd care if they know'd who we was. Wherever that was you just come from, that will do fine. Mona left?

Edgene Yeah. She's gone—

Peteman —and the house quiet. Take me there. Where you was.

Edgene Man, I'm sick.

Peteman We talkin' *years*, brother. I ain't had no music bumpin' up right. I need some whiskey, a woman and a dark, dirty corner, Jesus, it's creepin' out my bones. C'mon, 'Gene. Let's get us some quick livin'.

Edgene I ain't sayin' no more to count me out! Why you all ridin' me? Damn!

Silence.

Peteman This about your woman. *(Beat)* Shit. I felt it. I felt it. What happened to "passin' through," gettin' me some dollars and headin' on out? *(Silence)* Muthafucker, don't play with me.

Edgene Hey, hey. She likin' you, right? I tole you I'm talkin' to her. She easygoin'. Just let me do this and you'll get what you—alright?

Peteman *(Friendly)* Alright. Alright. You keepin' it good with Peteman. Shit, you got to keep it good.

They give "dap."

'Cause you fuck with me, man, I'll kill you.

Act Four

Scene 1. The Promotion of Fools[13]
Patterson Music Room / Edgene's Paint Studio - Evening, Spring, 1957

Thomas waits on the piano bench. The lights of the willow tree beam and shimmer as Asa sits next to him, playing his concerto.

Simultaneously, Lights up on Edgene's paint shed. He drinks heavily. Mona poses near him, seductive, nude, and beautiful.

Edgene I slept out here last night and dreamt I died in 1972 in Baltimore. I froze outside a bar. I eased into death. Nuthin' loud at all. Kinda liked it. *(Beat)* Come to me.

Edgene motions for his model. Lights down on Mona John as Melody races over, a shawl loosely wrapped over her naked body.

Asa stops suddenly on the all-too-familiar note, looking over his shoulder as if someone called his name. He exits, staggering toward his destination. The lights flash and freeze, illuminating the air.

Thomas No!

Thomas leaps to his feet. Steven enters.

Steven Thomas! I can set my watch by you. Sorry to have kept you waiting.

Thomas I always tell my children, "Nothing good ever comes out of being late."

Steven Oh, well… Yes, I guess you're right there. *(Beat)* Have a seat. Please.

Melody looks at the piece and rewards Edgene with a kiss. His hands journey to the shawl. Lights down in the shed as he pulls it away.

Thomas I say that to Miss Melody, too. It's not like her to be late. Is she on her way down? *(Silence)* Is everything alright?

Steven Thomas, I'm afraid we have to have somewhat of a serious discussion today. Would that be alright?

Thomas I've been part of this family for over twenty years, Mister Steven, sir. You can talk to me about anything.

Steven Your strengths continuously point out our weaknesses, Thomas. Our family is so busy being involved with the goings-on of this town—galas and Melody's performances, then the business—we're never in tune with one another. We're always on the go—

Thomas —and you've been blessed because of it. The fruits of your labors are more than evident—

Steven —thank you, but what I'm... We experience breakdowns in our communication far too often. Because we're family, we take for granted the next person knows what we're thinking and will carry the ball the rest of the way. Such as in this case. Several weeks ago, our family made the decision we would not be taking you with us to Europe this summer, and in fact, we informed Melody we would shortly no longer be in need of your services. My sister, I suspect, being a woman of the most delicate sensibilities, never told you.

Thomas No, Mister Steven. She didn't.

Steven Right now she's out running some girlish errand, I'm sure, because she didn't have the courage to be in the house knowing you and I were to have this conversation. Melody was supposed to give you notice nearly two months ago, Thomas. To give you time to prepare her for our trip overseas, which now, is not too far around the corner, and for you to solicit new clientele. Because of that oversight, my father is prepared to give you something to tie you over in the meantime.

He offers Thomas an envelope.

Thomas You don't have—

Steven We insist.

He places the envelope in Thomas' hand. The lights of the willow tree slowly begin to diminish.

Thomas Mister Steven—

Steven Yes?

Thomas Did I do something, Mister Steven?

Steven You're an excellent teacher, Thomas. Very talented and your music—

Thomas My music, sir?

Steven The song you've been teaching our Melody. It's a wonderful piece. And my sister won't be playing that anywhere.

Thomas Of course, Mister Steven.

Steven Is the amount we gave you enough? We wouldn't be offended if you looked inside.

Thomas opens the envelope.

Thomas You are fair, Mister Steven, sir.

The lights on the willow tree go out.

Steven Let me offer you something to drink before you make your walk home.

He goes to a table to pour some water.

Thomas You're a very loyal son, Mister Steven.

Thomas exits. Lights down on the Patterson music room.

Scene 2. Thy Bed From Underneath[14]
Trenton Kitchen - Evening

We hear the sound of a car engine revving and failing repeatedly. Lights up on Rena in the kitchen. She is dirty and holds the stolen picture.

Rena *(Unsettled)* Chile waddn't lyin'! Gracious! What time is it? Reared up in Chattanooga: Couldn't find my way through the thick of the woods out back. Never seen such black. So still… *(Beat)* Shouldn't be blunderin' about the woods, no count. Especially a colored woman. With stolen merchandise. A nudie picture, no less. *(She frowns)* Oh, Edgene.

Peteman enters, his shirt and hands covered with axle grease. His hand aches. Rena hides the picture.

No luck, young buck? *(No response)* You ain't given me two words of respect since bein' here in my house. Guess that just how y'all is in New York, mmm? *(Silence)* Hmmm-hm. Don't touch my table cloth.

Rena exits. We hear a car pull up behind the house. Mona John and Edgene enter.

Mona John Yay is yay and nay is nay. No confusion, no holdin' people guessin'. You can't deny the Lord's wisdom when he talkin' to you. Ooh-wee, it shakes my brain up sometimes: We be makin' plans, but God make purpose. *(She inhales)* Gracious, Ruby got it smellin' fine in here. What she make, biscuits?

Peteman They coolin' on the counter over there. Where y'all comin' from?

Mona John Wednesday night is Bible Study, Mister Peteman, and Lord have mercy, it was a good one. You gonna have to come with us some night.

Peteman I'm busy into the evenin'. Fixin' Ruby's car.

Mona John There's Sunday mornin', too—

Peteman —I'm fixin' her car.

Mona John Just an invitation. It will always stand. I'm gonna run to the bathroom and rinse my face real quick 'fore I jump in one of them biscuits. Got a little warm in that church for my tastes.

Mona exits.

Edgene Where Ruby?

Peteman Why?

Silence.

Edgene Ruby a good girl. A real one.

Peteman She's upstairs recoverin': I touched her knee. I can't have me no good girl?

Edgene walks over to the basket of biscuits, helping himself. He breaks his biscuit, and it crumbles, a large piece falling onto the floor.

Sloppy. *(Edgene turns)* All this walkin' about, goin' to church. You know, self-righteous Negroes be the first ones to rat us out.

Edgene Us?

Peteman Muthafucker—*me*.

Edgene It a church house, man—

Peteman It ain't *this* house. What if somebody from that church wanna drop by an' visit? *(Beat)* Nigga. You really think you rulin' me.

Mona John enters. She goes to the sink and pours a glass of water.

Mona John Ooh-wee. Yes. That much better. Feelin' like a person again.

Peteman Make one of us.

Mona John Pardon?

He approaches Mona John and stands dangerously close to her. He rinses his hands in the sink.

Peteman It hard labor: that car. Don't think she don't bite back. Look at here. *(He shows her a scrape on his forearm)* And here. *(A rip on his shirt)* I'm breakin' her in real good, though. Actually thinkin' she startin' to like it now.

Mona John Mister Peteman, you gonna have to come on down to the church buildin' with us soon. We have first Sunday potlucks each month, you know. It be real good eatin', too. Food for your soul, then some good church lady potato salad for your belly.

Peteman You see me the church type, Miss Briggs?

Mona John All men, if they desire, are the church type.

Peteman What it like there? What y'all be talkin' about?

Mona John Jesus. The Truth. Rightfully dividin' God's purpose.

Peteman Yeah, Jesus. My boy.

Silence.

Mona John What you mean?

Peteman Same crime: guilty of bein' too clear for niggas. It make a nigga jealous knowin' you can do what nearly nobody on the planet can do. I relate to your Jesus real good with that one.

Mona John I—okay.

Peteman Folks can't wrap they minds around it, so they fear it. Like Edgene. Ain't got it. So far from it, it like nose holes to ass holes. It real regular, too: not havin' it, that… clarity. Your yay be yay? All that pew warmin', sittin' up at that church house: you got it or your don't. Right man?

Edgene turns and sits.

Peteman Now, c'mon now. You know I'm playin'.

Mona John Everything alright?

Peteman I get too rough. When my body worn down. You willin' to make me some ice, Miss Briggs?

Mona John Of course.

Mona goes to the freezer.

Peteman I think your man got some odds with me. 'Cause I'm Jesus-like.

Mona John Christians are Christ-like.

Peteman I'm sure y'all is.

He laughs and takes the compress.

Thank you much. It will help the ache.

Mona John The car do that?

Peteman Oh no. This? This sumthin' old. Got it from this nigga. Remind me kinda lot like Edgene. Over a pretty lady. A lot like you. Woman liked me, didn't like him, so he pulled a knife on me. Don't know why he didn't think cursin' me out could do the trick. I mean, I got feelins.

Mona John I see that.

Peteman So, I took the knife the only way I could. *(He holds up his hand)* Clean through. I took it, pulled it out, and…what's the word, Edgene? Uh, *converted* him.

Mona John Jesus.

Peteman *(Laughing)* He called me Jesus.

Mona John Edgene—

Peteman *(Singing)* Edgene!

Ruby enters.

Ruby No, y'all eatin' them biscuits already? They too hot. Let 'em cool first.

Peteman No, they just right. Hot suit them just right.

Ruby Yeah?

Before the silence becomes suspicious:

Mona John Sorry. I was tryin' to cool it in my mouth just now. No, you right. Way too hot.

Ruby Let me get you a marmalade. Or I got this peach jam—

Peteman Oh, yes. A man can get used to this!

Mona John No, Miss Ruby. If we want sumthin', we grown folk. We can get it out the icebox ourselves. *(To Edgene)* Yeah?

She elbows him.

Edgene Yeah.

Ruby Peteman? I…I'm feelin' much better now. You know, with earlier and all. I'm okay now. You okay?

Peteman Perfect. A little hot in the kitchen for me, though, Miss Ruby. Thinkin' I'm gonna get back in that car engine. Why'nt you come with me: Shine some of your light on me with a smile? Cut through all the dark?

She smiles.

There she go, y'all ! *(To Ruby)* Come with me.

They exit.

Mona John *(Calm)* You got me here lyin' in your sister's house like everything fine when it seem real clear, it ain't fine. What'd I just see?

Edgene A Negro down on they luck, where you been? Glad Ruby cheerin' him up right now. It's good. Seein' a woman workin' to lighten her man's load. Don't see that much.

Mona John What you owe him? *(Silence)* What you owe him?

Edgene sits. He pulls a flask from his coat pocket and swigs.

You had that in the church?

Edgene It ain't mine.

Mona John I don't care whose it is. Money? Is that it?

Edgene Why it gotta be that? Ruby sittin' here lonely, and I got a friend, that's all. They look pretty happy to me.

Mona John I ain't givin' you no money, Edgene.

Edgene I ain't ask you!

Mona John This why you come back?

Edgene You think that? *(Beat)* I need to drink this, and I need you to—to just be with me. Can you do that?

He swigs again.

Mona John I can't walk this walk with you.

Edgene Of course. My girl brand new. I love it. I get it.	**Mona John** *(Overlapping on "I love it.")* That right. That right.

Edgene Yeah, that dress brand new. Hat new, too, but you lookin' the same. Lookin' at me the same. I remember that look.

Mona John And what look would that be, Edgene?

Edgene You covered for me. You spit a lie out real easy. *(Beat)* You saved from what? I'm feelin' you tryin' to get saved from folks like me. But I know you. From before. Now you lookin' down your snoot at me?

She heads to the door.

Half them Negroes partytin' with us on Saturday was singin' "Hallelujahs" on Sunday mornin' with peppermint in they mouths to cover the whiskey on they breath. We'd laugh at 'em as they walkin' out the church. Remember?

Mona John I do. We were a boy and a girl, and everything was a laugh. Even God.

Edgene And we was honest how much we hated all that bullshit.

Mona John *(Overlapping on "much")* Honest?

Edgene We with each other in ways we can't be honest with nobody else.

Mona John Honest.

Edgene You and me the only folk walkin' around with enough know-how to call it like it is. No sugar-coatin', no "hopin'-you-like-us-tomorrow" holdin' us back from callin' folks out.

Mona John You called me out, Edgene?

Edgene What you mean?

Mona John I don't remember you ever callin' me out. You *love* me? You should have called me out, but you was gone. God had to uproot me through the most terrible of ways, and that was the only way my eyes could turn inward. We weren't brave. We laughed at folks 'cause we didn't have enough courage to admit we just don't like gettin' up early in the mornin' when we don't have to. That we don't want to spend our money on nobody but ourselves. That we don't like givin' up sumthin' when we ain't gettin' anything out of it and don't ask us for nuthin' or make me change. We weren't honest. We never looked at *us*. *(Beat)* You're the hypocrite, Edgene. Sittin' here in this crazy house, with some crazy plan that gonna tear your life apart and it is crazy, 'cause right now I am more grateful to you than I have ever been in my life. Runnin' with you done managed to make an honest woman of me after all.

Edgene Damn, it's quiet. *(Beat)* Tell me what to do.

Mona John kisses him on the cheek and turns to leave. Edgene quickly grabs her, kissing her deeply and passionately.

Mona John No, Edgene. Come off it.

Edgene I ain't garbage. I ain't…

He grabs her breast and goes in for another kiss. She slaps his face. They both stand apart for what seems like an eternity before Mona breaks to leave through the front room. She stops in the doorway.

Mona John I'm goin' out this way to the car. *(Silence)* I'm gettin' in the car.

Edgene Where you goin'?

Mona John I won't disrespect your kitchen.

Edgene We can disrespect in your car?

Mona John exits. Edgene approaches with a few hesitant steps, then quickly races after Mona John.

Act Five

Scene 1. He Wasteth and Chaseth Them Away[15]
Trenton Backyard - Day

Lights up on Mona John and Ruby on the porch. Mona watches Ruby shuck corn. In the background, we hear the revving and failing of Ruby's car engine.

Ruby Love can happen. Out of nowhere it can happen. It take on shapes and forms and stuff, but once it in you, it don't go nowhere. You and Edgene just peculiar.

Mona scoffs. Silence.

Mona John That real pretty corn you got.

Ruby Mister Thompson sell it out his truck by the lake. Gonna finish shuckin' it, then gonna fry it up for dinner. Peteman say his granny used to make him fried corn when he was comin' up. Thought it would surprise him nice.

Mona John I think he'll be quite pleased.

Mona hums. Ruby laughs.

What?

Ruby Nuthin'.

Mona John C'mon now. What?

Ruby You.

Mona John What about me?

Ruby You funny right now. Hummin' when you wanna be talkin'. Nobody else wantin' y'all the way you wantin' each other, Mona. Make me kinda tired watchin' all these flips.

Mona John Edgene's in love with Edgene. And I'm in love with my problems. *(She chuckles)* We ain't got it in us to make room for one another.

Ruby Plenty women wantin' Edgene's love, Mona, and you go kickin' it back. Don't you think he handsome—?

Mona John I ain't blind—

Ruby —and smart. And funny. Dress good. He listen to you half good when he want to, too. Dance real nice. Give yourself permission.

Mona John To do what, Miss Ruby?

Ruby What's deep in you…for the person you love. Love is sudden permission. Just remember that. When you gets scared, remember that.

Mona John That's why I'm leanin' on the everlasting arms. I guess some of us know love like an instinct or sumthin'. The rest of us gotta be trained. *(Beat)* Love get you in a mess of trouble you ain't careful. You got to be careful, Ruby.

Ruby stops shucking her corn. The engine revs and fails.

I know it feel good havin' somebody in your heart, but one thing I've had to learn about love: What you see is what you get. The heart be talkin' real strong sometimes to the point you can't hear what your brain tellin' you. So, sometimes, that why the Lord give us friends. We friends, yes?

Ruby You the best friend a girl could have, Mona.

Mona John Good. 'Cause I listen to what you tell me and you ain't got no reason to lie. I ain't got no reason to lie to you…Because we best of friends.

The engine revs and fails.

Ruby Mona. Whatever it is…   **Mona John** You my…Ruby—

The car engine revs again and hums. From behind the house:

Peteman Ooh-wee! I got her!

Peteman races over. Rena enters onto the porch.

I got her! I got her! She purrin', y'all! Ruby!

Ruby You did it, Peteman?

He picks her up and spins her around. Her hands linger.

Peteman I tole you I could do it, didn't I? I tole you!

Rena That thing ain't run in over three years. How'd you fix her?

Peteman Time and hard work, but she come around. Let me take y'all for a spin. Short one down the road.

Ruby scrambles to put her things away. Thomas enters onto the porch.

Ruby Daddy, he fixed it! He fixed my car! *(Beat)* It Saturday. You need a ride?

Edgene enters.

Edgene *(Somewhat groggy)* What goin' on out here?

Ruby Peteman fix my car, Edgene! Daddy, we'll drive you to the Pattersons.

Thomas I'll walk.

He goes inside.

Edgene But, I'm hungry.

Ruby *(Calling out to Mona John, who has gravitated to the willow)* You gonna come with us, Mona? We got room for one more!

Mona John It such a pretty day. Thinkin' I might stay out here for a while and enjoy the Lord goodness.

Noticing her, Edgene tucks his shirt.

Ruby Alright. You be here when we get back?

Mona nods. Ruby and Peteman run behind the house. Rena follows:

Rena Hold on, gal. Where you think you goin'?

A few moments later, we hear the dénouement of the car as it heads into the distance.

Mona John The quiet real nice, hm?

Edgene It's okay. You look real pretty. Never thought anything could be beautiful under this tree. Granddaddy under this tree.

Mona John I didn't know that.

Edgene Yeah.

Mona John I came to see you. You been on my mind.

Edgene Can I kiss you? Can I just…just…

He embraces her, their bodies pressed against the willow trunk.

You bad about runnin' off, Mona. Not hearin' from you these past days got my imagination goin' terrible. Thinkin' all sort of things I didn't like. Like maybe…maybe you wished we hadn't done nuthin'. But you know, we in love, so there ain't nuthin' wrong with us gettin' in the back of your car, or any other place. Just wanted to say that. You know, speak that out loud for you to hear.

Mona John Why?

Edgene Why, 'cause…you mine.

Mona John Edgene, the other night…I was holdin' back.

Edgene *(Loaded)* But not for long.

Mona John I ain't talkin' about us in the car. I'm talkin' about us bein' right with each other, and good with God and I ain't come right with you. Not yet, and you the one I gotta come right with.

Edgene Where you goin'?

Mona John I'm out front. Stay here and wait for me.

She exits. Edgene leans against the willow. He turns around and studies it: a silent communion. Mona returns. She holds Asa by the hand. Mona John removes his hat.

Mona John I ain't ever tell you—

Edgene It all right. Ruby mention him, how you take him, and that sumthin' a little wrong wit em, yeah? She say he slow?

Mona John *(Overlapping on "mention him")* Ruby?

Edgene It alright. I made her. I wanted to know why you was so…so different to me.

Mona That what you see?

Edgene What you mean?

Mona When you look at me. At him. That's all you see? *(Beat)* After you left, my daddy sent me to LaFayette—

Edgene To your Auntie's.

Mona John I had saved for Baltimore. Remember that? Not a fair trade, I don't think. And no dancin', drinkin', no fightin' or cursin' died it down.

Edgene I ain't mean to leave you all alone.

Mona John You. *Didn't.* You didn't. I didn't know. And when I did, I didn't care. Daddy said I brought him such shame. He sent me away when he knew, but partyin' in LaFayette's just as good as here. I ain't sure what I done. If it was the wild livin', or fallin' around drunk, but when he was born…he ain't even cry. I didn't name him for two weeks. I just laid there in my auntie bed lookin' at him lookin' right through me. Me smilin' didn't matter. None of my face games. I didn't want to touch him. She make us when he was strong enough take a walk along the flower road, and as I was carryin' him, I thought about just settin' him down in the brushes by the creek, like the little baby Moses. Moses and the Law and God and he was so heavy in my arms. What kind of woman…? He was so heavy. I turned around and saw just how far away from the house I had walked. I had gone too far. I sat in the grass, didn't care that the red ants were havin' a good time on my legs. Each fire bite they gave me, I had it comin'. I can't tell you how long I sat there, but it was like I came to when there was one on his little face. I flicked it off before it could bite him. Didn't realize I had done it until I heard the little snap of my fingers sendin' it through the air. The sun was goin' down on us and if I wasn't goin' to get up then, I wasn't ever goin' to get up. So I took off my underslip, and tied him to my back. It was night when I walked through the door, and my auntie say she was startin' to get worried, but thank God I had made it home. She had dinner waitin' for me, and made me pray before we ate. I had never said a prayer before. Not a real one.

Edgene *(Re: Asa)* He don't do nuthin'?

Ruby races from behind the house to the side of the shed. She finds a gas can that has been living among the flower pots, etc. Mona and Edgene do not see her.

Mona John He just look.

Edgene Well…I'll just look right back. *(He crouches over and studies Asa)* He a good lookin' boy. You been takin' real good care of him. He play outside?

Mona John He just look.

Edgene Well, I ain't mad at you, if that's what you wonderin'. We all do what we gotta do.

He heads to the house. She follows. Asa moves to the piano beneath the tree and strikes some keys.

People got to survive. I ain't mad about that.

Mona John Where you goin'? Please don't walk away. Ed!

Edgene Listen. Just…Okay, he mine. I hear ya. What you wantin' from me?

Mona John It's just, you know, it ain't right. You not knowin' you got a boy walkin' around. I mean—that—you should know him. A boy should know his daddy, yeah? Just—just, Edgene? Edgene.

She stumbles. He catches her.

Edgene Woah, woah, woah. What the matter with you?

The piano continues to play, like raindrops. Rena approaches. She spots Ruby eavesdropping and hides herself.

Mona John Please. I'm bein' honest. I'm honest. It waddn't ever supposed to be like this. *(She breaks)* You don't know what it feel like, someone lookin' straight through me like I ain't even here. An empty face that your face, Edgene. And God put it there for me to see all day, and I did it, I made him this way.

Edgene Don't be talkin' foolishness like that. You ain't done nuthin', Mona. It is what it is. That how he turn out.

Mona John He do this to me, Edgene!

Edgene Who?

A car horn honks. We hear Peteman giggling in the distance.

Peteman *(Offstage)* Hurry up with that gas can!

Ruby runs behind the house before Mona John and Edgene see her.

Edgene! Edgene! Get on down here, chump! Help us push this thing!

Mona John Ed—Ed, listen. We can—together, we—

Edgene releases her.

Peteman *(Offstage, singing)* This thing run out of gas. Mona! Drive Ruby to the gas station!

Silence.

Edgene I needta....

Mona places Asa's hat on his head, etc.

Where you goin'?

Peteman *(Offstage)* Mona!

Mona John *(Shaking her head)* Why'd I think—? Why—

Peteman *(Offstage)* Edgene! Come on. This thing weigh a ton!

Thomas enters onto the porch. Mona John and Edgene freeze.

Edgeeeeene!

Thomas *(To Edgene)* Someone's callin' you.

Edgene Yessir.

Edgene flees.

Thomas I heard...Was that you?

Mona John Sir?

Thomas The—uh...

Mona John No, Mister Thomas. It was...Ruby was...callin'...

A car horn honks.

Thomas They're waitin' for you? *(No response. Re: Asa under the tree)* Is that a boy back there? You need somebody to watch him?

Mona John Sir?

Thomas I'll watch him. 'Til you get back. No trouble.

Mona John Well, I—I got some other things to take care of.

Thomas Do 'em. Not forcin' you, now. Won't take him without your permission.

Mona John You've my…permission.

Thomas Alright then. I forgot to tell everyone my schedule changed today. Good thing, too: helpin' you out.

Mona John Yessir.

Silence.

Thomas They're waiting on you.

Mona John Yessir.

Mona runs. We hear her car descend down the driveway.

Thomas approaches Asa beneath the tree.

Thomas Was that you?

Rena steps from her hiding place.

Rena Thomas, go lightly now.

Thomas *(To Asa)* May I sit with you?

Rena Listen, now. There's more to this boy—

Thomas sits. A long silence. The silence is filled with love. Rena stares.

Rena There's more…

The sky becomes a dreamscape as father and son begin the concerto. The tree twinkles. The music is richer and fuller with both sets of hands. Mesmerized, Rena slowly approaches. They reach the familiar note and then silence.

As if something solid has hit her, Rena gasps and grabs her chest. Ringing.

Scene 2. Better Than Secret Love[16]
Trenton Living Room - Evening

"Blueberry Hill" plays on the gramophone. Rena lays on the sofa, fanning herself. Ruby, dressed in a simple summer dress, clumsily sways to the music.

Lights up on Edgene exiting his paint shed, checking to see if the coast is clear. Melody steps out clumsily, a little buzzed, and kisses him before taking flight. Edgene watches her.

Thomas enters the living room, catching Ruby practicing her dance.

Ruby Oh! I'll turn it down.

Rena Done asked her twice. Don't know what to think of you young people and music. Wouldn't know good music if it came up and bit you on the bump.

Thomas Mona back yet?

Ruby Unh-unh.

Thomas It's getting late, don't you think? Edgene paintin'?

Ruby I didn't know you were here. *(Silence. Re: the music in the room)* Yeah, I oughta…

She shuts the record player off. Thomas studies her clothing.

You hungry or sumthin', Daddy? I didn't cook. Was puttin' the baby down, but I can make you a sandwich…if you hungry.

Thomas You goin' somewhere?

Ruby Mister Peteman takin' me out for a drive in my car... *(No response)* It runnin' fine now that we put some gas in that thing. It stopped right in the middle of the road when we took it for a first run. I don't know, I guess the gas in it just dried up all that time it was sittin' dead in the back of the house. But now that we filled it up, it's runnin' just fine, Daddy. Peteman washin' it up real good by the lake. It gonna look like a brand new vehicle! Make me excited to think about people seein' us drivin' around in what look like a new vehicle. It's excitin'.

Thomas Ruby.

Ruby Yeah, Daddy?

Thomas Last time I looked, I was still your father. And any man that wants to take my daughter from this house is supposed to first come by me.

Ruby Daddy, you know Mister Peteman.

Thomas I do.

Edgene enters the living room and makes a start down the hallway.

Ruby Edgene! I was tellin' Daddy about how there so much good goin' on right now.

Edgene Mona back yet?

Ruby She say she be right back. You was workin' on your masterpiece just now, yeah?

Edgene Yeah.

Rena Y'all mind? I'm feelin' worn.

Ruby I knew it would be. Good things happenin' today… *(She turns to face Thomas)* I didn't even know you was back from practice, Daddy. You know, I was lookin' at pictures earlier of stars in some gowns from Paris and thought about you walkin' around on brick streets, people mumblin' French. Goodness gracious, what if you brought one of them dresses back for me to wear? I don't know if I would be even brave enough to touch it. *(She laughs alone)* It's a ticklish thought…to think. *(Beat)* But when'd you get back from the Pattersons?

Thomas Just now.

Edgene I thought you met up earlier.

Thomas Ruby, what about what I said to you? You're supposed to be goin' out where tonight?

Ruby I don't know. We just drivin'.

Edgene You goin' out with Peteman? When?

Ruby Now.

Edgene You tell nobody?

Thomas If he supposed to be takin' you out "now," where is he? How you know he ain't take your car and drive off with it? You give him the keys?

Ruby *(Self-doubting)* Yeah.

Thomas Gracious.

Rena Thomas, leave the chile alone.

Thomas He could be half way to Augusta with your brand new polished car, and you gave him a full tank to do it, too.

Ruby He wouldn't do that.

Peteman enters the kitchen. He carries a bouquet of wildflowers.

Rena Sister, he's a plannin' negro, that's exactly what he'd do. Don't half speak—

Thomas Had you asked me, I never would have blessed it. Had you asked me, I would have put him out of here months ago. But y'all so busy doin' whatever it is that you're grown enough to do—

Edgene *(Overlapping on "busy")* What'd I do?

Thomas —that you don't have any regard for the order of things, the way thing's supposed to be. You're impatient and you want what you mind and nevermind what Daddy or anybody else in this house think because Ruby's goin' to do what Ruby's goin' to do.

Ruby turns to Edgene.

Edgene *(Shrugging)* I wouldn't have given him my keys.

Peteman enters the living room.

Peteman *(Re: flowers)* Saw these on the way back. Had to pick 'em for you. *(To Edgene)* How you doin', man? Nice shirt.

Peteman "fixes" Edgene's collar.

Edgene Where uh…you and Ruby goin' out?

Peteman Well…Where you want to go, Miss Ruby?

Ruby Maybe see a picture at the drive-in?

Peteman That good?

Ruby Twenty-third Street. Yeah, that good.

Peteman Okay. Yeah, that's what we'll do—see us a New York movie.

Ruby Oh, Peteman, can we?

Thomas Y'all got money for a New York movie?

Ruby Daddy, please.

Thomas I may be old, but I'm not a fool. I know what goes on in drive-ins. Ruby's not going.

Ruby Well, then we can—

Thomas No, you can't. Peteman—Good Lord in Heaven! Does anybody even know what this Negro's first name is? He's comin' in here marked up without a dollar to his name talkin' about how he's taking Ruby off in the middle of the night. Why? She payin'?

Rena Son.

Thomas Why you want to take Ruby? There are young women all over this town. Why you want to take Ruby?

Rena *(Interjecting on "all over")* Thomas.

Thomas All the women in Chattanooga, why you wanna take Ruby?

Ruby Mister Peteman, maybe we should let the car run, in case it want to act funny before we go?

Peteman exits.

Thomas You defy a father's wishes.

Ruby I honor you. I honor you everyday. Just a few hours, let me have sumthin'. Please, Daddy.

Thomas What do you know about this man?

Ruby He Edgene friend.

Silence.

I love you, Daddy. And I'm gonna go. Just for a little while.

Thomas storms into the kitchen. Rena follows.

Rena Thomas.   **Ruby** Don't do that, Daddy. Please.

He begins to prepare a meatloaf sandwich.

Ruby All I want is a New York movie. I want one.

Edgene I'm paintin'.

As he walks away:

Ruby I'll tell you about it when I get back! I promise!

Like a lost boy, Edgene wanders into the kitchen and takes a seat at the table. Ruby grabs her sweater and leaves.

Thomas *(Fixing a sandwich)* I was a good…son. An excellent son.

Rena Yes, baby.

Thomas To both my parents. That was when I knew what to do, because it's better being a son than a father. *(He takes a bite of his sandwich)* It's good meatloaf. *(As if something hurts him)* It happens quick. I don't know where it came from, how it got in me, but I am fast to obey.

Rena We love…against our judgement. Our souls lie in tellin' us we should carry on. And we end up far away from what we intended.

Thomas When I was little, I thought I was a good boy, doing what they'd ask of me before they had to ask.

Rena Because we see we're needed. We make sure we're there. 'Cause we love.

Thomas I thought that made a good child. I thought…when your Grammy died, I thought I was doing what a good child would do. "Help Daddy. Give Momma some honor."

Rena No—

Thomas And Ruby: She was there. So obedient and fast. Cleaning away the mess, wiping his hands. Hiding the mess as I asked of her: just like a very good girl.

Rena No—

Thomas She understood the need to shape it, so they'd have peace, and you'd all have a future. And it worked: our thinking.

Rena No.

Thomas You all grew up. I look at you and your shirt is clean. You're healthy. But we don't talk.

Rena Stop talking.

Thomas At all. And I don't know if I would change that. If I could. I don't think that should change.

The front of Rena's blouse begins to seep blood. Ringing. She weeps.

Scene 3. Her Ways Are Moveable[17]
Edgene's Paint Studio - Night

A special up on Rena in another plane. As she speaks, Ruby, disheveled, searches the window sill of Edgene's shack. She finds a key and enters. She walks among Edgene's paintings and stops at a wall mirror, studying herself. Edgene enters, flask in hand, and finds his seat behind the easel.

Rena I see. I see. His face. He comes. So dark. So terrible. And gorgeous. So black. His skin. My love. Light shines. The sound. So loud. My ears. They ring. Then pain. Oh, why? My heart. This burns. My love. Oh, God. Oh, God. I love you.

Lights down on Rena. The ringing fades.

Edgene You sneakin' now? How was your date with Peteman? No movie? Shoot! Been waitin' up to hear about it. Maybe the next one?

Ruby attempts to fix herself. Edgene notices the rip on the shoulder of her dress.

He's a muthafucker after all, hunh? But you alright though. You alright, yeah? Yeah, we're alright. Hmph, I wondered what was wrong with you, wantin' to go with him and all, but you kept hollerin' you wanted your New York movie, so I left it alone. *(Beat. Then smug)* So, he don't make you happy no more?

Ruby You been in here all night?

Edgene Can't sleep. Dammit! *(He smacks his brush against the easel repeatedly)* Dammit! Dammit! Dammit! All that talk you do about New York. God, Rube, I can feel all my dreams tappin' me on the back of my neck, waitin' for my hands to get it all figured out so that the dreams can start to happen. My dreams are frustrated, waitin' on me! *(Beat)* I'm drunk.

Ruby You wanna go to New York?

Edgene What do people know about art here in Chattanooga? Shit, what can *I* know about art down here in Chattanooga? New York—that's where the artists go. You say it yourself. There or Paris, but I don't know no French.

Ruby I see the pictures of the city up there, and how the womens dress and walk about. They beautiful, and they go to music clubs and dance on stage with feathers in they hands.

Edgene Them's the whores, Ruby. Gosh you're dumb.

Ruby *(Sharp)* Don't do that.

Edgene What?

Ruby Don't make me listen to your dreams while you laugh at mine. Don't do that. *(Beat)* They beautiful and they send it out across the room, past and through all the men watchin' 'em. And when they move and wave them fans of theirs, they fannin' the music through the air. They're all sparkles and beauty and love and they don't even have to open they mouths 'cause they already have every ear standin' at attention, just waitin' to hear they slightest request. That's what beauty is, Edgene. That's what it does.

Edgene begins to paint her as she speaks.

Edgene Go on, Ruby. I'm listenin'.

Ruby *(As if she hasn't heard him)* You are? *(Beat)* They have they hair pinned up on the top of they heads, Edgene, and they have jewels in it to fasten the curls. Jewels in they naked belly buttons, on they shoe buckles, crushed up in they eyeshadow, and everyone watchin' them is just so in love. *(She begins to weep. It escalates into horror)* He took my car, Edgene.

He…My body…froze up, and he…I tried. I really tried, but I froze up. I disgust him. And I have no right, draggin' him around, bein' ugly and nappyheaded. Stupid—

Edgene He's a lie, Ruby.

Ruby He's the truth. You the lie, 'cause you my brother you and love me, but I look around this room, at all the women you paint and who you touch and you know you wouldn't ever touch or paint a woman like me, 'cause I ain't got no beauty. My hands are rough from cookin' and cleanin' and workin' in the garden and I have no hopes of anything beautiful ever happenin' to me. You, you have beauty: You drawn to it, and you want to capture it and you gonna find it, and that's why you lock me out. You don't want nuthin' ugly comin' around your work, 'cause ugly's got no right to it.

Edgene goes over to his sister and holds her close. She lifts her face and kisses him, her mouth starved and clumsy. He pulls away. Ruby kisses him again, and Edgene lets her. She places his hands on her body.

Act Six

Scene 1. A Sweeping Rain[18]
Trenton Kitchen - Day

Magazine pages stick to the willow tree. Its roots are exposed: Someone has dug up the earth.

Ruby sits at the table, shaking her head. She is dirty.

Thomas enters. Both he and the kitchen are a mess. He carries a basket of vegetables.

Thomas Rain drowned half of what the weeds didn't get. Beetles ate up holes in the rest. *(Beat)* Ruby?

Silence.

Ruby Everything was fine before, waddn't it, Daddy? We was okay. A dead car was just fine for us. Good. Then they come to us. Outta nowhere, talkin' so sweet.

Thomas Ruby, we've—

Ruby He put his tongue in my mouth, Daddy. I acted like I hated it. I had to. The two of us was so comfortable, and I knew waddn't gonna be nobody else for me. But who love me like him? Forgive me. I—Edgene—

Edgene enters from outside. Ruby fixes her eyes on him: a secret.

Thomas You livin' out there these days?

Edgene Hunh?

Thomas I'm asking you a question. With words. Not grunts. You haven't been seen around the house going on days now.

Edgene *(Opening icebox)* Just…just finishin' sumthin'.

Thomas The masterpiece. Yes. Well, when you're finished transforming the known art world, I could use your help around here. Surely you noticed your sister has decorated the tree. Did that instead of cookin' today if that's what you're lookin' for. I don't know what Peteman's got to do with the rest of us havin' food in our belly 'less she's tryin' to punish us for that Negro bein' gone. *(To Ruby)* I'm leavin' this stuff here on the counter. Keep what you will. You hear me? Ru? *(Silence. To Edgene)* We need a woman here. Look at us. Pathetic. That Mona John of yours—we barely gettin' by as is and she sticks us with that brat.

Edgene He ain't a brat.

Thomas Don't talk. Tear up the house. Groanin' when you touch 'em. Soil hisself. Only thing quietin' him my piano. Might as well tie him to it. The boy ain't got a lick of sense. What you call that?

Edgene He just missin' his Auntie Mona, Pop. Kids do that. 'Til Mona come back, we're what he got.

Thomas Fix your sister up.

Edgene I think she just…need to be alone.

Thomas *(As if she's deaf)* You want us to leave you alone? Ruby?

Ruby Alone? Ain't you listnin'? I'm married now. And all y'all can't fit. I tried it. Edgene and— **Thomas** *(Overlapping on "And all y'all…")* You see this? This what you been missin' out on!

Ruby What we gonna do? Peteman can't come in and see all you men here. A baby in the back room. It don't look good. It don't look good! It don't look good!

Edgene Daddy—!

Ruby You gotta leave. People talk. What we gonna say?

Edgene I—?

Ruby *(Impatient)* 'Cause you gotta be gettin' along, Edgene!

Edgene I ain't goin' nowhere—

Ruby It don't look right, you men here with me, and now a baby walkin' around: I'm a woman! People'll start thinkin' things!

Edgene Where we gonna—?

Ruby *(Hugs Edgene)* Oh, no. What did I do? I'm so sorry. I'm so sorry.

Thomas Ruby? Compose yourself.

Ruby I can't tell, Edgene. Please, don't make me tell.

Edgene I—uh. What you talkin' about?

Ruby The baby.

Thomas If you know something about that burden in the back room, let it out. Do us all a favor.

Silence.

Ruby *(Carefully)* He's…special. Ain't that right, Edgene?

Edgene Yes.

Ruby And he need a home. A family. Family is everything. Family and a home and—and love is everything.

Thomas Peace and quiet mean something, too. All this mayhem. Everything broken. Us. You. Looking all broken.

Ruby No, we love each other. We love each other so, don't we? But, how we explain we love each other when you leavin'?

Thomas Nobody's leaving!

Ruby Stay. I'll talk to Peteman. I can't have you unsure about the love I got for you. I love you, Edgene.

Edgene *(Visibly shaken)* I ain't gon' nowhere!

Ruby *(Grooming herself)* Let me clean myself. And make you some cornbread. I gotta get y'all's whisker hair out the bathtub. Here, sit down.

Thomas *(Insistent)* Take her to the washroom, Edgene. Fix her up.

Edgene I—I—what the hell she even talkin' 'bout? Dirty hair in the cornbread: What the hell she talkin' about?

She weeps.

Ruby I gotta tell you. About the baby. Please don't be mad.

Silence. A gradual laughter escapes Thomas.

Thomas What she talking about? What she mean? *(Beat)* Peteman? You 'spect me to believe that? Under my roof?

The basket of fruit falls to the floor.

Ruby Don't send me away.

Thomas seizes her viciously.

Thomas What you know about folks makin' babies?

Edgene Let her go! Let her go!

Ruby He love me. He love me. He love me.

Thomas releases her.

Thomas Edgene, what this girl talkin' about? What she meanin', boy?

Edgene She just tired. Shut up, Ruby. Shut up!

Edgene Daddy. She—she just tired…I'm believin'.

Silence.

Thomas Then I'll be believin' that, too. Yeah. You go get some rest, Ruby. I'll finish perusing your garden, 'fore I head to work. You let me know when supper ready. *(Edgene starts to speak, but Thomas shakes his head sharply)* You done enough. Finish puttin' all of this in the trash. *(To Ruby)* That right, Ruby?

Ruby Yes, Daddy. This is all...trash.

Thomas leaves. Ruby gently approaches her brother. She rests her head on him.

Ruby *(Apologetically)* I can't cook dinner for y'all tonight. I gotta get dressed and go on out. *(He hugs her)* Edgene?

Edgene Hunh?

Ruby That juke joint you go to? You—you tell me where it is?

Edgene Ruby—

Ruby Peteman take me dancin'.

Edgene You can't do that, Ruby. Ruby. *(Long pause)* Peteman didn't...? Did we...? You talkin' about the baby...in the back, right?

Ruby Please, Edgene. I gotta tell him we sorry.

Silence. Edgene goes to the counter and scribbles directions on paper.

Edgene Here.

Scene 2. O Naïve Ones[19]
Trenton Living Room / Kitchen / Edgene's Studio - Afternoon

Special up on Rena. She changes out of her blood-soaked clothes. She is putting on the outfit she wore at the top of the show.

Special up on Ruby. She is changing clothes: her idea of glamorous.

Special up on Mona John. She is taking off her clothes, pinning up her hair.

Mona John This is beautiful.

Ruby This feeling.

Rena Ain't nuthin' like tonight.

Mona John You always reminded me—

Ruby I didn't know—

Mona John I was—

Rena I remember—

Ruby So beautiful.

Rena Come to me.

Mona John It's too hard, worryin' 'bout what people say.

Ruby But this feel better.

Mona John Feel freer.

Rena Walkin' under the stars.

Ruby In high-heeled shoes.

Rena To find you. The music real faint in the distance.

Mona John I am here now.

Rena I'm comin' to see you. My God. What's wrong with me? I know better.

Mona John I'm crazy!

Ruby I'm bad! But I gotta see—

Rena Your face. The end to this…story.

Ruby Come to me.

Mona John I'll make up the rest.

Rena I'll patch the empty up with bits of blankets—

Ruby Fresh baked bread—

Mona John An imaginary husband killed in the war. So I can move—

Ruby Close to what I need.

Rena Excuses. But I remember now. Us. What always was. And the vision that had been inside of me—the wisdom.

Mona John The dream. Inside of me.

Ruby Your touch.

Rena I had laid it down. For you.

Mona John I lay you down.

Rena I had laid you down. Like you hadn't hurt me.

Ruby Because of love.

Mona John Stupid. Always.

Ruby Love.

A man appears in the shadows behind Ruby. He is obscured, but it appears to be Peteman.

Rena Stupid. Stupid. But the vision comes now, and I pick it back up again, and I remember it fully.

Ruby I'm seein' you tonight and we will be special. We will dance.

Lights down on Ruby.

Mona John And be seen. And envied. And perfect.

Rena And you will hold me. I've missed you.

The man moves toward Rena. She turns. It is Asa. They kiss passionately. Lights down on Asa and Rena.

Mona John Make me forever.

Mona, glamorous and seductive, drapes across a chaise lounge. A flash. Lights down.

Scene 3. A Repeated Matter[20]
Edgene's Studio / Trenton Living Room / Kitchen - Evening

Lights up in Edgene's paint shed.

Melody studies Edgene's current painting.

Melody Who is she?

Edgene It's broad daylight.

Melody Who is she?

Edgene Your voice—

Melody No one saw me. I was careful. *(Beat)* You got any whiskey?

Edgene Not today.

Melody Liar.

Edgene Of course I am. But not today.

Silence.

Come here. *(He pulls her close and kisses her)* That's better yeah? Don't see nobody in here, do ya? It's nobody. What? Whatcha thinkin'?

Melody It's good.

Edgene Yeah?

Melody Fantastic, actually.

Edgene I don't—

Melody I had hoped it would be me. That you'd get it. With me.

Edgene Gave her your hands. Come look at it.

She approaches.

Melody Doesn't look like a real person.

Edgene No?

Melody Looks like one of my bad dreams. I look at her…I want her in my collection, just to feel safe knowing she's locked in paint. I've never seen anything like this in my life. You will be coveted. *(She watches him paint)* I've become possessive of you. Did I embarrass myself?

Edgene Absolutely.

Melody Shoot. And it's still in my body, the thought of someone naked before you, making love to you the way I make love to you. Someone possibly better at it than I am. *(She grabs a small painting)* Are you a collector of women?

Thomas comes from behind the house carrying another basket of rotting vegetables.

Edgene I don't turn away a gift.

Melody You—!

She laughs. Thomas stops and walks toward the shed.

(Considering) Is that what women are—gifts? My grandmother crochets me sun bonnets each year for my birthday. The last one was orange.

Edgene *(Amused)* Oh, yeah?

Melody I never wear them…because I never want them. They're more a representation of what she can do than a display of affection. But, some gifts are better than others, don't you think? And some women? When my family returns to Chattanooga, I won't be with them. Do you think about it?

Edgene Of course I do. I mean, yeah. I think about it.

Melody Would you come? If I sent for you?

Edgene I…Wow, I don't…Pop…

Melody I have a father, too, Edgene, but you and I are far too exquisite. We are young and have desire. We are alive. Look at what you've created! We should go to France where we can walk about in broad day light. The night is romantic, but it's becoming cruel now, don't you think?

Edgene Sounds like a dream. *(Long pause)* Right now, my thoughts are comin' to me in…like foggy flashes, like a dream. There's sumthin' underneath…Sumthin'…funny happened the other day. We were in the living room. Pop said he was with you, but you were here. With me.

Melody What are you asking me?

Edgene French people comin' to see what I create wasn't my dream. That was Pop's dream.

Melody Edgene—

Edgene Are you stealin'? You are. You're not? Is he still teachin' you? *(No answer)* When you came over here the first time—

Melody It was to give him something I thought would mean the world to him, because for years he's meant the world to me.

Edgene You throw him away like he's nuthin', wasn't ever nuthin'! He pushed me and all us, us *blood*, aside so that he could work his dreams with you. He dreamed of Paris. Of you playin' what he taught you.

Melody So loyal. Every day I've been here, the music I gave you hasn't moved from that broken down dresser in the corner. *(Beat)* I couldn't tell him we were letting him go.

Edgene You con job.

Melody We're the same—

Edgene violently jerks away from her touch. She steps back. Silence. She looks around at the many paintings.

How did I just become your enemy? You're better with whiskey.

She exits, taking a moment to collect herself. Thomas steps from his hiding place. She doesn't see him behind her. He watches her walk away.

Edgene steps out, looking in the direction of her departure. He turns around, staring into his father's face.

Edgene Pop—

Thomas I'll see you later on, okay, Son?

Thomas goes into the house. Edgene returns to his shed. He lifts his masterpiece from the easel, studying it closely: a black woman holding her head in pain. Much red. She has very large hands. Long, skinny fingers. Her face is hidden in her hands. She is slouched over. We see a glimpse of her breasts, thighs, hips, pubic region: a pained position. The painting bears a familiarity to it. We, the audience, recognize traces of the many women who have influenced Edgene.

Lights up on Asa entering the living room. He makes his way to the piano.

Edgene kicks his leg through the canvas. Lights down on Edgene.

Asa touches a key. A light twinkles in the willow tree.

Ruby enters: a failed attempt at glamorous.

Ruby Was that you, baby? *(No response. She laughs)* Goodness, what wrong with me? Hold on right there. I'll be back.

Asa begins to play the familiar tune. More lights, but this time the twinkling is within the home, then the sky, then the world.

Ruby turns around: a twinkling boy. She removes her hat. As Asa reaches the familiar break:

Stop that!

Asa keeps playing, the song taking a never-before-heard turn.

Stop that!

The music swells and swells until the world disappears into a violently shimmering dreamscape. The world transforms into a starry night. Only the characters and the willow tree are visible. A sudden loud bang! The sound of a chair falling backward.

Lights up on Thomas in the kitchen. He stands over Rena laying dead in a pool of blood.

End of play.

End Notes

About the Creation of Edgene's Paintings

The easel should not be exposed to the audience during the painting of Edgene's lovers. Neither do we need the frontal nudity of the actresses functioning as models. The audience's imagination is the engine supplementing the creation of the paintings.

I envision the masterpiece is comprised of each of the women. Red for the bloodshed. Piano fingers. Perhaps "pretty hair" and "small feet" like Mona John, etc. Every production will interpret this differently.

About Rena

After the first scene, no one (except Melody) should interact directly with Rena. Actors should respond to surrounding statements and stimuli, and Rena's interjections can inform the climate of the room. She is "sensed" rather than experienced. Timing is integral.

About Asa

The music brings Asa into remembrance (a pseudo-resurrection). When Asa reappears in the 1950s, he is seen as a child. All interactions should be framed accordingly. Thomas senses the music within the child, remembering sentiment, but does not physically see him as his father, Asa. Rena gradually remembers / experiences Asa as something other than a child as her memories "refocus" him before her very eyes. She is the only one to experience him as a man when he reappears. He is never to appear in children's clothing.

About Children

No actual children should be used in this play. The adults are children and the children are adults.

Proverbs

1. Proverbs 1:8-9: My son, hear the instruction of thy father, and forsake not the law of thy mother: For they shall be an ornament of grace unto thy head, and chains about thy neck.

2. Proverbs 13:12: Hope deferred maketh the heart sick: but when the desire cometh, it is a tree of life.

3. Proverbs 30:9: Lest I be full, and deny thee, and say, who is the Lord? Or lest I be poor, and steal, and take the name of my God in vain.

4. Proverbs 18:24: A man that hath friends must shew himself friendly: and there is a friend that sticketh closer than a brother.

5. Proverbs 31:31: Give her of the fruit of her hands; and let her own works praise her in the gates.

6. Proverbs 6:20: My son, keep thy father's commandment, and forsake not the law of thy mother.

7. Proverbs 3:12: For whom the LORD loveth he correcteth; even as a father the son in whom he delighteth.

8. Proverbs 14:28: In the multitude of people is the king's honour: but in the want of people is the destruction of the prince.

9. Proverbs 10:4: He becometh poor that dealeth with a slack hand: but the hand of the diligent maketh rich.

10. Proverbs 25:15: By long forbearing is a prince persuaded, and a soft tongue breaketh the bone.

11. Proverbs 7:7-9: And beheld among the simple ones, I discerned among the youths, a young man void of understanding, passing

through the street near her corner; and he went the way to her house, in the twilight, in the evening, in the black and dark night.

12. Proverbs 3:3: Let not mercy and truth forsake thee: bind them about thy neck; write them upon the table of thine heart.

13. Proverbs 3:35: The wise shall inherit glory: but shame shall be the promotion of fools.

14. Proverbs 22:27: If thou hast nothing to pay, why should he take away thy bed from under thee?

15. Proverbs 19:26: He that wasteth his father, and chaseth away his mother, is a son that causeth shame, and bringeth reproach.

16. Proverbs 27:5: Open rebuke is better than secret love.

17. Proverbs 5:6: Lest thou shouldest ponder the path of life, her ways are moveable, that thou canst not know them.

18. Proverbs 28:3: A poor man that oppresseth the poor is like a sweeping rain which leaveth no food.

19. Proverbs 1:22: How long, O naive ones, will you love being simple-minded? And scoffers delight themselves in scoffing and fools hate knowledge?

20. Proverbs 17:9: He that covereth a transgression seeketh love, but he that repeateth a matter separateth very friends.

Acknowledgements

This book was made possible by the Women's Project. Julia Miles' foresight and ambition in creating that organization, along with the many remarkable artists who have brought that vision to life over the years, were very much a part of the inspiration for this book.

We are very grateful to the current staff of the Women's Project, with Julie Crosby at the helm, who served as our publisher and brought us together through the Lab program. Julie's work to revitalize the organization and her determination to bring great new writers to the stage has been inspirational. And her help on everything from contracts to contacts proved essential. Associate Artistic Director Megan Carter convened a tremendous and savvy mix of artists for the 2008-2010 Playwrights Lab who are represented in both volumes of this anthology. We thank Megan also for her thoughtful Preface, and Karron Karr for her administrative support.

Outside of the Women's Project, inspiration and support came from many fronts, first and foremost from the publishing working group led by Alexis Greene at the first gathering of 50/50 in 2020 at the Julia Miles Theater in August 2009. Alexis provided vital early encouragement and information about the publishing process. We also benefited from The League of Professional Theatre Women's publishing workshop, run by Stephen Squibb of NoPassport Press.

NoPassport's founder, the playwright, essayist and translator Caridad Svich, later provided invaluable practical support and encouragement.

Sally Oswald and Jordan Harrison's *Play: A Journal of Plays* expanded our vision of how plays might live on the page.

Many thanks to Theresa Rebeck, for generously allowing us to publish her speech, "A Thousand Voices," as our preface. It was first presented at the annual ART/NY Curtain Call presentation at the Laura Pels Theater on March 15, 2010.

Sincere thanks go to those who contributed essays and interviews for each of the plays: Gabeeba Baderoon, Isaac Byrne, Jorge Ignacio Cortiñas, Stella Feehily, Connie Grappo, Dyana Kimball, Chris Mills, Denyse Owens, Ken Prestininzi, Louis Scheeder, Lloyd Suh and Jessica Thebus.

Our profound appreciation goes to Gretchen Van Lente for taking on the enormous and meticulous task of proofreading both volumes.

Thanks to Ash Shairzay for design guidance.

And last but not least, thanks to all the members of the 2008-2010 Women's Project Lab. It was always invigorating to be in the room with you, to learn from you, to discuss both work and life, and to share an occasional glass of wine. We look forward to seeing your names in lights.

Women's Project 2008-2010 Playwrights Lab Member Bios

Bekah Brunstetter

Bekah Brunstetter's plays include *OOHRAH!* (Atlantic Theater), *Miss Lilly Gets Boned* (Lark Playwright's Week) and *You May Go Now (A Marriage Play)* (Finborough Theatre, London; NY IT Award for Best New Play.) She is working on commissions for Naked Angels, Ars Nova, and the Roundabout Underground. Member: Primary Stages Writer's Group, Women's Project Lab, At Play Productions. MFA, The New School for Drama. www.bekahbrunstetter.com

Carla Ching

Born and bred an Angeleno, Carla Ching's full-lengths include *TBA* (2g/Milagro Theater-CSV), *Dirty* (Finalist: 2006 Cherry Lane Mentor Project and 2008 Victory Gardens Ignition Festival), *Big Blind/Little Blind* (Ma-Yi Labfest 2008) and *The Sugar House at the Edge of the Wilderness* (NAATF workshop 2009). Shorts include "Dissipating Heat" (finalist for the 2005 Heideman Award from Actors Theatre of Louisville) and "The Further Adventures of Little Goth Girl." Member: Ma-Yi Writers Lab and Women's Project Lab. Fellowships: 2008 Urban Artists Initiative fellowship, 2009-2010 Teachers & Writers Collaborative Fellowship. Nominee: 2009 Wasserstein Prize. MFA, Actors Studio Drama School. Artistic Director, 2g.

Alexis Clements

Alexis Clements is a writer, performer and pamphleteer currently based in Brooklyn, NY. She has received a Dramatists Guild Fellowship, the 2004 Washington Theater Festival Literary Prize, two Puffin Foundation Artist's Grants, and a Ludwig Vogelstein Foundation Grant. Productions include: *Place ReImagined* (NYC); *Your Own Personal Apocalypse* (NYC); *The Interview* (Edinburgh Festival); and *Pieces* (Washington, DC & Iowa City, IA). Publications include: selected plays in *KNOCK Magazine*, short stories in US and UK collections, and articles in *Nature*, *The Brooklyn Rail* and *The Guardian*. MSc, Philosophy & History of Science from the London School of Economics & Political Science. BA, Theatre Studies, Emerson College. www.alexisclements.com

Nadia Davids

Nadia Davids is a South African playwright and scholar. She has written five plays, including *At Her Feet* (2002) and *Cissie* (2008). Her work has been produced in Africa, Europe and North America and is studied at a range of universities on all three continents. She is the recipient of a Fleur de Cap Theatre Award (*Best New Director*, 2003) and was nominated for the Noma Award (2007), two African PEN Awards (2006, 2009), and a Fleur de Cap Award (Best New South African Play, 2009). She teaches at Queen Mary, University of London.

Laura Eason

Laura Eason is the author of fifteen plays, original work and adaptations. Produced full-lengths: *Sex with Strangers* (Steppenwolf, Chicago), *When the Messenger is Hot* (59E59, NYC; Steppenwolf; Theatre Schmeater, Seattle), *Area of Rescue* (Andhow Theatre, NYC), *Around the World in 80 Days* (Baltimore Centerstage; Kansas City Rep; Lookingglass Theatre, Chicago), *The Adventures of Tom Sawyer* (Hartford Stage), and *Rewind* (Side Project, Chicago), among others. Publishing: Playscripts, Smith & Kraus and Broadway Play Publishing. Affiliations: Affiliated Artist, New Georges, NYC; Women's Project Lab, NYC; Ensemble Member and former Artistic Director, Lookingglass Theatre, Chicago. Originally from Chicago, Laura lives in Brooklyn, NY. www.lauraeason.com

Christine Evans

Christine Evans' productions include multi-award winning *Trojan Barbie* (American Repertory Theatre, 2009; Playbox Theatre, U.K. 2010); *Weightless, Mothergun* and *All Souls' Day* (Perishable Theatre); *Slow Falling Bird* (Crowded Fire, San Francisco; Metro Arts, Brisbane) and *My Vicious Angel* (Belvoir St. Theatre; Adelaide International Festival, Australia). Honors include the RISCA Playwriting Fellowship, two MacDowell Colony Fellowships and the Jane Chambers Playwriting Award. Christine is a Fulbright alumna, holds an MFA and PhD from Brown and teaches playwriting at Harvard. Her plays are published by *Theatre Forum*, NoPassport Press, Smith & Kraus and Samuel French (2010). www.christine-evans-playwright.com

Charity Henson-Ballard

Charity Henson-Ballard, actor and emerging playwright, lives in New York where she is a member of Rising Circle Theater Collective. She received her Master's in English with a concentration in Renaissance Literature and Psychoanalytic Theory from UMASS Amherst, and a Master's of Fine Arts in Acting from NYU. Charity conducts actor coaching and playwriting workshops using critical approaches to language performativity and the utilization of the complete actor instrument. Her current projects include *Pete the Girl* and *Muddy the Waters* (full-length), which was originally showcased at the World Financial Center in collaboration with Women's Project and River to River Festival, 2009. www.charityhensonballard.com

Kara Manning

Kara Manning's plays, including *Mind the Gap*, *Killing Swans*, *afterdark,* and *Sleeping Rough*, have been performed or developed via the Royal Court Theatre, Hampstead Theatre, the O'Neill Playwrights Conference, Playwrights Horizons, Rattlestick, NYTW, LAByrinth Theater. She is the 2007 recipient of the Princess Grace Award in playwriting. Member of the Women's Project Lab and MCC Theater's Playwrights Coalition. Playwright-in-residence with the Royal Court Theatre's International Residency, Page 73 Productions' 2008 Yale retreat and Women's Project's 2009 Voice & Vision retreat. Recipient of the 2000-2001 Jerome Foundation, Affiliated Writers Program grant. Graduate of Columbia University's MFA playwriting program.

Lynn Rosen

Lynn Rosen has had plays produced or developed at many theaters, including: Women's Project, Centerstage (Baltimore), The Working Theater, The Lark Play Development Center, New Harmony Project, The New Group, New Georges, Geva Theatre, Ensemble Studio Theatre, The Studio Theatre, Todd Mountain Theater Project, Willow Cabin Theatre Company and several productions in Germany. Commissions from the EST/Sloan Foundation and New Georges. Named one of "50 to Watch" by *The Dramatist* magazine, Weissberger Award nominations, a member of the Women's Project Lab, EST, Dramatist Guild, The Fire Dept., and a New Georges and Lark Affiliated Artist. She is originally from Gary, Indiana.

Crystal Skillman

Crystal Skillman is the author of the plays *Birthday, Nobody, The Telling Trilogy* (Rising Phoenix Rep, Dir. Daniel Talbott), *The Sleeping World* (Developed by Flux, Woodshed Collective, Lincoln Center Directors Lab) and *Hack (*Vampire Cowboys Saloon Series, The Brick Too Soon Summer Festival 2010). Currently, Crystal has also been commissioned by the Vampire Cowboys to write a new play for an upcoming season. You can also find her work published in *Plays & Playwrights 2008*, *Poems & Plays*, as well as Smith & Kraus. Member: Women's Project Lab, RPR, EST, The Pack, Dramatists Guild.

Andrea Thome

Andrea Thome is a Chilean-Costa Rican, Wisconsin-born mutt who grew up navigating the multiple landscapes and languages that now inhabit her plays. Her dramas, comedies, translations and video satires have been presented by organizations including: Lark Play Development Center, INTAR, TerraNova Collective, El Museo del Barrio, NYU, Yale, Cherry Red Productions (DC), the Bay Area's Yerba Buena Center for the Arts, Brava!, Latina Theatre Lab and Stanford University. Andrea co-directs the satire collective FULANA (www.fulana.org). She regularly teaches youth and college students, and directs the Lark's U.S.-México Playwrights Exchange. She is a member of New Dramatists.

The text of this book is set in Perpetua, designed in the 1920s by Eric Gill, an English sculptor, sign painter and type designer. Based on the designs of old engravings, the font was first used in a limited edition translation of *The Passion of Perpetua and Felicity*, printed in 1929. In that same year Gill set his own book, *Art Nonsense and Other Essays*, in Perpetua. The titles and front matter of this book are set in Gill Sans, also designed by Eric Gill in the 1920s. In making Gill Sans, Gill was inspired by Edward Johnston's Johnston typeface for the London Underground. Gill Sans rose to prominence in the late 1920s when it began to be used throughout the train system in England on railway station signage, train timetables, advertising posters and restaurant car menus.

This book was designed by Alexis Clements.

Volume 2 Available Now!

Featuring:

At Her Feet by **Nadia Davids**
Conversation by **Alexis Clements**
Le Fou by **Bekah Brunstetter**
Sleeping Rough by **Kara Manning**
TBA by **Carla Ching**
Undone by **Andrea Thome**

Buy your copy today at
www.outoftimeandplace.com

www.ingramcontent.com/pod-product-compliance
Lightning Source LLC
Chambersburg PA
CBHW022045160426
43198CB00008B/132